Y0-CCH-134

THE RISE OF A REFUGEE GOD
HONG KONG'S WONG TAI SIN

THE RISE OF
A REFUGEE GOD

HONG KONG'S WONG TAI SIN

GRAEME LANG & LARS RAGVALD

HONG KONG
OXFORD UNIVERSITY PRESS
OXFORD   NEW YORK
1993

Oxford University Press

Oxford   New York   Toronto
Kuala Lumpur   Singapore   Hong Kong   Tokyo
Delhi   Bombay   Calcutta   Madras   Karachi
Nairobi   Dar es Salaam   Cape Town
Melbourne   Auckland   Madrid
and associated companies in
Berlin   Ibadan

Oxford is a trade mark of Oxford University Press

First published 1993

Published in the United States
by Oxford University Press, New York

© *Oxford University Press 1993*

British Library Cataloguing-in-Publication Data

A catalogue record for this book is available from the British Library

Library of Congress Cataloging in Publication Data
Lang, Graeme.
The rise of a refugee god: Hong Kong's Wong Tai Sin/by Graeme Lang,
and Lars Ragvald.
p.   cm.
Includes bibliographical references and index.
ISBN 0-19-585755-0. — ISBN 0-19-585744-5 (pbk.)
1. Wong Tai Sin (Deity)
299'.5142113—dc20
I. Ragvald, Lars, 1942–.
II. Title.
92-47422
CIP

Printed in Hong Kong

Published by Oxford University Press (Hong Kong) Ltd
18/F Warwick House, Tong Chong Street, Quarry Bay, Hong Kong

Preface

CHINESE folk religion has a way of capturing foreign academics, and so was I captured, during a stay in Hong Kong in 1984. I had gone there during a sabbatical leave from teaching at Memorial University, intending to study small textile factories, but I was just then beginning to turn my attention to the sociology of religion and was more intrigued by the local temples. One in particular caught my attention — a large temple to the god Wong Tai Sin.

My visit to this temple, as it happened, was during the Chinese New Year period, and on my arrival at the gates of the temple I was caught up in the dense crowd and pushed along into the courtyard in front of the main shrine, where the sights and sounds of mass worship assailed the senses with the smoke from thousands of incense sticks and the incessant rattling of containers full of bamboo divination sticks, as worshippers knelt before their offerings of food for this god, seeking his help and advice. Intrigued, I began to try to find out more about the history of the temple, but very little had been written about Wong Tai Sin. It soon became apparent that this god was popular only in Hong Kong, and only since the 1950s. This especially fascinated me, since my main interest, within the sociology of religion, was in explaining why some new religious movements become successful while others remain small and obscure. I decided to try to explain why Wong Tai Sin had become so popular. My initial contacts with the organization which managed the temple produced much useful information, but sooner or later I would need help in tracing the origins of the cult inside China.

Fortunately, I had met Lars Ragvald at the Universities Service Centre in Kowloon. Lars's primary interest was in the recent social and cultural history of Guangdong province, and he agreed to participate, devoting some of his research time in 1985 to searching for the original temples to this god in Guangdong province. (None now existed, but he found the ruins of all three of the original temples to Wong Tai Sin in Guangdong). We divided the labour, with Lars mainly working on the origins and fate of the cult at several sites in Guangdong and reading the relevant Chinese sources, and I working mainly on the growth of the cult in Hong Kong and its offshoots in Macau and New York.

We are still fascinated by the history of worship of Wong Tai Sin, and some of the mystery which drew us into the study of this cult still remains. Perhaps readers of our book will be infected with the fascination which the project has held for us and will make further discoveries. Meanwhile, we hope that what we report in this book will be of interest to those who study Chinese religion, urban temples, the rise of cults, or the relation between religion and social change in Asia.

GRAEME LANG
Hong Kong
December 1992

Contents

Maps, Table, Figures, and Illustrations

Maps

Table and Figures

Illustrations (*between pp. 102 and 103*)

Acknowledgements

GRAEME LANG would like to thank Memorial University of Newfoundland for supporting research trips to Hong Kong in 1984, 1987, and 1989, and City Polytechnic of Hong Kong for supporting translation of nineteenth-century documents in 1991; the many scholars whose hospitality and interest in the research were so greatly appreciated, and whose work was a source of ideas and inspiration, including Choi Chi-cheung, David Faure, James Hayes, Graham Johnson, Ambrose Y. C. King, P. L. Kwok, Rance P. L. Lee, Bernhard H. K. Luk, Shiu Hon Wong, and Siu Lun Wong; the Chairman of the Sik Sik Yuen, Wong Wan Tin, for his kindness in opening the doors of the temple and the Sik Sik Yuen to a foreign scholar and helping him to understand the recent history of the Sik Sik Yuen; and the directors and members of the Sik Sik Yuen whom we interviewed during our research. Special thanks are due to Leung Fuk Chak and Peter W. K. Lo, who generously shared their special knowledge and insights about the history of worship of Wong Tai Sin, and without whose help and friendship this research would have been much impoverished.

Lars Ragvald would like to thank Stockholm University and the Royal Academy of Letters, History, and Antiquities for supporting research trips to China in 1985 and 1987, and the University of Lund for research trips in 1990 and 1991; the district public offices of Xiqiao and Fangcun for their understanding and assistance; Xie Hua of the Fangcun Cultural Affairs Bureau; Li Rui-xiang of the Guangdong Provincial Academy of Social Sciences; and the many scholars with whom he discussed this research in China and in Sweden.

We would both like to thank Dr Patrick Hase, who generously shared his knowledge and experience of the local society with us, helped us at several stages in the research, and provided many useful comments on an early draft of the book.

Romanization

NAMES of places, persons, and organizations in Hong Kong are written using Cantonese-based romanization: locally adopted spellings where these are available, and the Yale University system for romanizing Cantonese (Huang 1962) for the rest. Most place names and terms which do not need to be romanized in Cantonese are written in the pinyin system. The Glossary provides the written Chinese for many of the terms and names used in the text.

1   Introduction

THE rise of a new god has happened many times in human history, but such cases are usually shrouded in mystery. Somehow, a god known only to a handful of people becomes the god of tens of thousands or sometimes even millions of worshippers. For the student of comparative religion, this process, which has occurred on every continent and in every culture, is very important. We cannot understand the gods until we understand how they escaped their obscure beginnings.

The rise of a new god is also very rare. Most gods rose from obscurity to fame in the remote past and we seldom understand why. Who knows about the earliest stages in the worship of Zeus or Apollo, or Aphrodite or Athene, or El or Yahweh? Who knows why they were brought to life, and why they finally became huge and powerful in the minds of thousands of worshippers. We can only speculate, basing our ideas on scraps of literary and archaeological evidence which often date from hundreds of years later, and which are always inadequate. We can almost never confidently reconstruct what really happened.

But new gods which have suddenly become very popular in the recent past offer much better prospects. Documents which may illuminate the origins of the god's cult still exist, information on the surrounding society is still plentiful, and we can interview people from among the first few generations of believers. The sudden rise of a new god is rare, but when it occurs, those interested in how such things happen must grasp the chance to study the early stages of the phenomenon before it passes. This book is about one such case: the recent rise of a god named Wong Tai Sin (Huang Daxian) from obscurity to fame in modern Hong Kong.

The Wong Tai Sin Temple in Hong Kong

Anyone visiting Hong Kong with an interest in temples will quickly become aware of the Wong Tai Sin temple, the largest of Hong Kong's many urban shrines. It is not only the largest but also the most convenient of the city's temples because it sits above an underground railway stop which has been named after the god. The temple was built in 1921 on a hillside near a small village more than a kilometre from Kowloon City, but it is now surrounded by high-rise apartment buildings and stands in the middle of one of the most densely populated districts in Hong Kong. Because the fame of the temple is so great, this residential district has been named after the god.

While most of the urban temples in Hong Kong attract a trickle of worshippers with only a handful of people inside at any given time, there are always scores of people worshipping at the Wong Tai Sin temple. The steady stream of worshippers swells to a flood during the Chinese New Year period, when tens of thousands of worshippers crowd into the temple each day. There is no other temple in Hong Kong which draws such huge crowds.[1] Because these crowds consult the god through oracles, there is also a huge demand for the services of fortune-tellers, who interpret the oracles for worshippers. Consequently, clustered around the temple in stalls and booths, is what may be the largest single concentration of fortune-tellers in Asia. Most temples in Hong Kong and Taiwan have only one or two fortune-tellers. The Wong Tai Sin temple, during peak periods, has more than 100 of these professional diviners.

'Ask and it shall be granted' (*you qiu bi ying*, or in Cantonese: *yauh kauh bit yihng*) is a phrase often used in Taiwan and elsewhere to refer to the powers of a god. In Hong Kong, this phrase is used primarily to refer to Wong Tai Sin — such is his reputation. In local slang, a person who has been very generous in answering requests for aid may be called 'Wong Tai Sin'. Soccer goalkeepers who allow easy goals may also be called 'Wong Tai Sin' by the spectators (any shot is rewarded with a goal). The god's fame has been carried far from Hong Kong by people emigrating to South-East Asia, Europe, and North America, and Wong Tai Sin is one of the very few purely Chinese deities to whom a shrine has recently been erected in North America.

Who is this god? Why has he become so popular in Hong Kong? Is it because of his great miracles? His profound teachings? His impressive doctrines? Let us first consider the god himself and his origins and history.

Like many other Chinese gods, Wong Tai Sin — literally, the Great Immortal Sage Wong[3] — was once a human who lived in

China many centuries ago. This, at least, is what his inner circle of devotees believe. Most worshippers do not know or care about his earthly life. They worship him because of his great reputation in Hong Kong for helping and curing people and showing them what the future holds. For these people, his present godliness is all important; his former humanity is of little interest.

However, an official account of his life on earth has been produced by the private organization which has managed the main temple to Wong Tai Sin since its founding in 1921. This organization, known as the Sik Sik Yuen, has published this account in the form of a brief 'autobiography' of the god, written in the first person. Members believe that this autobiography was dictated by the god to a Taoist medium while the Taoist was in a trance. The medium wrote it down, as he received it, using a stick with which he drew the characters on a table. Although the Sik Sik Yuen no longer uses spirit-writing to receive messages from this god, they believe that the 'autobiography' is a revelation from Wong Tai Sin. This autobiography, which relates the life-story of the human named Wong Cho Ping who eventually became the god known as Wong Tai Sin, runs as follows:

I was originally a goatherd on Mount Jinhua, which lies to the north of Jinhua prefectural town in Zhejiang. . . .[4] To the north of Mount Jinhua there is a mountain called Mount Red Pine; I lived on this mountain. It was a place where people rarely came. The mountain-side was thickly wooded, and the clouds hung heavy over it. In the green-clad towering slopes, deep in a secluded valley there is a cave called Jinhua Grotto; it is one of the Thirty-six Grotto Heavens and Places of Good Fortune.

When I was young my family were poor, and we often did not even have chaff to eat. When I was eight years old I began to herd sheep and continued until I was 15, at which time I was fortunate to receive instruction from an immortal elder. He led me into the cavern, and there prepared the medicine of immortality by nine times transforming cinnabar. Thereafter I cast aside all wordly matters. My elder brother Cho Hei searched for me for more than 40 years without success, and it was only after he met a Taoist who was skilled in divination that he could find me, and we were reunited. My elder brother asked where my sheep were, and I replied that they were [grazing] on the eastern slope of the mountain. When we went to find them, all we could see were white stones lying all over the place. I called to the stones, and they all turned back into sheep! From that time onwards my elder brother took up Taoist practices, and he is now also ranked among the host of immortals.

My family name is Wong, and my given name is Cho Ping. I was born in the Jin dynasty and am a native of Danxi [near Jinhua]. Since I lived in seclusion on Mount Red Pine, I am also known as 'Immortal Master Red Pine'. However, I am not the same person as the immortal with this name who accompanied Zhang Liang on his travels.[5] If I did not make this clear, then no one would know anything about it; thus I have set down this autobiography.

The autobiography is inscribed on a large plaque behind the main altar in the temple. Such first-person accounts dictated by a god through a medium are probably not uncommon in cults which use spirit mediums to speak for the gods.[6]

In the case of this autobiography, however, a secular source has been found for the account (Wong 1985): a fourth century work by a famous Taoist theorist and writer on Chinese medicine named Ge Hong (284–364 CE).[7] In his book *Biographies of Immortals* (*Shenxian Zhuan*),[8] Ge Hong briefly describes the lives of 84 Taoist hermits and seekers of immortality. His account of the life of Wong Cho Ping, whom he places in the Jin dynasty (266–316 CE), runs as follows:

Wong Cho Ping came from Danxi. When he was 15 his family had him tend sheep. A Taoist, seeing that he was good-natured and conscientious, took him to a stone cave in the Jinhua Mountain. For 40 odd years Cho Ping stayed there without thinking of his family. His elder brother Cho Hei searched for him for many years in the mountains but without success. Once in a market-place he saw a Taoist. Cho Hei beckoned him and asked, 'My brother Cho Ping who was sent out to tend sheep has not been seen for more than 40 years. I don't know where he is or whether he is dead or alive. Would you please find out by means of divination?'. The Taoist said, 'On the Jinhua Mountain there is a young shepherd by the name of Wong Cho Ping. Doubtless he is your brother'. When he heard this, Cho Hei followed the Taoist in search of his younger brother. He found him. The brothers told each other of what had happened during all the years they had been apart. Cho Hei then asked his brother where the sheep were. 'Not far from here on the eastern side of the mountain', Cho Ping answered. Cho Hei went over there and looked for them, but he saw only white stones. He went back and said to Cho Ping, 'There are no sheep on the eastern side of the mountain'. Cho Ping said, 'The sheep are there but you, my brother, could not see them'. Cho Ping together with Cho Hei went over again to have another look. Cho Ping shouted to the sheep to rise and all the stones turned into tens of thousands of sheep. Cho Hei said to his brother, 'You have now attained perfection in the secrets of the Tao [the Way]. Can I also learn to do that?' Cho Ping said, 'Only if you are eager to learn the way will you attain perfection'. Cho Hei then abandoned his wife and children and stayed with his brother to learn the way.

The passage ends with a reference to medicines perfected by Cho Ping and states that people who have taken this medicine have managed to become immortal. Cho Ping, it is also said, eventually changed his name to Chisong Zi (the Red Pine Master) and Cho Hei changed his to Lu Ban. Ge Hong's account is quite clearly the source for all later accounts of Wong Cho Ping,[9] and for the details in the 'autobiography' of Wong Tai Sin. It is also the only contemporary account of the life of Wong Cho Ping.

On the surface, the autobiographical account is not very impressive. It offers only two extraordinary features in the life of this otherwise obscure hermit. Firstly, Wong Cho Ping says he learned the art of refining cinnabar into a drug which helped him to achieve immortality; and secondly, he turned some boulders on a hillside into sheep. This second miracle has clearly impressed some people, it has been depicted in drawings and woodcuts, and has been carved into a large plaque at the back of the main altar in the Wong Tai Sin temple (showing boulders sprouting legs and sheep's heads as they are transformed into sheep at Wong Tai Sin's call). But the miracle is not very inspiring,[10] and no other miracles are attributed to Wong Cho Ping during his life on earth.

His more profound achievements are what really ensured his reputation among Taoists: Ge Hong reports that Cho Ping developed cinnabar (mercuric sulphide) into a drug which could produce immortality. This experimentation with cinnabar preoccupied many Taoists, with intense interest in the substance dating from as early as the first century CE (Williams 1960:169; Welch 1965:97). The Taoist alchemists expended great efforts searching for drugs and potions which would prolong life, indefinitely if possible (Ge Hong himself spent some of his later years in this quest for immortality). The pursuit of immortality had begun centuries earlier, helped immensely by the patronage of emperors who hoped to escape the earthly death of other mortals (Welch 1965:98–9).[11] The use of arcane potions was only one of the methods used in this quest, and probably not the best way. Cinnabar is actually a poison, and some of the hermits were no doubt 'translated into the heavens' by cinnabar more speedily than they had hoped.[12] Nevertheless, the use of chemical potions retained its appeal, and stories of hermits who had allegedly perfected such a potion and become immortal were related by chroniclers.

Cho Ping evidently succeeded in cultivating his inner qualities during his years as a hermit. His power was so great that finally he was able to perform miracles, of which the turning of boulders into sheep was merely one manifestation, recorded only because his brother finally arrived to provide a witness to these powers. Early Taoist writings, attributed to Chuang Tzu and dated about the third century BC, had described the powers of one who has perfected himself in 'the Way': he 'does not eat the five grains, but inhales air and drinks dew. He can mount the clouds and drive flying dragons; he can save men from disease and assure a plentiful harvest. He is immune to flood and fire.' (Welch 1965:91).

Although such depictions by the early 'philosophical Taoists' were perhaps intended to be taken allegorically (as Welch argues), they were accepted by later Taoist writers and magicians as descriptions of the kinds of powers actually available to the Taoist adept who had truly achieved perfection. Wong Cho Ping thus demonstrated to all, by his miracle of the boulders-into-sheep, that he had indeed mastered 'the Way'. Such a great sage could serve as a shining example for later Taoists with similar ambitions. This, no doubt, is why Cho Ping's life was described by Ge Hong.

However, there is not much in the life of Wong Cho Ping to inspire devotion. He ignored his family for 40 years and lived as a hermit in the mountains. When his elder brother finally caught up with him and decided to pursue the same life as a seeker of immortality, he abandoned his wife and family just as Cho Ping had abandoned his parents and siblings. Wong Cho Ping made no attempt to bring his discoveries back to his countrymen, or to teach anything to anyone. His quest was an entirely self-centred one — to cultivate the mystical powers of 'the Way' and to experiment with potions so that he could escape death. In addition, Wong Cho Ping is only one of many hermits and seekers of immortality recorded in the Taoist chronicles who allegedly achieved what they sought. Yet none of these other ancient Taoist adepts are widely worshipped in Hong Kong, while hundreds of thousands of people flock to Wong Cho Ping's temple each year to ask for his favour and advice. We must conclude that it is not the life of Wong Cho Ping which has inspired them. Wong Tai Sin, the immortal sage who once lived on earth as Wong Cho Ping, is now far more than the sum of the parts of Cho Ping's life.

As for doctrines, there are very few associated with Wong Tai Sin. The Sik Sik Yuen believes that Wong Tai Sin's teachings can be summarized in the formula 'To act benevolently and to teach benevolence'.[13] Worshippers are generally aware of this ethical injunction. The Sik Sik Yuen has also claimed, in a chant or prayer published in one of its booklets, that Wong Tai Sin helps the poor and needy, and some worshippers are also aware of this claim. But most worshippers pay little attention to such material. They visit the temple and petition the god because of his great reputation for giving advice and help to his worshippers. This reputation is based on stories, which have swelled into a generally held conviction among believers, that the god gives accurate predictions about the future to sincere worshippers, and that he helps to guide and protect them. For most worshippers, the ethical doctrines of the god are much less important. These doctrines are not found anywhere in the life of Wong Cho Ping, and appear to have been credited to him quite recently, probably by the founders of the cult of Wong Tai Sin at the end of the last century.

If the popularity of Wong Tai Sin cannot be ascribed to any features of his life or his teachings, what is the cause of this popularity? How did he conquer Hong Kong with apparently so little spiritual capital?

First, we must consider the possibility that Wong Tai Sin was already a popular god in China, and was simply brought down to Hong Kong by the waves of immigrants who flooded into the colony from the 1920s onward, and that his current popularity simply reflects their fertility and their success in passing along belief in this god to their children and grandchildren. Indeed, most Chinese gods worshipped by large numbers of people in Hong Kong are very old gods, who were either already present in the coastal villages or were brought to Hong Kong by immigrants from China, and are worshipped by large numbers of immigrants because they were already familiar with these gods and accustomed to worshipping them in China as their ancestors had done for many centuries.

Wong Tai Sin was indeed worshipped in China for many generations, but clear historical evidence for worship of Wong Tai Sin exists only in the Jinhua area, far to the north of Guangdong province. His cult in Jinhua may have begun as early as the Jin dynasty, in the fourth century, and he was probably worshipped in the region without interruption until the end of the Southern Song dynasty in the thirteenth century (Wong 1985). Temples to

Wong Tai Sin in the Jinhua area were evidently rebuilt in the fifteenth and sixteenth centuries.[14] However, there is no evidence of widespread worship of Wong Tai Sin outside Jinhua, and no evidence of widespread worship even in the Jinhua area from the seventeenth century until the early twentieth century.

Wong Tai Sin, then, is different from other gods worshipped in Hong Kong. As far as we can tell, none of the people who grew up in China and later moved to Hong Kong had ever worshipped Wong Tai Sin in China. Indeed, we discovered that the god had only become very popular in Hong Kong since the 1950s, and after interviews with elderly worshippers of Wong Tai Sin who had grown up in China and moved to Hong Kong, we have come to believe that people who grew up in China before the 1950s had never heard of this god before moving to Hong Kong.[15] The hundreds of thousands of people who worship Wong Tai Sin have encountered him only in Hong Kong. We cannot explain this god's prominence in Hong Kong, then, by referring to his prior status in China. There are other ways in which gods have risen to prominence in various cultures. Do any of these apply to Wong Tai Sin? The following are some of the routes which can be identified.

Sometimes the principal god of a relatively small group — a clan or small kingdom, for instance — has become the chief god of a much larger number of people as the clan or kingdom conquered other groups and supplanted the native religion of these groups through various social, cultural, psychological, and political processes. But Wong Tai Sin never rode on the coat-tails of conquerors to gain his position in Hong Kong.

Even without conquest, sometimes the political dominance of a group can help that group's god to rise over other gods. For example, the political dominance of a clan or lineage in a village may allow the god of that clan to become the chief god of the village; or the patron god of the dominant group in an alliance of clans or villages may become the chief god of the alliance.[16] But Wong Tai Sin, as far as we know, was never the god of a particular clan or village, nor did he ever become the chief god of a political alliance of clans or villages, either in China or in Hong Kong.

Politics can lead to the rise of gods in other ways. The history of religion in China includes a number of cases in which the State mandated the posthumous worship of State heroes — exemplary officials, for instance, or heroic military leaders — in order to promote loyalty and service to the State and its rulers, and these new 'gods' have sometimes been accepted eventually by the masses as their own gods.[17] Although Wong Cho Ping was formally honoured by an emperor during the southern Song dynasty, he achieved fame, outside the Jinhua area, only 800 years later, and only in Hong Kong. The Hong Kong government, of course, never sponsored any such cults.

In the absence of State support for a god, rich patrons who believe a particular god has helped them can greatly assist the god's rise to prominence with their donations for the building of temples. In such cases, the luck involved in sickness and recovery, sometimes combined with the cunning and good timing of an enterprising priest, can lead to a sudden increase in the fortunes of a god.[18] As we shall see in Chapters 2 and 3, wealthy patrons were indeed important in the early stages of Wong Tai Sin's cult. However, such occasional donations cannot drive an obscure god to the heights of prominence achieved by Wong Tai Sin in Hong Kong without some other powerful social forces capable of sweeping large numbers of people into the new god's embrace. What were these forces?

We have found that the popularity of Wong Tai Sin in Hong Kong is closely linked to the history of a single temple in Kowloon. Thus our account belongs, in part, to the category of studies of the rise and decline of temples.[19] The explanation of Wong Tai Sin's rise to prominence in Hong Kong is complex, and cannot be attributed to any single factor. His success depended on the way groups of people reacted to plague, revolution, war, political turmoil, and massive urbanization during the period between the 1890s and the 1970s. The story is complex, but it is also dramatic. The history of this god's rise to fame is closely bound up with the profound upheavals which affected Hong Kong and south China during the last 100 years.

Before documenting the rise to fame of this god in Hong Kong, we must go back to the obscure beginnings of this cult at the end of the nineteenth century. How did the cult get started and what happened to the worship of Wong Tai Sin inside China which led to its extinction there during the twentieth century?

2 The Origins and Fate of the Cult of Wong Tai Sin in Guangdong, China

OUR research seemed to show that Wong Tai Sin's success as a god had occurred only in Hong Kong. Worship of Wong Tai Sin in Guangdong before 1915 must have been very localized, or very small-scale, or very short-lived. Nevertheless, we were curious about the Guangdong origins of the cult devoted to this god. How did it begin? When, and why, did a group of people inside Guangdong begin to worship this obscure god? If they had built temples to him in Guangdong, what had happened to these temples? What had happened to the worshippers? In regard to the founder of the Hong Kong temple, what had been his role in the cult in China, and why had he left China and moved to Hong Kong in 1915?

For the history of worship of Wong Tai Sin, however, we had only the Sik Sik Yuen's own official account of its history, which begins with the opening of the first Wong Tai Sin shrine in Hong Kong by Mr Leung Yan Ngam in 1915. This account was compiled by the Sik Sik Yuen after interviews in the 1960s with elderly members, including the son of Leung Yan Ngam, Leung Gwan Jyun (who died in 1971). These interviews must have produced much information about the Guangdong origins of the cult, but none of this material found its way into the official history of the Sik Sik Yuen. Fortunately, we managed to find out quite a lot about the origins of the cult of Wong Tai Sin in Guangdong province, and we also learned when and why the cult was extinguished inside China. Our findings are described in this chapter.

The Founder

The man who brought the cult of Wong Tai Sin from Guangdong province to Hong Kong in 1915, and set up the first shrine to this new god in the colony, was Mr Leung Yan Ngam. Leung had evidently started to worship Wong Tai Sin 18 years earlier, in 1897, in Guangdong province. Prior to 1897, we do not know of any worshippers of this god in Guangdong in the nineteenth century.

Leung was born in 1861 in Rengang village, near the base of Xiqiao Mountain in Nanhai County.[1] This mountain, an extinct volcano rising from the coastal plains of Guangdong, is famous in the region for its Taoist temple and for the herbs and herbal medicines grown in the area. Leung's father was a merchant who made his living selling these herbal medicines. Leung was educated in Rengang village, and grew up steeped in the lore of herbal medicine and Taoist medical practice. However, he did not immediately follow his father into the herbal medicine business. Instead, he got an appointment as a clerk in the Chinese Maritime Customs in Guangzhou. If he had not done so, the cult of Wong Tai Sin would probably never have been created.

Leung in the Customs Service in Guangzhou

Leung was in his early twenties when he joined the Customs Service, which had been established to monitor and tax imports into China. He remained for about 15 years, but at a low rank. Almost all of the upper ranks of the Customs Service were then occupied by non-Chinese foreigners recruited by the Inspector-General, who in Leung's time was the Englishman Robert Hart. Promotion to these upper ranks was still virtually impossible for Chinese employees of the Service.[2] Since upward mobility in the Customs Service was effectively barred to Chinese employees such as Mr Leung, the more ambitious among them must have begun to look around for other opportunities once their standard of living had reached desirable levels. Perhaps Leung also became restless. One of his grandsons also recalls hearing a family story that Leung felt uneasy about some of the activities expected of a minor official,[3] and that this had something to do with his later turn toward religion.

But if Leung was dissatisfied with his job in the Customs Service and beginning to think about alternative careers, he was not yet ready to leave his secure position and try something much riskier. It was the medical crisis in Guangzhou — the bubonic plague epidemics of the 1890s — that evidently led him to return in his mind to the rich tradition of Taoist religio-medical lore which he had absorbed in his native village, and probably also led to his religious encounter with the god Wong Tai Sin.

The Plagues

The bubonic plague hit this region of south China in 1893, and reached epidemic proportions in 1894 in Guangzhou. It was first noticed in the southern part of Guangzhou, and within ten days it had spread throughout the city. In the three months following the onset of the plague, it has been estimated that between 200 and 500 people died from the disease each day (Sinn 1989:159). At least 20,000 people died within a few months. Some refugees from Guangzhou crowded into Taipingshan on Hong Kong island, and this area soon became the epicentre of the plague in Hong Kong, where up to 100 people died each day at the peak of the epidemic (Perera 1987). Four months after it had begun, the epidemic was over, but a trickle of cases continued to occur, and the plague reached epidemic proportions again each year, by June or July, throughout the 1890s (Simpson 1902).

Neither the cause of the plague, nor its means of transmission, were yet understood. It was only at the turn of the century, when a Japanese doctor identified the rat-flea as the means of transmission, and research in India identified the plague bacillus as the cause, that the disease was truly understood, and its virtual elimination became possible. But until this time, the population of Hong Kong and of Guangzhou was made desperately anxious as the death rate increased all around them each summer. Victims of the disease tried whatever medicines they could afford, and every conceivable kind of treatment must have been tried by someone. Some plague victims travelled to Guangzhou hoping for better medicine there.[4] The plague also caused a desperate search for cures among those who were not yet bedridden, but suspected or feared they had caught the disease.

Some sought the help of the gods for medical help and for relief from the plague.[5] One way of getting help from the realm of the gods was to ask for special medical prescriptions from the Taoist immortals, who during their earthly lives had supposedly perfected the art of making potions which produce immortality. These prescriptions could be obtained through 'mediums' who regularly received messages from these gods and immortals through a kind of spirit-writing known as *fuji* (Cantonese: *fugei*).

In this form of divination, the god communicates with humans by controlling a stick in the hands of one of his devotees, who writes the god's messages with the stick on a table. Messages from ancestors and illustrious deceased persons could also be received by this method. Special personal qualities are required of the one who is to serve as the channel for the god's messages, however, and few people are thought to have the qualities or the 'inspiration' necessary to do it. Mr Leung was one of those persons. It was during this period that Leung began to receive messages from the god Wong Tai Sin. Apparently, Leung and a group of friends met occasionally in the evening in Guangzhou to engage in *fuji* sessions. This was evidently a common practice among educated persons. There are records of such divination sessions among the educated class as early as the Song dynasty (Chao 1942:13). The literati were intrigued by the opportunity to communicate with military, political, and cultural notables of the recent past, and when the civil service examination system was revived during the Song dynasty, educated persons also increasingly used divination to ask whether they would be successful in the very arduous and difficult examinations, and even to try to find out what questions would be asked in these exams (Jordan and Overmyer 1986:40). At other times, the spirits might be asked to predict one's fate in life, or to heal illness.

Some officials also resorted to such sessions for guidance during times of political stress, and one emperor during the Ming dynasty rewarded or penalized various persons according to the messages produced by his *fuji* team (Chao 1942:11). A viceroy of Guangdong province, who reportedly consulted the spirits through *fuji* during the Second Opium War (1856–60), received a message that the war would end quickly, and later became notorious among his countrymen for his resulting passivity.[6] In short, the practice of *fuji* was not uncommon among officials and the intelligentsia as a way of getting advice or predictions which might help them deal with their problems. (Smith 1991:228–9).

Mr Leung's grandsons believe that it was in 1897 that he and a few of his close friends became the first generation of followers of Wong Tai Sin. They did so because they were impressed with the god's messages — especially the medical prescriptions. It was also during this period that Leung received, by *fuji*, the 'autobiography' of Wong Tai Sin quoted in Chapter 1. The gods eventually dictated that the *fuji* writings should be compiled and published, and sufficient donations were eventually collected to meet expenses. The book, in two volumes, was titled *Jing Mimeng*, which, by its title, called upon the population to '*Awake [from] Illusory Dreams!*'.[7] Mr Leung wrote a preface to one of the volumes, recounting the god's success in curing many people with these prescriptions.

Jing Mimeng, however, contains very little specifically medical material. In common with most other compilations of *fuji* writings published by sectarian groups (see Jordan and Overmyer 1986), its editors were mainly interested in publishing the gods' general pronouncements to the world about morality, virtue, filial piety, and the importance of benevolence and proper conduct. The population were also frequently accused of living in a dreamworld (hence the title) in which they were guided by greed and desire, heedless of the retribution of heaven, which (if they did not listen) would continue to afflict them with plagues and other disasters, and thus 'shock them awake'.

The more personal messages produced in *fuji* sessions are often copied down from the *fuji* records after the session by the followers to whom they are addressed, and we have obtained several manuscripts which include some *fuji* messages dealing with illness (though none earlier than 1913). They are too complex to analyse here, but it is clear from these documents that the gods would frequently 'consult', and call in other gods and spirits in cases of diseases which were especially difficult. The diagnosis often focused on defects of behaviour or character which had to be remedied before a cure could be expected. Mr Leung was without doubt very skillful both in diagnosing and treating illness with the medicines available to him, and in appreciating the illnesses against which these medicines would be helpless. Through him, the gods also expounded frequently on virtue and piety, whenever the followers did not have very specific or pressing questions to ask. It is these pronouncements, addressed often magisterially from the gods to the population at large, which formed the main corpus of *Jing Mimeng*.

The revelations, according to a preface, were received at a shrine called the Shenliutang (Deep-Willow Hall), located at Panyi Pushan (Panyi Bodhi Hill/Mountain). We have not been able to identify this site, but it was probably a private or semi-private house-shrine in, or very near, Guangzhou. Eventually, Leung not only provided prescriptions by *fuji*, but he also convinced his circle of supporters to donate money to provide free medicine to some worshippers after they had received the god's prescriptions. Thus, they would accumulate merit by performing good deeds, as advised by the gods. This must also have helped draw people to the shrine.

For Mr Leung and his friends, the outbreaks of bubonic plague in Guangzhou added extra urgency to their consultations through *fuji* with the supernatural world of gods and spirits, and indeed the earliest *fuji* writings produced within Leung's circle contain a number of references to the epidemic. While Leung evidently had much success with the god's medical diagnoses and prescriptions for more ordinary illnesses, even the gods were frightened by the violence of the plague and the terrible deaths which it caused, and the desperation of the crowds seeking to avoid such a fate. One of the messages, from Wong Tai Sin himself, is surprisingly emotional:

Today crowds of people come to the altar. Today I will have no spare time. When I see the people around the altar I am really frightened. I put my head down and can't help but cry (*Jing Mimeng*, hereafter JM, I:60).[8]

While worshippers clearly wanted cures from the god through *fuji*, the god himself — or his human spokesman, the *fuji*-master — was awed by the plague and not at all confident:

The plague is like an arrow. Once released, it cannot be held back. The plague is like a flood which has overflowed the barriers. It's hopeless to try to stop it (JM, II:12).

But the cause of the plague could be explained. The disaster was not a random act of nature:

[The plague], which produces such a horrifying scene [of crowds of people desperately beseeching the god] is actually caused by the wrong-doing of the people. It is due to their misbehaviour that Heaven sends this kind of epidemic disease to fill up this whole region (JM, I:60).

Wong Tai Sin's messages, received through *fuji*, made this point repeatedly:

Listen, disciples: I have known of these events even before they happened. Such evil will overwhelm the whole of humanity. It all comes from the wrong-doing of the people. . . . I regret to see that the world is becoming immoral. I wonder why people still don't know the proper way to behave. I'm giving you a message about your wrong-doing as clearly as if I were hitting you on the head with a stick, but still you're in a daydream (JM, I, 60–61). (Compare De Groot 1964; 1302–6).

What were these evil deeds? A number of passages identify the kind of immoral behaviour which was causing this disaster. For example:

Nowadays, . . . [even] among brothers there is suspicion and murder. Indecent sexual behaviour, theft, lies, and fraud are common. These acts bring people nearer to death. How can such people pursue immortality? (JM II: Preface).

The smoking of opium was also condemned in *Jing Mimeng*, just as it was also frequently condemned by the gods in other *fuji* revelations produced in Guangdong in the 1890s.[9] The use of *fuji* to produce moralistic writings has been well-described for Taiwan *fuji*-cults by Jordan and Overmyer (1986).

The circle of *fuji* devotees which clustered around Mr Leung was not exceptional. The same forces and cultural tendencies produced a number of other folk-Taoist *fuji*-cults during the 1890s which were quite similar.[10] Leung's group was not the earliest of these (although it may have been one of the first to migrate to Hong Kong).

Reviewing spirit-writing cults in other societies, Jordan and Overmyer (1986:288) suggest that they are especially likely to occur during large-scale social disruptions. Certainly the conditions in late nineteenth-century China were deeply unsettling for many of the country's citizens. Some educated people hoped to import Western science, technology, and ideologies to deal with the country's problems, but many others were committed, as a result of their education and training, to a vision of the classical virtues and of a strong Confucian State. They hoped to bring renewal and recovery to China through a return to the values which, they believed, had once made their country strong, united, and proud. If they also believed that the gods and deified heroes of the past hovered nearby, fretting over the state of the country and eager to call their countrymen back to the glory of the past which they had created, it is hardly surprising that a number of *fuji*-masters were more than eager to serve as their spokesmen.

It is worth noting that in other cultures, shamanism has often provided a way for leaders and would-be leaders to gain authority for their efforts to guide and lead their fellows against the shocks of rapid social change or colonial invasion, and that these shamans typically served as mediums for the pronouncements of illustrious ancestors or culture-heroes (Lewis 1989). There are many points of comparison with the *fuji*-mediums in Guangdong in the 1890s.

While most of the *fuji* material in *Jing Mimeng* does not address the political conditions of the time, some passages show that the *fuji*-master and his circle were deeply concerned to try to generate a spiritual rebirth through a return to traditional morality by each citizen. The gods worry about the country, and Wong Tai Sin is portrayed as a patriot:

> The strong neighbours, Europe and America, look upon China like a tiger. The dismemberment of China will happen soon [if this situation continues]. . . . In the past, various famous men, including Ge Hong, fled to various parts of the country to escape from oppression or to find refuge, but these places are all occupied now by the Europeans and there are no more places for refuge. If all people had in their hearts faithfulness and filial piety, their hearts would be protected [against evil], and thus their bodies, and their homes and families, and thus also finally the State would be saved and China would be a happier land (JM, II: Preface).[11]

There are not many such passages about the political conditions of the time. The *fuji*-master was kept busy with messages directed toward his immediate followers. To provide variety, a large number of gods and famous figures from the past visited the altar. They advised followers according to their particular expertise and character. Some of these figures suggest as much about the audience as about the gods. For example, a famous general lectured the group about how to fight battles and serve the emperor, suggesting that military men were among the audience. Women also attended, and the daughters-in-law were sometimes scolded about mistreatment of their mothers-in-law, while as wives they were advised to be respectful and obedient to their husbands. The deep conservatism of the *fuji*-master is evident in some of these passages.[12]

The *fuji*-master also found it necessary to respond to disturbances among his followers, or around his shrine. Sometimes Wong Tai Sin responded with irritation to visitors who questioned his medical competence or his unexceptional poems, or who alleged that the shrine was not producing real messages from the gods. Many messages from the gods were also directed toward the inner circle of followers — they were exhorted to attend the shrine regularly, and scolded when they stayed away. Leung held their attention for two years with such messages.

By 1899, there were enough followers and patrons that it was decided to set up a temple in a more open area, near the city, so that worshippers could more easily come to visit and petition the god. This was evidently the first free-standing temple to Wong Tai

Sin in Guangdong. It was constructed just across the river from Guangzhou, in a district known as Huadi, in what is now a suburb of Guangzhou called Fangcun.

The First Temple to Wong Tai Sin, in Huadi District, Fangcun

According to a preface in *Jing Mimeng*, this temple was opened in 1899 and was called Pujitan, which means 'the altar (shrine) for providing universal help [to those in need]'. The success of the original shrine, and the demand for prescriptions and messages from the god, had evidently led the gods to transfer their presence to the larger site. The *fuji* operation to obtain medicine prescriptions was transferred to the new shrine, and some herbal medicines were given out free of charge. At some point, a set of fortune-poems and medical prescriptions was compiled which allowed the shrine to provide the god's answers, using fortune-sticks, to a far larger number of worshippers than could be accommodated with the much more demanding *fuji* procedure.

This temple was rebuilt, on a larger scale, in 1904.[13] Interviews with several elderly people who knew the rebuilt temple well indicate that the new site was more than 1 hectare and possibly as large as 2 hectares, with several buildings and interspersed gardens. The buildings included living quarters for temple staff and one or more resident Taoists, and probably a dining hall where vegetarian food was eaten, with quarters for women who prepared this food. Inside the gate, in the temple itself, stood statues to both Buddhist and Taoist deities, with Wong Tai Sin occupying a central position.[14] The statue of Wong Tai Sin was made of clay and covered with gold (possibly painted with gold lacquer).

The location of the temple was — it seems to us — carefully chosen to get the best balance between cost of land and convenience to worshippers. It was across the river from Guangzhou, in an area which was then mostly under cultivation. According to an elderly worker living in the area, most of the visitors came by boat. They landed at a dock or quay on the Huadi River, near where it runs into the Pearl River opposite Guangzhou, and walked up to the temple. The number of visitors was high on the birthday of the god, and one elderly resident remembered that on such occasions a considerable stretch of the riverside around the rear gate of the temple would be clogged with boats.[15] A lane ran from the quay to the main entrance of the temple and was called Ci An Jie (Temple Bank Street). Probably the intention in building the original temple on this site, and in connecting it to the quay on the Huadi River, was not only to draw worshippers from Guangzhou, a short boat ride across the Pearl River, but also to attract some of the people travelling across the Pearl River and then up the Huadi River to the manufacturing centre of Foshan.

The reconstruction of the temple on a much larger scale in 1904 was partly due to a medical 'miracle' accomplished by the temple. The Commander-in-Chief of the provincial naval units, Li Zhun,[16] had consulted a number of doctors in Guangzhou about an eye disease, which his mother had recently contracted, but nobody could cure her. Then he heard that Wong Tai Sin of the Huadi temple was an effective healer. He personally brought his mother to the shrine to ask for a cure. Not long after the medicine was administered, she recovered from the disease. To thank the god, Li Zhun initiated a campaign to rebuild the temple, using his influence to mobilize the merchants and people of Huadi and Guangzhou to donate money for the project.[17] Li Zhun himself was evidently in charge of all the preparations as well as the reconstruction. The approaches to the temple were also improved, and the dirt road leading to the entrance was paved with stones.

But Mr Leung left for his native village sometime during this period, and commenced to find sponsors to build a new temple there. The influence of Mr Leung in the Huadi temple must have been completely overshadowed by Commander Li Zhun and all the merchants he rallied to the task of rebuilding the temple. Indeed, in several passages in *Jing Mimeng*, the god expresses his irritation at proposals to build a new temple, though he stops short of opposing it (JM II:45–6). Perhaps Leung decided to withdraw and start another operation rather than remain and be relegated to the background by the powerful new sponsors. The crowds at the shrine also caused some tension, and the messages on one occasion scolded two followers for shouting at the crowds, and then refusing to come to the shrine the following day. It is interesting to note that some of the followers were pressing for the god's permission to try wielding the *fuji* stick, which the god refused on every occasion with the explanation that only the current *fuji*-master (Leung) had just the right characteristics for the job (JM I:14). Nevertheless, the followers persisted (JM II:69), and Leung may have felt that his control of the group was slipping.

Interestingly, at about the same time that Leung was evidently deciding to return to his village, Wong Tai Sin announced that his task at the temple was now completed and that he would soon leave. He had given his messages to the world, and tried to lead and guide his followers and to save mankind from sin. The heavenly Jade Emperor, who authorized Wong Tai Sin's return to earth to help save the world in 1897, now called him back to heaven three years after he had first begun to speak to them through *fuji* (JM II: 56–7). Wong Tai Sin's followers asked him not to leave. But he must leave, he announced, and they must accept this. A passage refers to the tears of Wong Tai Sin as he leaves them (JM II: 58), which may also be the tears of his followers, and perhaps of Leung himself. In any case, Leung, the *fuji*-master, thus elegantly departed from the group on the heels of the god, making subsequent revelations from Wong Tai Sin all but impossible, and preserving his status as the god's sole spokesman.

Political developments may also have influenced Leung to leave Guangzhou. According to his grandsons, Leung finally quit his government post because he and many others had lost confidence in the Qing government, and sensed that the dynasty was about to fall. He also is said to have received a message by *fuji* that there would soon be great turmoil in China and in Guangzhou. The prediction was certainly accurate. Before following Leung back to his village, we will relate the subsequent fate of the Huadi temple, and of its successor built nearby.

Temples and The Revolution of 1911

The revolution of 1911 brought to power a group of revolutionaries hostile to folk-Taoist temples such as the one in Fangcun. There had been some attempt to control folk temples, and some conversions of such temples to secular uses, in the late Qing period (Yang 1961:325, 368–9; Duara 1991:75–6), but the assault on folk religion really began in earnest only after the Republican revolution. Viewing folk religion as full of useless superstitions which retarded modernization, many officials of the new regime moved against local temples. The earliest and some of the most aggressive actions were taken in Guangzhou, where in 1911 some Chinese Christians smashed shrines and decapitated statues in the temple of the city god and in several other major temples in the city, dumping some of the statues in the river (Rhoads 1975:255).

Elsewhere in China, though to different degrees depending on the local officials, temples were converted to schools, offices, and other secular uses (Yang 1961:326,329; Esherick 1976:246; Franck 1925:258). In Guangzhou, there were several waves of such confiscations in the decades following the revolution of 1911. We know that in addition to their general hostility towards folk religion, some Republican officials were also hostile to the practice of some temple-keepers of accepting money in return for providing medical prescriptions from the gods.[18] This, it seems, was precisely what the temple-keepers at the Fangcun temple were doing. Thus, it is not surprising that the Wong Tai Sin temple in Fangcun did not escape the attentions of the authorities during these campaigns.

The Fate of the First Temple to Wong Tai Sin

The temple was confiscated by the municipal government during the first decade of the new republic. According to Mr Leung's grandsons, the military commander of Guangzhou confiscated the temple some time prior to 1920 so that the site could be used for the construction of an orphanage. Lars Ragvald was told in Fangcun that this event occurred around 1919. According to this account, the mayor at that time belonged to the radical faction of the Nationalist Party (Guomindang) and took strong action against traditional religion. The temple, however, was not immediately demolished.[19] In 1922, the head of the Guangzhou police district, Chen Jinghua, banned the worship of the god, and the gold-coloured statues were removed from the temple, broken in pieces, and thrown among the bamboo trees.[20] An orphanage was built on the site using contributions from overseas Chinese in Thailand, but was later closed due to lack of funds. The buildings survived until the arrival of the Japanese armies which captured Guangzhou in 1938. During the confusion of the Japanese occupation, some local people apparently used the opportunity to tear down the remaining buildings on the site to obtain construction material.[21] The Japanese army also destroyed some of the buildings along the river to build a fort and some blockhouses. After 1941, when guerilla activity in the area increased, they destroyed many other buildings around the fort to provide better defence against attacks on land or along the river. They may have used the half-empty area where the temple once stood as a headquarters for their military police. Elderly residents say that many people were executed in the area during the war.

After the war, the orphanage was rebuilt by the municipal government. Although almost nothing of the old temple remained, some local people continued to go there to burn incense for many years after 1949. But by the early 1970s, this became impossible: a coffin factory was built on the grounds of the former orphanage, enclosed by a wall around the buildings.[22] Only workers, cadres, and people on official visits to the coffin factory were allowed inside the gate. By the 1980s, only a few elderly people in the area still remembered the old temple.

A few pieces of the temple had survived the destruction. For instance, the pillars which once held up the gate of the temple had been left on the ground and eventually buried under earth and debris after the old buildings were torn down, but they were unearthed during the construction of the coffin factory in the early 1970s. When Lars Ragvald arrived, he found these pillars neatly arranged on the ground for the workers to sit on. In another corner of the factory compound there were remnants of the portal and also parts of pillars carved over with well-made and attractive ornamentation. In 1985, on Ragvald's first visit to the site, nobody in the factory knew that these relics had once been part of a Wong Tai Sin temple.

By 1987, everyone in the factory knew. Ragvald's visit in 1985 had apparently made the local cultural bureau aware of the location of this temple.[23] The visit also led to an article in a local newspaper about Wong Tai Sin and his connection to the site of the factory. The workers of the factory proudly showed Ragvald this article in 1987. The factory manager also appeared to be pleased at the thought that the temple might be the original site of the successful and famous Hong Kong cult of Wong Tai Sin. He and many of the workers seemed to think that if such a relationship could be established it would help them in selling more coffins to Chinese abroad. However, up to 1991, no attempt had been made to restore any part of the temple, or to do anything with the few remaining pieces of it lying around inside the grounds of the coffin factory. While these few remaining traces of the origins of the cult of Wong Tai Sin in Guangzhou have survived (barely), the god is no longer worshipped there.

Before becoming extinct in this area, the cult of Wong Tai Sin was briefly revived in the 1930s, in a second temple built in Fangcun not far from the first one.

The Second Temple to Wong Tai Sin in Fangcun

In 1934, more than ten years after the destruction of the first temple and the conversion of the site into an orphanage, a second, smaller Wong Tai Sin temple was built about half a kilometre further inland from the river.[24] This second temple was made possible by a change in government, which brought to power a young general who became, for a few years, the warlord of Guangdong. His name was Chen Jitang, and his wife was apparently a believer in Wong Tai Sin.

Chen, a career military officer in the Nationalist armies, had come to power in 1929 as the military Commander of the region, and quickly consolidated his political power as well, ruling Guangdong almost as an autonomous region with only loose ties to the Nationalist government in Nanjing. Unlike the first generation of civilian revolutionaries, he was not hostile to traditional religious practice. Indeed, he believed in fortune-telling, palmistry, and geomancy, and according to one report, 'before deciding on a senior appointment he would have the candidate's physiognomy studied by an expert to see if the man would be reliable' (Boorman and Howard 1967:162). Chen also courted the support of the many believers upset at the destruction of temples by supporting their restoration.[25] Evidently many temples were revived in the early 1930s as a result of this policy. Chen Jitang's wife, Mo Xiuying, who was a believer, provided the money for the second temple and employed the artisans who built it. She is fondly remembered for this by elderly people who still live in the area. It was much smaller than the first temple: only about 0.2 to 0.25 of a hectare, with three low buildings. At the entrance there had been an inscription identifying the temple as the Jinhua Fenyuan (the court or sub-hall of Jinhua, the mountain where Wong Cho Ping had become a saint). There was also a large portrait of the warrior god who protects the Buddha.[26] A statue of Wong Tai Sin, about 2 metres high, had stood in the centre of the the main hall, flanked by statues of Wei Zheng[27] and Lu Dongbin. Like the statues in the old temple, these statues were made of clay and painted with gold lacquer. This duplicated the arrangement and appearance of the statues in the first Wong Tai Sin temple.

There was a dispensary at the temple from which medicine was administered according to the god's advice, received through divination. There was also a herbal doctor who attended at the temple.[28] The herbal medicines came from a medicine shop in Guangzhou. There was also a well nearby called the 'Saint Wong Well', which was supposed to possess healing power. Local residents interviewed by Lars Ragvald claimed that some people were healed by water from this well.

The temple evidently thrived during the 1930s, and conducted major celebrations of the birthdays of Wong Tai Sin and (on a smaller scale) of Lu Dongbin. For Wong Tai Sin's birthday, large numbers of people would gather at the temple. From early morning till late at night worshippers would chant scriptures and have vegetarian meals. Buddhist monks and nuns and Taoist priests were invited to set up altars and hold their ceremonies for seven days and seven nights. There would even be performances of Cantonese opera. Elderly local residents recall that people from other parts of Guangdong province and from Hong Kong and Macau would come for these ceremonies.

The Fate of the Second Temple to Wong Tai Sin in Fangcun

Chen Jitang lost power and was forced to flee not long after the completion of the new temple, and his policy of supporting temples was stopped. However, the Wong Tai Sin temple built by his wife survived. Japanese occupation of Guangzhou in 1938 did not greatly affect the temple. The Buddhist statues in the temple and the Buddhist warrior god at the gate linked the temple to a venerable religious tradition which the Japanese respected. People continued to worship there, and indeed, when a cholera epidemic broke out in Fangcun in 1940, the temple provided medical services and offered some free medicine to the poor, while the Taoists prayed to the gods for help. This activity produced a favourable impression among local residents, which they still recalled nearly fifty years later. The civil-war period in the late 1940s adversely affected the temple's operations, but worship there continued, and the people in charge of the temple remained in contact with the Wong Tai Sin temples in Mr Leung's home village and in Hong Kong.

The Communist victory in 1949, however, doomed this second Fangcun temple. It was much too recent to be worth preserving as a historic site, as with other temples in the city. Hence, it was vulnerable and without protection when the new Communist

Map 1 Wong Tai Sin Sites Near Guangzhou, China (Rengang, Fangcun, Chishi Yan, Mt. Luofu)

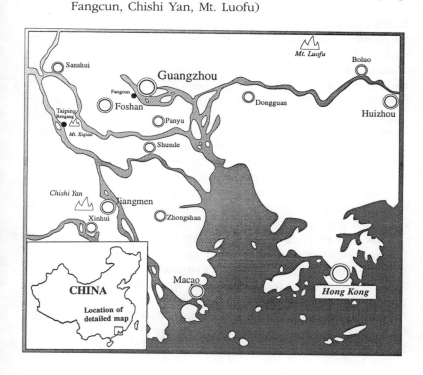

government began to move against temples and religious organizations. Worse, it was closely associated with a well-known Nationalist warlord and anti-communist. In the early 1950s, then, the temple suffered the fate of many other temples during that period: it was closed and confiscated by the government, the statues were torn down, and the buildings converted into a factory and dwellings.[29] The Saint Wong Well was filled in by the government in 1957. In 1985, people in the area, including some of the people who now live in these buildings, remembered the temple well, but no one worshipped Wong Tai Sin openly.

The third of the three major temples to Wong Tai Sin which once existed in China, and the one which lasted the longest of the three before it too was destroyed, was the one which Mr Leung built in his home village.

The Wong Tai Sin Temple in Rengang Village

Leung had left his job with the Customs Service and returned to his native village, named Rengang, located a few kilometres to the west of Xiqiao Mountain. It consists of two hamlets separated by a hillock, with only the one facing toward Xiqiao Mountain inhabited by the Leungs. In this village, in 1901, Leung commenced to build a second Wong Tai Sin temple (the first being the temple built in Fangcun several years earlier). According to villagers interviewed by Lars Ragvald in 1985 and in 1987, this new temple, which was named the Puqing Tan (or 'universal blessing/joy altar'), covered an area of more than 1 hectare, and consisted of six or seven buildings with interspersed gardens, with an artificial lake in front of the temple. It was several years before all of these structures were completed. Mr Leung supervised the work, and outside craftsmen were employed on the project.

Some very rich people who had been cured had provided money for the construction of these buildings. A large sum of money was donated, for instance, by a rich man from Gangtou village[30] in Sanshui county, who had been cured. The land on which the temple stood apparently included some land owned by Mr Leung's family. According to villagers, some further land was provided by other local families of Leungs to make up the large plot needed for all of these buildings.

The building at the front of the site, facing the lake, was the main shrine of the temple, and like the Huadi temple it contained a gold-covered statue of Wong Tai Sin. This statue stood alone in the main shrine room (unlike in the two Guangzhou temples, in both of which Wong Tai Sin was flanked by statues of Lu Dongbin and Wei Zheng). In the rear part of the building, on the second floor, there was also a small statue of Lu Dongbin. Near this building there were five other buildings including a medicine dispensary, a Guanyin shrine, and a shrine to Wong Tai Sin's parents.[31]

Interestingly, and in sharp contrast to the two Fangcun temples, there were no Buddhist deities except Guanyin at the Rengang temple. Perhaps the operators of the Fangcun temples felt the need to give their temples added respectability by including gods from the venerable Buddhist tradition; this might give the temple some protection from the hostility of some authorities and intellectuals toward folk Taoist temples and cults.[32] In Rengang, Leung and his associates in the temple project may have felt less need for these

Buddhist 'guardians'. In any case, it is clear that this temple was much more thoroughly focused on Wong Tai Sin than were the two Fangcun temples. The function of the temple as an outlet for the purveyance of herbal medicines was also more prominently featured in the arrangement of the buildings.

There was a large medicine shop or dispensary near the temple entrance, containing a statue of Wong Cho Ping's brother, Wong Cho Hei. Some of the medicine was given free of charge to poor people, but those who could afford it were expected to pay. There was no standard fee, and everyone paid as much as they thought proper. The medicine was not produced in the village, but was brought in from outside and was considered to be of good quality.[33] To find out what medicine should be used to cure a particular illness, the prediction stick method was used. Numbered sticks in a container were shaken until one dropped on the ground. Each number corresponded to a different prescription slip, and hence the numbered stick represented the god's prescription for the petitioner's medical problems.

There was a pavilion for the interpreting of fortune sticks. Leung, by this time, had compiled a complete set of fortune-poems and of medical prescriptions, and worshippers could now obtain the god's advice about their problems and their illnesses simply by shaking out a fortune stick and consulting the designated oracle in the book. Fortunately, the book which contained these prescriptions has survived in the possession of the Leung family, and we can examine the prescriptions which were provided.

The prescriptions are grouped into five categories (for men; for women; for children; for eyes; and for external ills). The worshipper specifies the category, and the god supplies the appropriate remedy. Many of the remedies are straightforward: take three measures of these ingredients, two measures of those, boil together, and drink the mixture.[34] Sometimes the prescription adds additional advice and diagnosis — for example: 'this illness might seem trivial, but you must be careful' — but the remedies are within the realm of the traditional herbal potions, which could be effective without any magical or supernatural actions and could thus be considered as 'secular' medicines.[35]

Some of the remedies seem to extend into semi-magical realms, even if natural ingredients are used. The ingredients might seem ordinary, but a special mystical property is added by their association with the god. For example, several remedies (such as number

38 in the eye category) advise taking 'Puqing tea', which was named
after the temple. Although it was ordinary tea, it acquired its healing properties by being 'blessed' by the god.[36]

In other remedies, the ingredients are not ordinary, and probably derive some of their potency from their extraordinary origins
or character.[37] For example, number 99 in the category of remedies for women says, 'there is some danger [in your illness], but
you can be saved; you are trustful. Take this medicine and you
will be cured: a cup of breast milk, a little urine of children, along
with five measures of [a medicine is specified], mix together, and
drink the mixture'. Number 71 in the children category advises,
'[procure a] bat, remove the organs, and mix with eggshell. This
will clear the "hot air". Each morning, take three measures of this
mixture, with congee [rice soup]'.

Sometimes the prescription-message acknowledges that the worshipper will find the ingredients extraordinary. For example, number 91 in the 'external' category says 'Your illness is strange, but
my prescription is even more strange: take some fresh cow dung,
add three measures of eggshell and one measure of white fungus.
Drink this together with alcohol, and you will know its power'.
(The power of such a mixture is beyond doubt).

Some of the prescriptions included drawings of charms, which
were to be worn (number 1 in the children category), thus protecting the wearer against evil forces which could cause illness,
or were to be copied onto paper and then burned to ash and the
ash ingested (number 64 in the children category). The remedy
typically specified the colours to be used in the charm (red ink on
yellow paper).

In some prescriptions, the remedy directs the patient to ingest
incense ash. For example, number 48 (for men) says: 'Take a cup
of clear water to the altar, drop [incense] ash [into the water], take
this home, and drink it'. This practice is still carried out by many
believers.

There are also some prescriptions which specify that a greater
adherence to religious duty is needed. Thus, number 3 in the children category tells the parent: 'you do not understand this child's
sickness. You are very anxious, so pray to the Monkey god (Chai
Tin Tai Sing) immediately. The day when you do good . . . the condition of the body will become peaceful again'.

Finally, the gods were quite capable of dismissing the worshipper's request for healing. For example, number 12 (eye category)

says, 'you cannot ask for the prescription because your heart is not right. You must repent and then you will be given a prescription. [For now] no prescription'. Even more blunt is number 73, also in the eye category: 'I know what is your intention in coming here. You want to test me. This is blasphemy! You want to see if I am true and powerful, and only then will you put your trust in me. Go away! Go away!' We must not assume that either the worshippers, or the traditional practitioners whom the worshippers consulted at the temple, would have followed such prescriptions blindly. During the process of consultation, prescriptions may be tailored to the worshipper's particular condition.

In any case, there were about ten people working at the temple, some of whom interpreted these prescriptions in terms of the precise medicinal combinations required. Local villagers assured Lars Ragvald that the Taoists who interpreted the prescriptions were quite skilled at recognizing common diseases.

Large numbers of people from the surrounding area came to the temple — mostly from northern Shunde, Nanhai county, and Gaoming and Heshan counties on the other side of the West River. These people came to worship, petition the god, and frequently, to get herbal medicines. The birthday of the god was an occasion for major ceremonies at the temple, but there were no Cantonese operas performed in connection with these ceremonies. It was not a village festival, and the temple was not a communal institution.

Indeed, like the Hong Kong temple, this village temple accepted private memberships which entitled members to special privileges, probably including messages by *fuji* rather than by fortune sticks. In other words, the member could obtain a somewhat more personal message from the god, and perhaps also the feeling of receiving a little more of the god's time and attention than would be available to non-members. Membership privileges also no doubt included special attention from the resident Taoists, and the right to don Taoist robes and participate in ceremonies. The membership fee was a donation of about 30 kilograms of rice.

During his first years back in his home village, and about the time that the construction of the new temple was completed (1903–4), Leung produced a new volume of *fuji* revelations and commentaries. Titled *Xing Shi Yaoyan*, or *Important Words to Awaken the World*, this volume continued many of the themes of *Jing Mimeng*. There were some interesting differences also. *Xing Shi Yaoyan* is more didactic, and addresses the world somewhat more impersonally. The gods do not express their emotions, or scold particular worshippers, or converse among themselves, as much as in *Jing Mimeng*.[38] It is very likely that Leung was under much less pressure to produce interesting and captivating messages for a circle of intensely interested followers watching every motion of his stick. Now he could reflect, and compose his messages without needing also to entertain.

In addition, the writer of these messages from the gods was also prepared to be much more openly critical of the military leaders. By 1903, Leung had watched China humiliated by foreign military powers after the so-called Boxer rebellion, and his revelations (from the spirits of famous generals) condemn the generals' lassitude and corruption, their padded regiments in which they took the pay of non-existent soldiers, and their lives of leisure. Perhaps he could not have been so outspoken while performing in or near Guangzhou, and with military figures occasionally in attendance at his shrine.

There are also several passages inserted by other followers, one of whom, for example, asks Wong Tai Sin whether he can contribute his reflections to the manuscript. The god generously agrees. The follower then tries to the explain the severity of the epidemic in Guangzhou by saying that the city is especially wicked, a place where 'the virtues of courtesy, wisdom, and benevolence are replaced by money, desire, and corruption'; people in Guangdong, he says, are generally discontented with their lot and avid for luxury, but Guangzhou, near the coast and more open to evil influences than the rest of the province, is the worst, and hence heaven ordered the worst plague for that city (*Xing Shi Yaoyan*:114). His view expresses what might be the disgust of the rural gentry, schooled in the traditional virtues, at the free-wheeling ways of the capital.[39] If Leung had been able to remain in the countryside, his literary output, already prodigious, might have expanded further, with new themes and more analytical critiques unhampered by the need to personalize messages and create conversations among the gods in order to hold the attention of patrons. However, his life in Rengang did not remain peaceful. The revolution of 1911 soon produced convulsions which rapidly extended outward from the cities, reaching even Rengang village.

During and after the revolution of 1911, conditions became chaotic in parts of the countryside, and there was a great increase in lawlessness, with armed groups connected with various factions, or operating independently, looting and extorting money wherever they could do so with relative impunity. All wealthy families were potential targets of such extortions. The Rengang temple had been prospering, and Leung was, in any case, probably wealthy from his years in the Customs Service. So it is not surprising that he also became a victim. According to family stories passed on to his grandsons, Leung was repeatedly harassed by 'bad elements' in the village, who attempted to extort money from him through threats and intimidation.

He may also have been frightened by the recent movement of hostile armies through this area, particularly in 1913, during the struggle for power which followed the revolution.[40] Leung must also have been badly hurt when the value of paper money plummeted during the political crisis and its aftermath in 1913 and 1914.[41] During this period, 'thousands of well-to-do people flocked to Hong Kong and Macau for safety, while business in Canton came to a virtual standstill' (Rhoads 1975:261). If Leung himself did not make this trip, he would certainly have heard about the much greater economic and financial stability of the colony from acquaintances who did go there and later returned to Guangdong; he probably began to think about a possible move to Hong Kong.

In any case, unsettled by the political and economic chaos and prompted by the threats of local extortionists, Leung consulted Wong Tai Sin for advice through *fuji*. The message which he received said that he should go south to set up a new altar to the god. So, in late 1915, he packed up a portrait of Wong Tai Sin and moved to Hong Kong. The Rengang temple continued to operate in his absence. Leung returned to the village in 1919, and again in 1921, after he had helped set up the new temple to the god in Hong Kong. He died in Rengang village in 1921.

The Fate of the Wong Tai Sin Temple in Rengang Village

In the 1930s the village had a population of about 250 people. Many of the adults had become members, along with some people from the adjoining hamlet. Altogether there had apparently been several hundred members, with more than 100 from neighbouring villages in the Xiqiao area and a similar number from Gaoming county across the river. (Since there are Leungs living on the Gaoming side of the river, and they are related to the Leungs living in the Xiqiao area which includes Rengang, it is possible that the visitors to the temple from Gaoming had become aware of the shrine through their Xiqiao relatives.) Elderly residents of the village interviewed by Lars Ragvald in 1991 recalled that the temple had flourished for a time in the 1930s. One of these villagers claimed that they had visited the temple, and that people had come from across the river, because Wong Tai Sin was reputed to be powerful as a healer and could protect their health. It seems that the god was still seen primarily as a divine medical practitioner, although the god's predictions about other matters were also sought. In any case, elderly villagers remembered only one fortune-teller at the temple, whose table was set up near the entrance as in most other temples in the region.

Up to 1949, the Rengang temple maintained contact with the Hong Kong Wong Tai Sin temple, which was then still managed by Mr Leung's son, and at least ten people from the Rengang group of believers would go to Hong Kong each year for ceremonies at the Hong Kong temple. Villagers in Rengang believe that some money was collected in Hong Kong and brought back to the village for further work on the Rengang temple in the decades after its construction. This seems plausible, since the Rengang temple was still the oldest and largest surviving temple to the god Wong Tai Sin. The new Hong Kong temple was still only an 'offshoot' of the main temple back in the village.

During the Japanese occupation of Guangdong in the late 1930s and early 1940s, however, the Rengang temple started to decay. Food was scarce in many areas, and many people in the countryside who had once patronized temples could no longer afford to do so. Also, public order broke down and people from the village started stealing parts of the temple to sell. The temple survived the Japanese occupation, but like the second Fangcun temple, it fell victim to the anti-religious policies of the Communists after 1949.

The temple was closed and the smaller buildings demolished during the government's 'campaign against superstition' in 1958.[42] Many of the bricks were apparently saved and used in building a shoe factory near the entrance to the village. Evidently, the destruction was completed a decade later during the Cultural Revolution, when a large number of temples — as many as 60 per cent of the remaining temples in Guangdong province[43] — were sacked or destroyed by zealous Red Guards. Mr Leung's grandsons believe, and local villagers have confirmed, that what was left of the temple was destroyed about 1967. The villagers remember that the main building was smashed with hammers. Some furniture and possibly some pillars from the temple survived and were used in other buildings, but the temple itself was completely destroyed. On the site, there are now only fields covered with stands of sugar cane and other crops.

However, there are still a few pieces of the temple lying around on the ground. During our visit to the village in 1987, the villagers showed us where these pieces lay. One decorated slab of stone was still lying in the weeds at the edge of the sugar-cane field near where the temple once stood. A villager related that by the time the demolition team had knocked down the last of the temple structures, they were too tired to carry the slab away. Since nobody wanted it for other construction, they left it on the ground. Another discarded pillar lay in a bamboo thicket nearby. A piece of furniture from the temple also survived: a chest of drawers with the name of the temple inscribed on both of its doors. In 1985, during Lars Ragvald's first visit, this chest was in the management office of the shoe factory which had been built near the village using bricks from the temple. But the most striking relic of the temple lay at the entrance to the village — a slab of stone some 3 metres long and half a metre wide, lying face down on the ground and partially covered with dirt and weeds. It had been the headstone above the entrance to the temple, and was still intact. On the slab, inscribed in relief in large characters, were the words 'Red Pine Wong Tai Sin Temple' with the date of construction (1901) inscribed in smaller characters. It is remarkable that this large slab of stone had been preserved when the rest of the temple had been smashed and carted away. Lying face down, it showed nothing which could offend passing cadres. Indeed, the villagers could point to it as evidence of their zeal in following the policy of eliminating feudal superstition. But we noted that after lifting the stone slab to show us the inscription, the villagers carefully placed straw under it before turning it face down again. The memory of the temple had survived in the village, and the elements of the cult seemed to await only a propitious time to be reconstituted once again into an active shrine to the god Wong Tai Sin. We suspected that the shrine would eventually be rebuilt.

Why Wong Cho Ping?

Although we managed to find answers to many of our questions about the origins and fate of the cult of Wong Tai Sin in Guangdong, one obvious question has not yet been addressed: why did Leung

Yan Ngam make contact with Wong Cho Ping, of all the possible Taoist saints and immortals who might have spoken to Leung through the *fuji* procedure? We know that Leung did not receive messages only from Wong Cho Ping, but also from a number of other gods and saints. Why did he pluck Wong Cho Ping from the obscurity of the old textbooks, bringing his long silent voice into the midst of the seances attended by Leung's friends in Guangzhou, and why, once Wong Cho Ping began to speak through Leung, did Wong become the centre of a new cult?

For the original group of believers in the 1890s, the reason for Wong Tai Sin's appearance was to save mankind from folly and sin. He had told them so in his *fuji* messages. For the secular social scientist, an answer drawn from the mind of a god is not quite satisfactory. As an alternative, the historian or the anthropologist or the sociologist would begin by looking for antecedents of the cult in the surrounding society. As far as we know, there was no cult devoted to this god in Guangdong province prior to 1897: no worshippers, no temples, no sacred texts, no teachers expounding the god's doctrines or miracles. Why, suddenly, did Leung begin to write messages from this god? If we suggest that Leung 'chose' Wong Cho Ping, we must look for an explanation for this choice. There are several possibilities: it is remotely possible that Wong Cho Ping had been known or venerated in certain circles in the region for many generations. We have found no concrete evidence to support this. However, Wong (1985) notes that the Ming dynasty official Wong Gung Fu (1573–1657), who lived for a time in the Xinhui area south of Xiqiao, had written a poem mentioning Wong Cho Ping. The possible influence of this poem on later generations of literati in this region is worth mentioning.

Wong Gung Fu, a native of Duruan village in Xinhui, had held several high positions during the reign of the last Ming emperor, and had fought the peasant rebellions in central China. Only when the dynasty was collapsing did he retire for a while to his home village. When the Manchu troops reached Guangdong he took a prominent part in the resistance. During his brief retirement he lived in a cave in a narrow valley, on or near a hill in the Guifeng moutains in Xinhui called Yangshikeng, or 'Sheep Stone Pit', so-named because it was thought to look like a flock of sheep. He is reported to have renamed the hill where he lived with the more poetic Chishi Yan: 'The Crag of Shouting [at the sheep]', evidently referring to the miracle in which Wong Cho Ping called to a flock of boulders, turning them into sheep. Wong Gung Fu may have encountered the legend of Wong Cho Ping years earlier, when he lived far to the north.

During his term of service as a Ming official, Wong Gung Fu had once been stationed in Pucheng in the northernmost corner of Fujian province, not far from Jinhua Mountain where Wong Cho Ping had become a saint, and where Wong Cho Ping was evidently still venerated in Wong Gung Fu's time. The people in Pucheng must have been familiar with the gods of Jinhua, and Wong Gung Fu may have become interested in the god at that time. There was apparently no shrine to Wong Cho Ping in the Guifeng mountains, nor any records of worship of Wong Cho Ping in that area. (There is now a shrine on the mountain to Wong Tai Sin, but it was built very recently with Hong Kong money: see Chapter 7). However, the references to Cho Ping in Wong Gung Fu's poem may have kept the memory of Wong Cho Ping alive in the region. Wong Gung Fu became famous as a patriot for his participation in the battles against the invading Manchu armies at the end of the Ming period, and there is a memorial hall to him on the mountain. His life and works are thus well-known to scholars in the area. His poem mentioning Wong Cho Ping was eventually inscribed on a rock on the mountain. The Chishi Yan is still considered to be one of the scenic spots of the Xinhui area, and its name contains a veiled reference to Wong Cho Ping which may have helped to sustain some interest in him in Xinhui. However, there is a gap of about 250 years between the time of Wong Gung Fu and the time of Leung Yan Ngam, and there is apparently no record of worship or veneration of Wong Cho Ping in the Xinhui region during this period. Some worshippers early in the twentieth century came to the Rengang temple from Gaoming and Heshan counties, not far from Xinhui county, and further careful investigations in these counties across the West River from Rengang might uncover some traces of Wong Cho Ping during the period between Wong Gung Fu and the late nineteenth century. More likely, they would turn up nothing at all.

It is also possible that there was some kind of minor worship of Wong Cho Ping in Leung's home village prior to his departure for Guangzhou in the 1880s to take up his post in the Customs Service. One of the stories which Lars Ragvald was told in Leung's village in 1985 was that there had been a scroll depicting Wong Cho Ping, hanging in a small second-floor room next to the gate of the village even before the new Wong Tai Sin temple was built in 1901. It had been there 'for a long time'. The scroll was considered powerful, and therefore many people came to see it (though only men were allowed to climb up to the little room to view the scroll).

The structure which contained this room was a type of shrine called a Wenchangge, meaning something like 'Pavilion of bright/ prosperous education'. The Wenchangge is usually built like a gatehouse or small pagoda at the entrance to a village. Indeed, the villagers simply called it 'the gatehouse'. Such shrines were common in Guangdong (there is a Wenchangge on Xiqiao Mountain, not far from the village). This type of shrine is normally dedicated to the civil god Wenchang. The phrase 'Wenchangge' was originally another name for Wenquxing, referring to a constellation comprising the upper six stars of the Big Dipper which exerts particular influence on literary geniuses. Wenquxing was later worshipped by Taoists as the god in charge of academic degree and official rank. In other words, there was a shrine in Leung's village which suggested a local devotion to the aspirations of scholars, literati, and would-be officials. Inside this shrine was a scroll depicting Wong Cho Ping. Wong may therefore have been seen as a figure able to help scholars and would-be officials.

We know that Leung was well educated enough to achieve a post in the Customs Service at a young age. We know that would-be officials trying to pass the civil service examinations often resorted to the *fuji* procedure for advice. We might speculate that in Rengang some of these *fuji* procedures elicited advice from Wong Cho Ping. Leung would undoubtedly have attended such sessions, and learned about Wong Cho Ping and his help and advice for people like Mr Leung. Perhaps his success in getting the post in Guangzhou had already given him a sense of obligation to this Taoist saint. Perhaps Leung turned to him again for advice during the plagues and political troubles of the 1890s?

The problem with this account is that nobody in the village could have any direct knowledge that the scroll of Wong had hung in the room above the village gate as early as the 1880s, before Leung left for Guangzhou. Further, Lars Ragvald was told in 1987 that Leung had actually brought the scroll to the village himself. If it hung in a room above the village gate before the temple was built in Rengang in 1901, it might have been placed there only a few years earlier. In other words, the story that the scroll had hung there for a long time, and was there before the temple was built, may only tell us that Leung returned to the village occasionally from Guangzhou, and had set up a small shrine to the god in the village after the founding of the first temple to Wong in Guangzhou in 1899. Only when he quit his job in Guangzhou and moved his residence to Rengang, did he commence to build a major temple near the village. This strikes us as a plausible explanation for what Ragvald was told by the elderly villagers.

We are inclined, then, to be cautiously skeptical about the idea that Wong Cho Ping was worshipped for a long time in Leung's home village or in this region prior to Leung's introduction of the cult in Guangzhou in 1897. It is at least as likely that he started the cult himself in Guangzhou and imported it back to Rengang. This still leaves us with the problem of explaining Leung's choice of Wong Cho Ping.

Wong Cho Ping's life was recounted first by the famous Taoist author Ge Hong, in his fourth-century work *Shenxian zhuan*, or *Biographies of Immortals*. The account of the god's life on earth as a human which is used in the main Wong Tai Sin temple in Hong Kong was clearly taken from Ge Hong's book, or from one of the later works which reproduced Ge Hong's version. Any literate, earnest Taoist living in Guangzhou would have had access to Ge Hong's book. However, Wong Cho Ping is given no special attention among the more than 80 Taoist saints whose biographies are sketched by Ge Hong. What would make Leung pay special attention to Wong Cho Ping? There are several possibilities:

First, it is interesting to note that Wong Cho Ping was included, 600 years after the time of Ge Hong, in a short encyclopedia called the *Shilei fu* (*Rhapsodies on [one hundred] Subjects*), which was compiled during the tenth century CE by Wu Shu (947–1002). The book consists of 100 rhapsodies on subjects ranging from heaven and the seasons to insects and plants. It also contains a commentary which quotes from a wide range of early literature, with many extracts being drawn from works which are now rare. The passage on Wong Cho Ping briefly summarized Ge Hong's account of the hermit who turned rocks into sheep.[44] Because of its concise form, the *Shilei fu* experienced considerable popularity among candidates within the imperial examination system. It would have been procured and read by many aspiring literati, and it is probably through this work, rather than Ge Hong's writings, that Wong Cho Ping became widely known among Chinese intellectuals of the Song, Yuan, and Ming dynasties.

A number of poems dating from the Song period also refer to Wong Cho Ping and were preserved in local histories, and in accounts by various writers of their travels in the area where Wong Cho Ping is supposed to have lived (see Wong 1985). No doubt some of these poets had become aware of Wong Cho Ping through the *Shilei fu*.

Wong Cho Ping's visibility to intellectuals was perhaps further increased in the twelfth and thirteenth centuries, when several Southern Song emperors were reported to have visited Jinhua Mountain or to have bestowed titles on Wong Cho Ping and his brother (Wong 1985).[45] The first of these emperors, Shaoxing (1131–62), had been forced to abandon the areas north of the Yangzi River after the Jurchen tribes sacked the original capital, and he established his temporary new capital in Hangzhou. He found himself in what is now Zhejiang province (indeed, not far from Jinhua Mountain), where a local cult devoted to Wong Cho Ping already existed. Evidently there was a temple to Wong and his brother in the area (Wong 1985). Wong Cho Ping was a local saint who had gained recognition in the already famous writings of Ge Hong. The new emperor may have found it expedient to bestow imperial favour on this local cult in order to build ties to the local population whose support he needed while he consolidated his regime. Perhaps he also hoped to prolong his life by praying for blessings on the mountain. He did not long survive the establishment of the new capital. Two later emperors who bestowed titles on Wong Cho Ping and his brother (in 1189 and 1262) probably also had a narrowly political motive: to curry favour with the local population by giving official State recognition to their religious icons.[46] Other local gods or goddesses have benefited from similar motives.[47]

The result of this attention to Wong Cho Ping by an encyclopedist, by poets, and by the imperial court is that Wong passed out of the Taoist literature and entered the broader historical and cultural record. The Southern Song was an extremely important era in the cultural history of China because of the flourishing of painting, poetry, and historiography which occurred during this period, and any well-educated person in nineteenth-century China would necessarily have become well-versed in Song history and culture. Perhaps it was through such studies that Leung first encountered Wong Cho Ping. It is also likely that Leung read the original account in Ge Hong, even if his interest in Wong Cho Ping was perhaps stimulated initially by the attention to Wong in other sources from the Song period.[48] Perhaps there is a better answer to the question of why Leung 'chose' Wong Cho Ping, but we have not found it. (Or perhaps, as believers assert, it was not Leung Yan Ngam who chose Wong Cho Ping, but Wong Cho Ping who chose Leung Yan Ngam).

In any case, Wong Cho Ping passed into oblivion in China within 70 years of the time he first began delivering his messages to the small group of anxious intellectuals in Guangzhou in the 1890s. By the 1960s, the cult of Wong Tai Sin had been completely crushed and dissipated inside China. No trace of open worship occurred, and no temples remained standing. Only the 'offshoot' in Hong Kong survived. To its history, and to the reasons for its eventual great success in Hong Kong, we now turn.

3　The Refugee God in Hong Kong

THE cult of Wong Tai Sin which had begun in the 1890s in Guangzhou, flourished briefly at a couple of locations inside China, and then died. There were never more than two active temples to Wong Tai Sin in Guangdong, and when these temples were destroyed, local followers gave up. The cult disappeared, except in the memories of a dwindling number of old people. An offshoot however, had taken root in Hong Kong, and by the time the last Wong Tai Sin temple in Guangdong was being demolished in the 1950s, the off-shoot was prospering. Within the next two decades, Wong Tai Sin would become famous. How did this happen? How did a single Taoist entrepreneur,[1] carrying a painting of an obscure Taoist saint down to Hong Kong in his search for a safer and less tumultuous life, start a chain of events which would eventually have a major impact on the religious life of hundreds of thousands of Chinese in Hong Kong? In this chapter, we will review the history of wor-ship of Wong Tai Sin in Hong Kong from 1915 to the 1980s. We will also try to explain why this god became so popular.

The Founding of the Temple: 1915 to 1921

As far as we know, Wong Tai Sin was obscure and largely unknown in Hong Kong before Leung Yan Ngam arrived from Rengang village in September of 1915.[2] Leung had no constituency of eager believers waiting for him to arrive and help them organize a temple. He had to start again from the beginning. He was not without funds, however. He rented a flat on the second floor of a building in the Wanchai district on Hong Kong island, and set up an altar to Wong Tai Sin in the apartment.[3] For an image of the god, he used a picture of Wong Tai Sin, which he had brought to Hong Kong from Rengang village. By March of 1916, he had opened a herbal medicine shop on the ground floor of another building nearby, and he moved the altar into the back of the shop. People buying herbal medicine at the shop could, if they wished, proceed into the back of the shop and ask this new god, Wong Tai Sin, for prescriptions for their ailments, so they would know what medicines to buy. For the next two and a half years, Mr Leung apparently performed *fuji* and sold herbal medicines out of this shop. We may assume that with his skill and his knowledge of herbal medicines, he gradually built up a clientele of regular patrons. We may also assume that there were some healings accomplished among some of his clients.

But in November of 1918, a fire destroyed the herb shop. In great despair, according to his grandsons, he returned to Rengang village. He was now 57 or 58 years old, and had only three years left to live. Perhaps he was ready to retire and live quietly in his ancestral village. However, his son, Leung Gwan Jyun, now 22 years old, had remained in Hong Kong. According to his sons, Leung Gwan Jyun had become a believer in Wong Tai Sin four years earlier, at the age of 18. He had been suffering from a severe skin disease, and his father advised him to consult the gods through the *fuji* procedure at the Rengang temple. Subsequently, through potions and charms prescribed by the gods and with the assistance of various supernatural figures, he had been cured, or experienced a marked improvement.[4] This young man was eventually to become the proprietor of the Sik Sik Yuen during its most difficult years in the 1940s. We do not know if he was already aware of this calling, but in any case, not long after Mr Leung returned to Rengang, his son and a few other believers wrote to Mr Leung and asked him to come back to Hong Kong and set up another altar to Wong Tai Sin.

Evidently, some of Mr Leung's clients missed his services. He was their intermediary to this new god, and the only man who could provide them with the god's herbal medical prescriptions and general advice. His grandsons relate that Mr Leung was deeply moved by their request and by his son's entreaties, and he soon returned to Hong Kong and set up another altar in a flat in Wanchai. Within two years, he had enough patrons to support the construction of a free-standing shrine outside the city.

In April, 1921, Mr Leung recorded a *fuji* message from Wong Tai Sin which decreed that a new shrine should be built. The message said that the god had chosen a site which was 3,600 paces from a pier. Mr Leung and one of his followers soon found the spot: a plot of land at the foot of Lion Rock Mountain near the village of Chuk Yuen (Zhuyuan), which was about the right distance from the Kowloon City pier. The plot of land was largely barren,

and was used at that time only for raising poultry. After lengthy
negotiations, Mr Leung rented the site from the owner.[5] Subsequent
fuji messages dictated the dimensions of the temple, the orienta-
tion of the buildings, and the date and time for the inauguration
of the new shrine. The god also informed his followers that the
shrine was to be called the Puyitan (adopting the formula of the
two Guangdong temples) and that the enclosure and gardens should
be named the Sik Sik Yuen.[6] Workers were hired, and built several matshed structures to house the main shrine and provide rooms
for the temple-keeper and for ceremonial functions.

The funds were provided mainly by four wealthy businessmen
with whom Mr Leung had become acquainted.[7] It is likely that
these men had been clients of Mr Leung's medical prescription
shrine in Wanchai, and had become believers as a result of the
benefits they believed could be obtained from these prescriptions.
The super-longevity achieved by Wong Tai Sin, and potentially
available to sincere believers, was probably one of the aspects of
the cult which appealed to these wealthy men. It also seems that
the early patrons of this new shrine were from Mr Leung's own
Nanhai county in China.[8] This fact may have played a role in the
ties which Leung had built up with these men. In any case, their
patronage was crucial for the success of the project. The work was
soon completed, and the shrine was inaugurated in July of 1921.

The image of the god used in the new shrine was evidently the
picture of Wong Tai Sin which Leung had brought from Rengang.
The use of this picture, rather than a gold-covered statue as in the
two Guangdong temples, eventually became an accepted feature
of the temple, and now strongly distinguishes it from other Taoist
and Buddhist temples in the region.[9]

Apart from the use of a picture rather than a statue, however,
it appears to us that Mr Leung modelled the new shrine after the
Rengang and Fangcun temples. It was evidently intended that the
shrine would offer special prescriptions and advice from the god
for members and their families, but would also draw clients from
nearby villages and urban areas. Like the Rengang temple, it was
situated just outside a village, and was intended to be both aes-
thetically and religiously appealing to people in the surrounding
district. Like the first Fangcun temple, it could be reached after a
boat ride from the city, with visitors able to disembark at a pier
and walk up the road to the shrine. It was farther from the water
than the Fangcun temple, but on the other hand it had a much

more impressive location, at the foot of Lion Rock with the entire vista of Kowloon, the harbour, and Hong Kong island stretching out before it to the south. The shrine was just close enough to the more densely populated areas of the colony to provide reasonable prospects of drawing villagers and urbanites as clients, while at the same time it was far enough away and on barren enough ground that the land would not be expensive to rent. In short, the site was carefully chosen to offer the best prospects of success with the funds available.

Mr Leung could not have known how profoundly lucky his choice of the site would turn out to be for the future of Wong Tai Sin in Hong Kong. He had placed the new shrine in a location in which it would benefit from the later influx of refugees into the area, but far enough away from the harbour and the urbanized areas that it was not threatened by urban expansion and redevelopment until more than 30 years later.

But Mr Leung did not live to see the shrine prosper. He returned to Rengang village a few days after the inauguration of the shrine, and died shortly afterward. Back in Hong Kong, his son, Leung Gwan Jyun, received a message by *fuji* that seemed to indicate that his father had died, a message confirmed when he received a letter from the village 20 days later.[10] Leung Gwan Jyun was on his own, but his father had bequeathed to him a new shrine, a core of believers in Wong Tai Sin, and some of the knowledge which he needed to follow in his father's footsteps.

The First Phase of Growth: 1921–1941

By 1924, the Sik Sik Yuen had attracted a number of new patrons, and nine new officials were inducted into the various posts in the organization, replacing all but one of the officials who had served from 1921 to 1923. Subsequently, the temple put on a 21-day ceremony to mark the birthday of the god, with the participation of a number of businessmen, and opened a clinic offering a limited quantity of free Chinese herbal medicine to the poor. The herbal medicines distributed free from the clinic were financed by contributions from worshippers and from other members of the Sik Sik Yuen. The opening of the clinic suggests that these donations and contributions were substantial.

Taoists associated with the new shrine also decided to track down the volumes of *fuji* writings produced during the first years of worship of Wong Tai Sin in Guangzhou in the late 1890s. The volumes were finally located, and some donated money was used to republish them. These volumes were, for a time, distributed to interested persons by the Sik Sik Yuen.

The Sik Sik Yuen evidently made a profit in most of the years which followed.[11] The population in Kowloon had already begun to grow steadily, and more than doubled each decade between 1920 and 1940 (Hughes 1951:8). In 1931, over half of Hong Kong's 817,000 Chinese had been in the colony only ten years or less, and more than a third had arrived between 1926 and 1930. The colony's prosperity, along with continuing turmoil in China, was what drew these people to Hong Kong. The Sik Sik Yuen's policy of offering herbal medicine prescriptions from the god, along with a limited supply of free medicine, brought a steady growth in visitors, especially among the newer immigrants. By 1928, the Sik Sik Yuen was prospering.

There were probably other Taoist entrepreneurs who came to Hong Kong during the 1920s, attracted by the greater peace and prosperity of the colony. For example, two Taoist monks from one of the major old Taoist temples in Guangzhou, the Sanyuan Gong, arrived in the late 1920s with the intention of establishing a new shrine somewhere in the colony. One of them had been the head monk in the Guangzhou temple, and was perhaps looking for a more peaceful and secure setting for his religious calling. Their friends and associates in Hong Kong eventually raised the funds to erect a shrine near the village of Fanling, in the New Territories, which was completed in 1933 (see Tsui 1991, Ch.7). Known as the Fengying Xianguan, it is now one of the two major Taoist temples in the New Territories. There were undoubtedly other religious entrepreneurs who scouted the possibilities in Hong Kong, or who tried to open a shrine but did not manage to get enough wealthy patrons or to find a suitable location.[12]

The group which founded the Fengying Xianguan evidently had good credentials, and were in any case not yet interested in appealing directly to the general public (Tsui 1991:96), but the Hong Kong Government seems to have become concerned about the influx of religious entrepreneurs eager to make a profit from the operation of shrines. Government legislation soon followed which was intended to exercise some control over these entrepreneurs. This legislation would eventually have a dramatic impact on the fate of the Wong Tai Sin temple.

The Hong Kong Government Acts to Control Temples

The Hong Kong Government had begun to take an active interest in the regulation of temples in the colony during the 1920s. In 1928, a new law was passed requiring that all temples must register with the government, and include an accounting of their ownership, management, property, revenues, and the uses of these revenues.[13] Ultimate control over all public temples in the colony was given to a newly established Chinese Temples Committee, and all temples were subject to expropriation by this Committee. Temple-keepers now had to pay an annual fee to the government for the right to operate a temple, and they had to bid against other prospective temple-keepers for this right. The Committee could delegate the operation of particular temples to the groups currently controlling them, if these groups were considered to be operating their temples on behalf of some substantial local constituency rather than purely for private profit, or could show that they had operated a temple for generations.[14] If the operators of a temple or shrine were not appointed by local committees, or seemed to be too blatantly venal in their practices, or if the shrines appeared to have been set up recently and entirely for profit, they were confiscated or closed. As a result of this bill, 200 temples were soon registered, and 28 temples judged to be 'purely business speculations' were closed down.[15] Several other temples were confiscated from their operators.

Why did the government take such a bold step? In some colonial regimes, such an act would have provoked instant rebellion. The key fact is that the government had the full support of the Chinese elite for this legislation, and indeed, it appears the Chinese elite had prompted it. They had probably been influenced by events in China, where the Nationalists had moved to control temples on the basis of the belief that much of folk religion was simply the exploitation of the gullible masses by charlatans, a waste of time and money, and a hindrance to the modernization of the country. This policy had led to the conversion of thousands of temples to secular uses between 1911 and the late 1920s. Nationalist intellectuals were not necessarily hostile to all of traditional Chinese religious practice, and some tried to discriminate between good (or tolerable) religion and bad religion. One government committee in Zhejiang province in 1928, actually made a list of the gods to be retained and those to be discarded. The acceptable objects of veneration included, 'great [and subsequently deified] men of the past who have contributed discoveries in arts and sciences, [and] those who can be held up before the people as examples of filial piety and justice for their emulation. Secondly . . . religious leaders who have founded religions on the basis of right and truth, and have been popularly believed by the people' (quoted in Day 1969:192). The gods to be discarded included the gods of the skies, the earth, the water, the harvest, thunder, plagues, and so on.[16] The committee commented that, 'the principle for confiscation of temples is that we should do away with old pre-historic religions which cannot be proved historically, or which have no contemporary meaning or value; and that we should get rid of evil religions, for example those quasi-religious, money-making cults' (Day 1969). The Chinese members of the elite in Hong Kong who supported the new legislation had precisely the same attitude toward these 'quasi-religious, money-making cults'. In introducing the bill in Hong Kong, Sir Shou-son Chow outlined its functions as follows:

It will tend to prevent religion being made a source of private gain, and it will, I hope, go far towards preventing the misuse of religion by adventurers who prey on the more ignorant members of the community . . . [and] assist genuine Chinese religion by helping it to get rid of adventurers who use it for their own selfish ends (Hong Kong Hansard, 1928, p.22).

Such temples would be closed, or else confiscated and the profits transferred to the Chinese Charities Fund. The members of the Chinese Temples Committee which would make these distinctions between good and bad temples, and allocate surplus funds from the operation of temples toward worthy communal projects, included representatives from the two major Chinese charitable organizations in Hong Kong, the Tung Wah Group of Hospitals and the Po Leung Kuk. The Po Leung Kuk was established in the nineteenth century to provide hostels for children and women, especially under age women, who might otherwise be pressed into prostitution or 'domestic slavery'. The Tung Wah Group of Hospitals had also begun in the nineteenth century as a charitable organization designed to bring hospital care and better medical services to the Chinese population in Hong Kong.[17] By the 1930s, it had become the largest charitable organization in the colony, operating hospitals, schools, and homes for the elderly. Its board of directors included some of the wealthiest members of the Chinese elite.

Their large role in the provision of services to the Chinese population gave them great influence with the Hong Kong Government, and both their charitable activities and their influence with the government gave them great status among the Chinese population.

The directors of Tung Wah must have shared some of the views of officials in China. By the end of the nineteenth century, the wealthy merchants and compradors who headed the Tung Wah had already become a kind of shadow government in Hong Kong, and had developed numerous relationships with government officials inside China. They sent relief funds from Hong Kong and overseas Chinese into China during famines, and sometimes dined with Chinese officials when the latter visited Hong Kong (Lethbridge 1978:64). In common with many officials in China, they preferred Confucian traditions to the folk-Taoist magic which was commonly purveyed from many temples. Indeed, each year, in ceremonies exactly like those carried out by officials in China, they went as a group to one of the local temples to offer annual sacrifices to Confucius (Lethbridge 1978:62). They were undoubtedly a more conservative group than the new Republican officials in Guangzhou and later, in Nanjing (many of whom associated Confucius with feudalism), and were not as hostile toward traditional Chinese religion as some of those officials. But they shared the latter's disdain for much of what we would call folk religion. There is little doubt that the Chinese Temples Ordinance of 1928 reflected in Hong Kong the influence of events in China on these wealthy Hong Kong Chinese leaders. As a result of their influence, then, the Hong Kong Government moved to regulate and control local temples much more extensively than it had been inclined to do in previous decades.

The Hong Kong Chinese elite probably had another, more pragmatic agenda. Under the new legislation, some of the surplus income from temples would flow into the charitable institutions controlled by these men. Indeed, apart from the closing of a few of the smaller shrines and temples, this was the main effect of the intervention, and the Tung Wah Group of Hospitals, whose chairman sat on the Chinese Temples Committee, was the principal beneficiary. Tung Wah now controls nine temples whose operations were delegated to it by the Chinese Temples Committee, and it receives the surplus income, after maintenance costs, from these temples. One of the temples, the Wenwu (Cantonese: *Man Mo*) temple, had been formally transferred to the Tung Wah's control much earlier, in 1908 (it was in this temple that the directors annually honoured Confucius).[18] Full-scale expropriation of temples did not occur until the elite had watched events in China and had been inspired to find ways to tap more of the income from temples for medical and charitable programs in Hong Kong.[19] As noted, the Chinese elite in Hong Kong may also have been concerned about the influx of aggressive religious entrepreneurs into the colony.

The Sik Sik Yuen proclaimed itself a private shrine, and thus was not in danger of expropriation. In theory, a private shrine had a limited clientele and was not open to the public, and hence could not be accused of exploiting the public. However, the distinction was never easy to make. The Sik Sik Yuen, for instance, included private members but also drew other clients from Kowloon and Hong Kong interested in free medicine or in herbal medicine prescriptions from the god. Hence, it was potentially at risk under the new legislation. Its status as a private shrine allowed it to hide its finances from the government, but its dependence on non-members and its evident prosperity must have made the Chinese Temples Committee very curious at least. Doubtless aware of the danger, the Sik Sik Yuen was careful to build up some goodwill in government circles by making some voluntary contributions to the Chinese Temples Committee Fund, beginning with HK$1,500 in 1928, the first year of the Ordinance. This amount exceeded the rents for 1928 for all but three of the temples controlled by the Committee, and gives some indication of the Sik Sik Yuen's success.

It seems to us that the success of the Sik Sik Yuen during the 1920s and early 1930s was largely the result of the temple's policies of offering medical prescriptions from the god, and giving away limited quantities of free herbal medicines. In 1933, the Sik Sik Yuen posted a series of regulations in the temple, inscribed on a plaque, which clearly show the importance of their herbal medicine service. (The inscription is reproduced in Faure, Luk, and Ng [1986:513–15]). The staff of the Sik Sik Yuen were admonished to be most careful in managing and monitoring the shop so that it would be successful. The members were reminded that they should donate money regularly, if possible, to support the services of the medicine shop. Although part of their fees and annual dues were already used for the purchase of the medicine given out at the shop,[20] they were also advised to donate money on a monthly basis, if they could afford it, to pay for temple ceremonies and for the herbal medicines. The regulations even assert that what Wong

Tai Sin himself cares most about is the medicine, or the provision of medicine (Faure, Luk and Ng 1986).

Although still ostensibly a private temple, by 1934 the temple was attracting enough worshippers so that the Sik Sik Yuen again feared government expropriation under the Chinese Temples Ordinance of 1928, so they closed the main temple to worship (Sik Sik Yuen 1971). At the same time, they managed to get the permission of the Secretary of Chinese Affairs to open for public worship during the month of the New Year. Thus the Sik Sik Yuen was able to continue to draw many worshippers from among the general public during New Year, while maintaining the fiction that it was a private shrine during the other eleven months of the year.

The Sik Sik Yuen continued to prosper, and by 1936 they had accumulated enough money to rebuild the temple. Although the main gates remained closed except during the New Year period, people still came to worship, and the worshippers attracted several fortune-tellers who set up their tables outside the entrance. These fortune-tellers were allowed to set up icons of the god, which allowed public worship at the temple to continue without formally violating the terms of the Chinese Temples Ordinance and inviting expropriation.

The war in China moved closer as the Japanese armies entered southern China and finally occupied Guangzhou in October of 1938. They took Shenzhen, near the border between China and the New Territories of Hong Kong, a month later. This invasion caused a sudden large influx of refugees into the colony (Wong 1970). Some of them moved into squatter areas in Kowloon.[21] Others crowded into existing tenements as families sublet rooms or portions of rooms to the refugees.[22] The temple may have attracted some of these newcomers. A student who visited the temple in 1939 wrote at the time that 'there is never a day when there is a shortage of people going to worship there'.[23] In 1939, the Hong Kong Government apparently notified the temple and several nearby villages that part of the land on which they stood was needed for a firing range to provide target practice for British troops. According to Leung Gwan Jyun's sons, Wong Tai Sin assured his worried followers by *fuji*, 'Don't worry, the land is mine'. The government never did confiscate their land for the firing range. Within two years, the British Government was swept out of the colony by the Japanese armies.

Effects of the Japanese Occupation

In December 1941, the Japanese invaded the New Territories and quickly forced their way into Kowloon and across the harbour to Hong Kong island. Within two weeks the British and Canadian units defending the colony had been completely routed, and the Japanese set up their own government. In 1940, prior to the Japanese invasion, the population of Hong Kong had grown to about 1,846,000, of whom about 750,000 were refugees fleeing the advancing Japanese army (Lethbridge 1969:78). But the hardships of the Japanese occupation drove hundreds of thousands of people out of Hong Kong and back to their ancestral villages. The Japanese regime instituted rice rationing early in the occupation, but the ration was inadequate, and corruption and long queues to get even the meagre portions allocated to civilians forced people to resort to the black market to get rice (Hahn 1946:360–1). Poor people could not afford black market rice, however, and thousands starved. Many people left Hong Kong for the countryside, only to find that food was just as scarce in many of the villages in rural Guangdong province. The Japanese also drove large numbers of people out of Hong Kong to further reduce the burden on the rice-rationing system. The harsh repression of the occupying forces — it has been estimated that the Japanese military and police executed over 10,000 Chinese during the occupation (Hahn 1946:121) — also drove many people out into the countryside to seek safety. By the end of the war, there were only about 600,000 people left in Hong Kong.

The temple's historical account during these years is preoccupied with the Sik Sik Yuen's interactions with the Japanese army. Their first encounters with the Japanese at the temple were not auspicious. In the first month of the occupation, some of the Japanese soldiers were passing the temple and saw several cars parked outside. They came into the temple and told Leung Gwan Jyun to give them whatever fuel he had. He replied that the Sik Sik Yuen had no fuel, and that the cars parked outside did not belong to the temple. The soldiers became violent, dragged Leung outside, and said they would shoot him if he didn't give them fuel. At that moment, the owner of one of the cars, who was inside the temple, came out and took fuel from the vehicles and gave it to the Japanese, who then left. All over Hong Kong people were having similar experiences, as the Japanese forcibly requisitioned food and supplies, often at gunpoint and frequently accompanied by threats, beatings, or worse. Leung must have been badly frightened by this episode.

However, Leung and the Sik Sik Yuen survived the war, and he came to believe that the god Wong Tai Sin had helped him and the Sik Sik Yuen in their subsequent encounters with the Japanese army. Events occurred which he and others in the Sik Sik Yuen interpreted as evidence of the god's power over the invaders, and which quickly became part of the 'miracle-lore' of the temple. The temple history (in Sik Sik Yuen, 1971) records the following events. In 1942, Japanese soldiers entered the temple grounds to look around, and noticed a sign which apparently offended them. They ordered Leung Gwan Jyun to remove it. He declined, 'in a gentle manner', and a soldier attempted to remove the sign himself. In doing so, he slipped and fell. Interpreting this as a sign from the god, he bowed to the temple-keeper and withdrew. A small victory, perhaps, but after his first encounter with the Japanese, this must have seemed to Leung to be a sign that the god was protecting his temple. (Stories of how an intruder into a temple is foiled by the deity may be quite common; see, for instance, Preston 1980:76).

In 1942, Japanese soldiers again arrived at the temple, this time to requisition the bamboo growing around the perimenter of the temple compound. Leung asked them to pay for it, and they agreed. Leung believed that they had not dared to take the bamboo by force because they feared the god. According to Leung's sons, Wong Tai Sin had instructed the temple-keeper by *fuji* in 1937 to plant 10,000 bamboo plants around the periphery of the Sik Sik Yuen, and it was this bamboo which the Japanese cut down and took away in 1942. Apparently they paid for the bamboo with rice, and the temple-keeper gave some of the rice to local villagers who were already desperately short of food, and kept the rest for some members and staff of the Sik Sik Yuen. The god's wisdom and foresight was shown in this incident.

In about June of 1943, the Sik Sik Yuen received a phone call from the Japanese district office ordering the person in charge of the temple to go to the district office and give an account of how Wong Cho Ping had become a god. Leung Gwan Jyun then presented the district officer with Wong Tai Sin's 'autobiography', using the version which his father had received by *fuji* in the late 1890s, in which the god recounted his hermitage on Jinhua Mountain and his miracle of turning the rocks into sheep. While the temple's history does not explain why the Japanese made such a request, it was probably the result of a new policy then being developed, which came into force in July of 1943, in which the General Association of Chinese Charities, organized under Japanese auspices, was given responsibility for managing more than 20 Chinese temples. These temples were to be leased to temple-keepers by tender, with fees and surplus funds allocated to the General Association of Chinese Charities, to be used for hospitals, emergency relief for the poor, and other local charitable purposes (Kwan 1984). This arrangement was clearly modeled on the control of temple income achieved under the Chinese Temples Ordinance of 1928. The Sik Sik Yuen had escaped confiscation under the original Ordinance, but now faced a new regime which once again presented a threat to its control over the Wong Tai Sin temple. Presenting the 'autobiography' to the Japanese, they hoped to establish the credentials of their god. After receiving the document, the Japanese district office informed the Sik Sik Yuen that they would send someone to have a look at the temple and the Sik Sik Yuen's operations, and ordered the Sik Sik Yuen to prepare a vegetarian meal for the visiting officials. This order made Leung very anxious. If the visit went badly, and the officials were unsatisfied, he and his staff could be expelled from the temple. He requested Wong Tai Sin's advice using divination blocks,[24] and received a reassuring answer (three affirmative replies from the god). The visit evidently was successful: the Japanese were apparently satisfied that the temple was a genuine religious institution of a private character, and hence not eligible for confiscation and management under the control of the General Association of Chinese Charities. Leung must have been greatly relieved, and again believed that the god had protected the temple from a potentially serious threat.

In 1944, Japanese soldiers entered the temple compound at night and ordered everyone to gather in the main temple so their ID cards could be examined. One frightened member of the staff escaped as the Japanese entered, but another staff member who didn't have an ID card was not able to slip out before the Japanese had rounded up all the staff. The consequences of harbouring an unregistered person could have been very serious. While the Japanese were interrogating Leung, however, the altar incense flared, casting a sudden red glow around the room. The Japanese broke off the interrogation and left immediately (Sik Sik Yuen 1971).

Whatever the reasons for the Japanese soldiers' actions in each of these incidents, the temple historians characteristically interpreted each favourable outcome as due to the god's intervention. The last and most important of these events occurred in January of 1945. The Japanese, evidently worried about defending the airfield, notified the Sik Sik Yuen and several nearby villages that they all had to move out within one month, and they would be punished if they failed to obey. It appears that the Japanese may have been worried that the Sik Sik Yuen and nearby villages might be used as bases from which guerillas could mount attacks on the airfield.[25] Leung Gwan Jyun and some villagers went to the Japanese district office to present a petition asking for an exemption. The Japanese district officer's response was to order Leung and the village heads to meet later near the airport.

The villagers went to the temple to consult the god about their prospects of avoiding relocation. Certainly they had good cause to worry. The nearby village of Po Kong had already been levelled by the Japanese during construction in 1942, when they had needed the land to rebuild and expand Kai Tak airport.[26] The Sik Sik Yuen had also lost its herbal medicine shop on Cheung On (Chang'an) Street, from which it distributed free packets of medicine, during this phase of construction. Leung had gone to live in the temple for the next three and a half years, while his son tended Leung's own medicine shop on Argyle Road, returning to the Sik Sik Yuen each night to sleep. The Sik Sik Yuen reopened their herbal medicine clinic next to the temple in 1943, but now the other remaining villages, and even the temple itself, were in danger. Leung and the villagers used the *qiu qian* procedure to ask the god whether they would lose everything and be forced to move, and got one of the 'good' *qian* poems, indicating a favourable outcome, so 'their hearts were set at ease'. Nevertheless, Leung and the village heads must have gone to their meeting with the Japanese officials with some trepidation, wondering how they would be rescued from Japanese designs on their land. At the meeting place near the airport, a car drew up and the Japanese official, on alighting from the car, slipped and fell. A second official, alighting from a second car, saw that the first officer had fallen, and went to help him, but he also fell. The Sik Sik Yuen's account states that they injured their faces, and were covered with mud. The two officials were no longer interested in the villagers, and wanted only to leave as quickly as possible. They informed the villagers that the matter would have to be postponed, and left, after ordering the people to go home. The writer of the account states that although the accidental falls of the two officials could be considered a stroke of luck, it was also evidence of the god's spirit manifesting itself.

Many years later, Leung told the Sik Sik Yuen's historian that he was always frightened by the Japanese army, but that he believed Wong Tai Sin had protected him and the temple during the occupation. Some of the villagers also had a new respect for Wong Tai Sin, and believed that this new god had indeed helped to protect their villages from the Japanese. A man who had lived in Chuk Yuen village during the war, interviewed by Graeme Lang in what remained of Chuk Yuen village in 1987, confirmed that before the war, nobody in the village had worshipped Wong Tai Sin, but by the end of the war, he and others had become believers. He described the incident of the two Japanese officers who fell, and went so far as to say that the god had pushed them. He was also impressed by the fact that the Japanese had never entered the village to loot, as occurred in some other villages, and attributed this to the god's protection. By being available to offer divination and provide reassurance after the Japanese threatened nearby villages, Leung and his staff had helped Wong Tai Sin to get credit for the salvation of some of these villages from Japanese plans to destroy them and evict their inhabitants.

Equally important, the temple itself had survived largely unscathed. Indeed, a Guanyin temple nearby, popular among surrounding villages as late as the 1930s, became derelict during the Japanese occupation and was not rebuilt after the war (Hayes 1983b). Apparently, the hardships of the war led many local villagers to lose some of their faith in the gods enshrined in their local temples, since these gods had been unable to help them (Hayes 1970:186).[27] The Wong Tai Sin temple was one of the few exceptions. Leung and a few temple staff had lived in the temple throughout the war, and by keeping the shrine active and dealing with soldiers who arrived to confiscate supplies and who might have camped in the temple, or sacked it, they preserved it while smaller local temples became decrepit. It was the events which occurred after the war, however, which were the key to its success.

Post-war Immigration

The population in Hong Kong rebounded immediately after the war. Large numbers of people who had left during the occupation returned from villages in China. There are no exact figures, but the following estimates were made by the government in 1952:

Table 1 Estimated Hong Kong
Population, 1945–1951

August 1945	600,000
End of 1946	1,600,000
End of 1947	1,800,000
Early 1950	2,360,000
Early 1951	2,060,000

(Source: *Hong Kong Annual Report*, 1951, p. 23)

Some of the refugees who had fled to Hong Kong in 1949 returned to their villages in 1950 and 1951 after the end of the fighting between the Communist and Nationalist armies, but in 1952 the border was closed by the new regime in China. There were now over 2 million people in the colony, compared to a pre-war total of about 1.5 million. The 1 million people who had returned to Hong Kong after the war found an acute housing shortage. Some of them managed to sublet rooms or portions of rooms in tenements in Kowloon. Many others were forced to become squatters.

The squatter areas provided desperately needed low-cost housing, and indeed there was a market for squatter housing which had a role corresponding to that in the private sector: some people built illegal structures on crown land, or on plots rented from local farmers, and then sold or rented these structures to others (Smart 1985). Over the next five years, another 500,000 refugees arrived, and many of these people also became squatters. Most of these squatters settled on hills and farmland just outside the urbanized portion of the Kowloon peninsula, in what was called 'New Kowloon'.

The temple was ideally located to benefit from this massive influx of immigrants into 'New Kowloon' after 1945. It is difficult to estimate the number of immigrants into this area, since the first major population census after 1931 did not occur until 1961. However, figures from the 1961 census show that population in the area between the temple and old Kowloon exploded after World War II. New Kowloon, including the area around the temple, grew from 22,634 to 852,849, a growth of over 3,600 per cent. More than half of this population had been born in China.[28] Most came in the years immediately before and after 1949, as refugees from the fighting between the Nationalists and the Communists, or as refugees from the new regime. One estimate by the Commissioner for Resettlement was that in 1947 there were 30,000 squatters in Hong Kong, but by 1949 there were 300,000 (Leeming 1977:163). Some of these squatters were from the Hong Kong area — they had been forced out of their dwellings by the high rents resulting from the post-war housing shortage in Hong Kong[29] — but most of them came from China. Chuk Yuen was one of the areas where large numbers of these people settled (Leeming 1977:160). It became more profitable for owners of farmland in the area to sublet to the immigrants than to raise crops on the land.[30]

The Wong Tai Sin temple, overlooking large stretches of these squatter settlements in the 1950s, filled a need for a major local shrine among this rapidly growing population eager for upward mobility. Many of these immigrants, especially those who had held professional, managerial, or clerical posts in China, had experienced downward mobility in their first months and years in Hong Kong, in the sense that they could no longer practice their former occupations and had to take whatever work they could get (Chung 1983; Hambro 1954:44). Many became manual workers. Those who had been manual workers or farmers in China tried to find work in manufacturing or construction in Hong Kong, but many of them were forced into becoming hawkers (Hambro 1954:5). There was no 'social safety net' in Hong Kong at the time, except what was available from local charitable organizations, and many of the refugees evidently arrived with little money. They must have been desperately insecure.

Those who lived in squatter shacks were also subjected to worse conditions than they had experienced in their dwellings in China. The shacks, built of wood, corrugated metal, and cast-off materials, would have been very cold in the winter and stifling in the summer. They were frequently built on hillsides, without easy access to wells or streams. In the rainy season they were in danger from typhoons and from mudslides set off by the torrential rains streaming down the hillsides cleared of trees and brush. The rest of the time they were in danger from the fires which broke out periodically in the squatter areas, often destroying hundreds of the closely packed huts and occasionally killing some of the residents. The residents in these huts were usually surrounded by strangers, and so they also worried about theft and their children's health and safety. They were chronically anxious, and driven by a strong desire to escape poverty and find a route to success.

Many of them believed, in a general way, that the gods could be induced to help those who bring offerings and petition them earnestly and sincerely. They had left their local temples and ancestral halls behind in China, and were too busy to travel very far to visit temples in Hong Kong. They would not, in any case, have been very attracted to temples which already appeared to have close ties to a local community. They were strangers, and needed a god whose attention was not already occupied with a well-established local constituency of believers. By good luck, in their very midst, well-maintained, not closely linked to any local community, and ready to receive any and all new worshippers, stood the Wong Tai Sin temple.

The size of the temple and the god's alleged powers as reportedly demonstrated against the Japanese must have impressed the immigrants. They heard the stories[31] and could see for themselves that the god had protected his temple. Wong Tai Sin, assisted by his fortune-tellers, began to become one of the most popular deities among immigrants.

With the exception of the Chaozhou,[32] ethnic differences among these immigrants do not seem to have led to much pressure for religious differentiation — for additional Wong Tai Sin temples catering to particular ethnic or linguistic groups. The Chaozhou minority have developed separate temples and ceremonies to a considerable extent in New Kowloon (Myers 1975, 1981).[33] The only other free-standing Wong Tai Sin temple in Hong Kong, apart from the main temple, is a private and very exclusive Chaozhou temple built in the early 1950s on a mountainside several miles to the west of the main temple (described in Chapter 6). However, other divisions amongst the immigrants do not seem to have led to any offshoots of the Wong Tai Sin cult or any rival temples. While the immigrants and refugees came from a number of regions in south-eastern China, and while some of the dialect differences were substantial, even among Cantonese speakers, no rival Wong Tai Sin shrines appeared. These people wanted supernatural help and advice. An impressive temple to a god with a reputation for recent local miracles stood nearby, and large numbers of them went to the temple to petition this god and to make their offerings, hoping that his reputed power and benevolence would provide some benefit.

If the god had not helped them, however, they might have drifted away. The fate of these immigrants during the decades after their arrival in Hong Kong would help to determine the reputation of the god to whom they prayed for help.

What happened to them after 1949? Firstly, the government resettlement program which began in the 1950s produced rapid construction of new housing estates near the temple to replace squatter huts, and evolved into the later government sponsorship of large numbers of modern high-rise public housing blocks. A majority of the population experienced a great improvement in their living conditions as a direct result of these policies. Secondly, the Hong Kong economy grew rapidly over the same period, benefitting all classes and producing a large increase in real income. By helping Wong Tai Sin's worshippers to achieve more security and a better life, these changes also helped Wong Tai Sin. Because of the importance of these changes, we will review each one briefly.

Rehousing the Refugees and Squatters

Four years after the initial flood of refugees into the colony in 1949 and 1950, most squatters were still living in huts and shacks jammed together on hillsides or in fields, usually without running water or electricity. The government's main response had been to designate resettlement areas, served with water supply and roads, in which huts could be built.[34] One of these hut-resettlement areas occupied a large area of barren ground behind the Wong Tai Sin temple. However, the people living in these huts represented only about 10 per cent of the squatters then living in Hong Kong. A thorough assault on the problem of providing better housing for squatters did not occur until a major fire in one of the largest squatter areas in 1953, which left 50,000 people homeless. The government soon began to build resettlement apartment blocks to house people from squatter areas. These seven-storey buildings were primitive by modern standards: they had communal taps and toilets, and each family had only one room, opening onto a communal balcony (Pryor 1983:24). However, the units were cleaner and safer than the squatter huts. The government built 28 blocks of these apartment buildings on the land immediately in front of the temple between 1958 and 1965. These blocks, called the Wong Tai Sin Estates, housed about 75,000 people. Thus, a large number of the people who had

Map 2 Wong Tai Sin District (1949 and 1963)

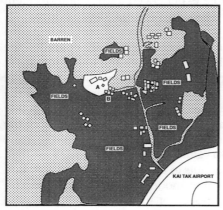

Wong Tai Sin District: May 1949

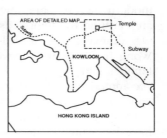

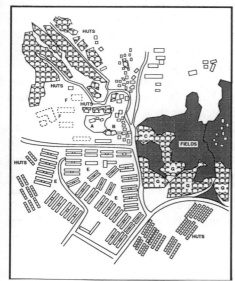

Wong Tai Sin District: January 1963

Key: A: Wong Tai Sin Temple
(perimeter is bamboo
trees)
B: Stalls of fortune-tellers
and sellers of incense
and paper offerings
C: Chuk Yuen Village
D: Resettlement buildings
(Mark I type: seven
floors)
E: Resettlement buildings
(under construction)
F: Houses and huts
(including shacks)

(*Note*: Maps are based on aerial photos in files of the Survey and Mapping Office,
Hong Kong Government.)

been living in huts, shacks, and tenement cubicles in the several square miles around the temple experienced a great improvement in their living quarters, and hence in their standard of living, by the 1960s.

In the 1970s and 1980s, the government gradually upgraded the older resettlement blocks with communal taps and toilets into more modern, self-contained apartments, or replaced them with fully modern high-rise apartment buildings. The transformation in the area around the temple as a result of these waves of construction was dramatic, and is well-illustrated by aerial photographs of the Wong Tai Sin District between 1949 and 1988.[35] By the 1980s, many families had experienced two 'great leaps' in the quality of their accommodations: from squatter huts to the early resettlement estates, and from resettlement estates into modern high-rise apartments.

Looking back, the housing policy of the government seems to have been highly successful at providing decent low-rent accommodation to hundreds of thousands of families who had previously been living in deplorable conditions. Very few cities in the world have been as successful as Hong Kong in providing housing to low-income people on such a scale.

However, during most of this period there was a continual shortage of public housing, and many people spent years on the waiting list,[36] watching others get better housing while they remained crowded together in their cubicles or their shacks. This period of change between the 1950s and the 1980s appears profoundly successful only when viewed from a great height — as in the aerial photographs. When viewed through the eyes of individual families, it was a time full of anxiety. Wong Tai Sin, however, was available to listen to the hopes and plans of thousands of these families, and to give advice and encouragement. Some of his worshippers even attributed their success in finally getting into better housing to the help of the god.

Growth in Real Income

In the 1950s and 1960s the textile and clothing industries in Hong Kong quickly expanded to supply the American market, and helped convert Hong Kong from a re-exporter of goods into a major producer. The manufacture of plastic and electronic products also grew rapidly. Construction of public housing estates provided thousands of jobs. The large number of refugees who arrived in 1949, and the steady flow of immigrants from China over the next ten years, provided cheap labour for this rapid industrial expansion.

By the mid-1960s, there was virtually no unemployment in Hong Kong. Indeed, there was a shortage of skilled workers which drove up industrial wages; real income roughly doubled between 1964 and the early 1980s (Youngson 1982:20). Unlike in some developing countries, low-income families in Hong Kong benefited strongly from this economic growth, since most families had several income earners who were able to find work in shops or in the thousands of small factories and workshops. The real income of all groups, including the poor, had increased greatly by the 1970s (Chow and Papanek 1979:15, quoted by Lau 1984:178).

Hong Kong's main industries also provided many opportunities for upward mobility. Since textiles, clothing, plastics, and even electronic components factories could be profitably operated on a small scale, most manufacturing establishments in Hong Kong have been small operations employing fewer than 50 workers (Kelly 1987:58). The number of these establishments increased rapidly during the 1960s and 1970s,[37] with many of them evidently owned by entrepreneurs elbowing their way up from the working class. Most families knew of people who had become rich in this way, and many people hoped eventually to start their own small factories or workshops.

However, the economy in Hong Kong fluctuated from year to year, sometimes drastically; few people in Hong Kong were ever very secure. If the principal income earners in the family became ill, the family's resources could be rapidly depleted, as in the family described by Salaff (1981:118). Small factories and shops frequently went bankrupt, and without unions or a very intrusive code of labour laws, workers were easily fired from their jobs. While the vast majority of the population achieved a much higher standard of living between the 1950s and the 1980s, the upward progress of any particular family was always highly uncertain, and attended by continual risk of failure or of being left behind. This situation was precisely the right situation for Wong Tai Sin to become important in people's lives. Their difficult lives, their uncertainty about their livelihood, and their anxiety to succeed, led tens of thousands of people to beseech the god for help and advice. Their eventual successes and the great increases in their standard of living led many of them to give Wong Tai Sin credit for supplying the help which, in their insecurity, they had so earnestly requested.

Probably the greatest increases in living standards during these decades were experienced by the refugees who had moved into huts and squatter shacks in New Kowloon during the late 1940s and 1950s. As many of these immigrants moved up in Hong Kong society, the reputation of the god who had helped them in their climb likewise spread.

Meanwhile, however, and unknown to most worshippers, the Sik Sik Yuen had faced a serious threat to the existence of its temple in the 1950s. The Sik Sik Yuen's response ensured the survival of the temple throughout the following decades. The survival and prosperity of the Wong Tai Sin temple thus cannot be fully understood without a closer look at the responses and the evolution of the Sik Sik Yuen.

4 The Evolution of the Sik Sik Yuen

IN the late 1940s and early 1950s, the temple had begun to draw many worshippers from among refugees and squatters. The Chinese Temples Ordinance was still on the books, however, and the newly re-established colonial regime soon noticed that the Sik Sik Yuen was more than just a private shrine. If it was not a private shrine, the Chinese Temples Ordinance gave the government the power to expropriate the temple, rent it to whoever bid the most for the right to operate it, and use the revenue for public welfare. The Sik Sik Yuen was in danger of losing its temple. The government was prepared to negotiate. The Secretary of Chinese Affairs invited the person in charge of the Sik Sik Yuen to a meeting at which it was suggested that the Sik Sik Yuen could formally apply to be open to the public during Chinese New Year, and that a 'reasonable application' would allow the temple to continue without government interference. The temple, however, was approaching a crisis.

The Crisis of 1956

In April 1956, the Department of Public Works, which at that time was responsible for the construction of resettlement estates, informed the Sik Sik Yuen that the land on which the temple stood was required for construction in connection with planned public housing blocks to replace squatter huts in the area. A new chairman of the Sik Sik Yuen saved the temple by proposing that the temple could become an important source of funds for the Tung Wah Group of Hospitals, the largest private charitable organization in Hong Kong.

Established in the 1870s, the Tung Wah Group operates hospitals, schools, an old-age home, and other charitable schemes. It also operates nine temples, whose management and surplus income were delegated to the Tung Wah Group by the Hong Kong Government through the Chinese Temples Committee. The government, of course, could legally have expropriated the Wong Tai Sin temple and torn it down to make way for resettlement buildings, or turned its management and surplus income over to the Tung Wah

Group. However, the Sik Sik Yuen saved itself by a stratagem which some members of the organization credit to the god Wong Tai Sin's wisdom and foresight.

Transition to a New Regime in the Sik Sik Yuen

A few months before the crisis of April 1956, the members of Sik Sik Yuen met to choose their officers. The process was carried out, as in some other temples in the area,[1] by divination (in this case, using divination blocks, or *bei bu*). Wong Wan Tin had just joined the group and yet was chosen by divination as the chairman, even though he was its most junior member. Against all precedent, the god passed over the entire list of more senior members to choose the one member of Sik Sik Yuen who had good connections with Tung Wah and would be in the best position to deal successfully with the government. Wong Wan Tin was a former Principal Director of the Tung Wah Group. He had joined the Sik Sik Yuen on the advice of his father, who perceived that the organization might have a very good future. Mr Wong's policies would help to ensure that the Sik Sik Yuen's future was indeed bright.

The deal Wong Wan Tin proposed was to use the popularity of the Wong Tai Sin temple to produce income for Tung Wah. The Sik Sik Yuen would open the temple to the public, charging a 10 cent admission fee at the gate, and all admission fees would go to Tung Wah for use in funding free schools. Further, Tung Wah would collect rent directly from the fortune-tellers clustered around the temple. The government accepted this proposal, backed as it was by Tung Wah, which included wealthy and influential Chinese on its Board of Directors, and by members of the Chinese Temples Committee.

The Sik Sik Yuen, however, was split over the proposal. Although Wong Wan Tin persuaded them to go along, the split remained, and some of the changes instituted by Wong Wan Tin must have deepened it.

Changes After 1956

The general nature of the Sik Sik Yuen changed after 1956, in the direction of a more secular, businesslike, and charity-oriented organization. These changes seem to owe a great deal to the direction of Wong Wan Tin. He appears to have had two main goals: to establish a system of charitable operations funded by the Sik

Sik Yuen and modelled in large part on the Tung Wah Group of which he had been a director; and to reorganize and modernize the Sik Sik Yuen so that its operations would be more businesslike, and not incidentally, also more impressive to the Hong Kong Government.

The first type of change — the expansion of charitable and educational activity — was highly visible. As early as 1959, the Sik Sik Yuen began to move into education by organizing a committee to sponsor and manage schools.[2] By 1992 the Sik Sik Yuen had sponsored three secondary schools, three primary schools, and three kindergartens, offering school places for about 8,000 students. Most of these were built by the mid-1970s.

In the 1980s the Sik Sik Yuen began to move into services for the elderly. As the proportion of elderly in the population of Hong Kong increased, as in all industrialized countries in recent decades, the importance of elderly services also increased (while the importance of funding schools is not as pressing as it was in the 1960s). The Sik Sik Yuen responded to the needs identified by the government, and shifted some of its focus to services for the elderly. Reflecting this change of emphasis, the elderly were featured in the Sik Sik Yuen's seventieth anniversary celebrations in 1991.[3] By 1992, the Sik Sik Yuen had opened five residences, five social centres, and a community centre for the elderly.[4] While much smaller than Tung Wah, the Sik Sik Yuen had become one of the major private charitable organizations in Hong Kong.

This rapid rise resulted not only from astute management by the new chairman, but also from the vast popularity of the temple. Much of the money disbursed by the Sik Sik Yuen comes from donations from worshippers. While petitioning the god, they stuff paper money into donation boxes in the courtyard directly in front of the temple; or if they wish to make a larger donation and have this donation acknowledged by the temple staff, they can walk across the courtyard to the offices of the Sik Sik Yuen, where they will be given a receipt. The money from these donations is not recorded separately in the Sik Sik Yuen's published accounts, but the increasing gate receipts (between 1956 and 1990, a total of over 31 million Hong Kong dollars had been collected from visitors' donations at the gates of the temple and passed on to Tung Wah[5]) can perhaps serve to indicate that such donations must be substantial. Some of this money was used for a complete reconstruction of the temple in the early 1970s.

The second type of change in the Sik Sik Yuen, toward a more secular, businesslike form of organization, was much less visible or well-known. First, the Sik Sik Yuen set up an organization between 1959 and 1961 which was eventually converted into a limited company (in 1965) in order to facilitate dealings with the government and to establish a corporate entity in which to vest control of the schools and other institutions. Leung Gwan Jyun, the son of the founder of the temple, and its proprietor during the war, refused to join the new company, and ceased to hold any official position in the Sik Sik Yuen after 1959, after holding office in the organization almost continuously since 1936. Several other long-time members also ceased to hold office after 1959. It seems likely that Leung Gwan Jyun's influence was much reduced after 1956.[6]

The transition to a more businesslike organization acceptable to the Hong Kong Government, and using temple revenues for philanthropy, were only partly accomplished by the changes introduced by Wong Wan Tin in the 1950s and 1960s. By the late 1970s, the temple's revenues were huge, and yet the organization was still run more like a private club than like a secular philanthropic organization. About 1981, Wong Wan Tin approached the Chinese Temples Committee regarding the need for further changes.

A series of consultations and reviews of the Sik Sik Yuen eventually led to the appointment by the Chinese Temples Committee of six additional directors of the Sik Sik Yuen in 1984, increasing the number of directors from 15 to 21. One of the new directors would be the chairman of the Tung Wah Group of Hospitals, since Tung Wah received a large amount of revenue from the temple and thus had a major interest in its management. The Sik Sik Yuen would benefit from the Tung Wah chairman's expertise in running a modern secular bureaucracy devoted to the public welfare. A second new director would be the government's Wong Tai Sin District Officer, who would serve as the community's representative on the board of directors and help the Sik Sik Yuen to relate its philanthropic spending to various social needs in the district around the temple. The third new director would be the Secretary of the government's Chinese Temples Committee. Three other directors would be chosen for their professional expertise in the various kinds of activities in which the Sik Sik Yuen was involved, such as education, financial management, and so on. In 1990, these three directorships were held by a school principal, an architect, and an accountant. Meanwhile, the Sik Sik Yuen hired a general secretary to manage the affairs of the Sik Sik Yuen. A retired government official served for a three-year term, and was eventually succeeded by his assistant, a young energetic graduate of the University of Hong Kong. These changes helped to move the Sik Sik Yuen further along the road toward the goal of a businesslike modern organization which would both foster and encourage the best of Chinese culture, and contribute substantially to the well-being of the community.

Another change in the character of the Sik Sik Yuen under the new chairman was the virtual elimination of divination as a form of decision-making. The *fuji* divination procedure is no longer used by the Sik Sik Yuen. It ended in the 1970s, after the current practitioner died. Until that time, *fuji* had been performed in a small shrine near the temple called the Feiluan Tai (Terrace/Platform of the Flying Phoenix),[7] which was considered to be, in a sense, the 'private dwelling' of the god. Partly for this reason, women were forbidden to enter. Here, Wong Tai Sin and other gods wrote their special messages to members and selected guests.[8] Now, this small shrine stands obscurely behind the Sik Sik Yuen's office building, ignored by worshippers (who are unaware of its significance), and seldom entered by members. Some directors say that the *fuji* is no longer practised there because no one at present has the qualifications or inspiration to do it. However, Wong Wan Tin has remarked that he stopped the practice because it was too susceptible to manipulation by the interpreter in order to make 'political' statements which are, of course, attributed to the god. He has firmly resisted pressure from some members to bring back *fuji*. No doubt he also wished to avoid the kinds of conflicts which can occur when the ostensible managers of an organization can be confronted with 'revelations' which may undermine their authority.[9]

Not all of the members have been completely happy with the secular character of the modern Sik Sik Yuen.[10] There is no doubt that some of them would like to have a more intimate nexus with the god, a more spiritual experience than they receive from participating on committees and overseeing accounts. Some of them participate in other Taoist organizations in Hong Kong which give greater attention to ritual, chant, and prayer. But the Sik Sik Yuen has held their allegiance, nevertheless, through the grandeur of its shrine and the importance of its activities, and through the prestige of membership in the organization which manages Hong Kong's largest and most popular urban temple.

In addition to eliminating *fuji*, the Sik Sik Yuen also eliminated the use of divination in the internal selection of directors and officers.[11] The god has thus been relegated to the sidelines in the day-to-day operation of the Sik Sik Yuen's affairs.

Of course, divination is still practiced at the temple by the fortune-tellers. They are the mouthpieces of the god, and interpret his messages encoded in the fortune-poems in booths outside the temple, as they have done since the 1930s. But the fortune-tellers rent their stalls from Tung Wah and have no formal connection at all to the organization which manages the temple. The Sik Sik Yuen profits from the public's demand for divination and its credulousness about the god's powers, and depends on the fortune-tellers to sustain their interest. Yet this symbiosis between the Sik Sik Yuen and the fortune-tellers does not prevent the organization from presenting an entirely businesslike and secular face toward the Hong Kong Government in order to minimize interference.

In part, the secularizing of the Sik Sik Yuen's operations also reflected the more eclectic religious views of the chairman. Although he is the head of an organization which is devoted to the worship of a Taoist deity, he is also at the same time, the Vice-President of the Hong Kong Buddhist Association. In this capacity he had contacts with the Chinese Buddhist Association after the restrictions on religion inside China began to decline from the late 1970s onward. At Mr Wong's invitation, the President of the Chinese Buddhist Association visited the temple, writing a poem which was inscribed on a decorative wall built on the grounds of the temple.

The Sik Sik Yuen schools are also eclectic rather than dogmatically Taoist. In the Sik Sik Yuen's high schools, a 'three religions' course is taught each year, and must be passed before students can advance to the next grade. The texts used include some cursory material on Wong Tai Sin, but devote much more space to teaching the history and doctrines of Buddhism, Taoism, and Confucianism. The Sik Sik Yuen has also built shrines in the temple compound devoted to Confucius and to other deities such as Guanyin, the Buddhist goddess of mercy. The teaching of the 'three religions' is a very old tradition in China (Overmyer 1976:133), and some sects have explicitly asserted that the three religions all point, in different ways, to a common core of truth.[12] The Sik Sik Yuen under its current leadership has associated itself with this stream of thought.

In effect, the Sik Sik Yuen has passed far beyond its original focus on one Taoist deity and on Taoist herbal medicines, and has become an organization devoting itself in part to the preservation of traditional Chinese religious culture. The values stressed are those traditionally mandated by that culture — the Buddhist emphasis on charity and benevolent acts, and the Confucian emphasis on education and respect for tradition. Most of these changes seem to have occurred since the late 1950s, under the regime of the new chairman.

The modern Sik Sik Yuen has 131 members (as of 1992), most of whom are businessmen.[13] Several of them joined because their fathers had been members. However, most of these people joined through business and personal network ties with members. Great wealth is not essential, but current directors whom we interviewed say that it is when one becomes wealthy that one will become interested in joining this kind of organization.

Donations to the Sik Sik Yuen from members are voluntary, but the Sik Sik Yuen has various ways to elicit contributions for its projects. During the New Year period, for instance, festive lanterns are auctioned to members. During the 1990 auction, nine lanterns were offered, each with a different name ('more children', 'wealth', 'long life', and so on). Chairs were set up inside the temple for the members and their families and guests, and while thousands of worshippers petitioned the god in the courtyard outside the temple, the directors inside gathered to bid for the lanterns. The directors first assembled in front of the main altar, wearing their ceremonial blue robes. Led by Wong Wan Tin, resplendent in red robes, they first knelt and bowed to Wong Tai Sin three times. Then they returned to their seats for the auction of the lanterns. The auctioneers conducted the bidding in a lively and good-humoured fashion, calling out ten counts at the top bid before awarding each lantern. The bids were competitive, but were not merely neutral quantities of dollars: they were always based on puns between the pronunciation of the numbers and other words in Cantonese having the meaning of good luck, wealth, and so on.[14] Thus, the winning bid for the lantern labelled 'wealth', was HK$26,800 (Cantonese: *yi luk baat*), which sounds in Cantonese like 'easy to make a fortune' (*yi luk faat*). All the winning bids used puns in this way. As each lantern was won, the winning bidder would rise to polite applause, bow to Wong Wan Tin, who bowed back approvingly, and then proceed to the altar to bow to Wong Tai Sin. The bidding raised about HK$250,000 for the organization, and indicates how the members and directors of the Sik Sik Yuen use some of their wealth, under the approving eye of the god, for the organization's purposes, and at the same time gain the recognition and approval of their peers for their generosity.

Of course, the reasons why people join such an organization are complex and seldom completely congruent with the organization's ostensible aims and ideology. Some current members have business relationships with each other, and doubtless some of their business relationships have been facilitated by their membership in the Sik Sik Yuen. Some wealthy individuals have probably achieved a greater measure of respectability than would otherwise be possible by investing some of their time and money in the organization.[15] The astute comments of Lethbridge (1978) in regard to the Tung Wah Group apply almost equally well to the Sik Sik Yuen — the Sik Sik Yuen offers an avenue of status-seeking and prominence for wealthy individuals, who can impress their own community both with the extent of their organization's activities and with the degree of recognition accorded to it by the government. The colonial government in turn needs the good will, co-operation, and charitable energies of wealthy Hong Kong Chinese businessmen, and hence both government and private organization collaborate to enhance each other's dignity and 'face' in the eyes of the public. High officials, including the Governor, have attended the opening ceremonies of various new buildings in the temple compound over the last 15 years, and praise in the accompanying speeches is invariably fulsome on both sides (see, for instance, the speeches reprinted in Sik Sik Yuen 1971 and 1981). The general public, even if only vaguely aware of these ceremonies, cannot fail to be impressed, and the reputation of the temple, and the god, is further enhanced.

The Clinic

The traditional-medicine clinic still remains at the temple. However, most worshippers do not visit the clinic to get herbal medicines. The number of free doses given out by the clinic has not increased significantly since the early 1960s, and has in fact declined in recent years.[16] Most people go to the temple for other reasons. The continued demand for herbal medicines and traditional-medicine consultations has kept the clinic in operation, but attitudes toward medical treatment in Hong Kong have changed greatly since the 1920s, and the Sik Sik Yuen has introduced several innovations at the clinic.

In particular, the increasing faith of the Hong Kong population in Western-style medicine,[17] and the need among low-income families for better access to doctors, prompted the Sik Sik Yuen to bring a doctor to the clinic each day from 1980 onwards. People who go to the clinic can now choose between a doctor and a traditional practitioner. The consultations with the traditional practitioner are still free, but the clinic charges a registration fee for each consultation with the doctor. In 1989–90 the doctors handled more than 58,000 consultations at the clinic, an average of about 200 people per day.[18] In the 1930s, the Sik Sik Yuen's officials were convinced that what Wong Tai Sin cared most about was the medicines. At the time, this meant traditional herbal medicines. Modern medical science has made some inroads into this god's traditional speciality. The Sik Sik Yuen, however, has kept pace with the changes in the attitudes of worshippers, and we can only assume that the god is not far behind.

The Sik Sik Yuen continues to evolve, and some of its current projects would amaze its founders. For example, one of these projects is to fund a 20-inch telescope and an observatory in the New Territories. When this is completed, it will be the only such instrument in Hong Kong. It will eventually be turned over to the government, but will be available for use by students from Sik Sik Yuen schools. The students will not be looking for gods as they peer through the telescope, but since science and technology are increasingly seen as crucial for Hong Kong's development, the Sik Sik Yuen is prepared to participate by funding one of the symbols of the twentieth-century scientific quest for knowledge.

In effect, the Sik Sik Yuen has now become a recent and prosperous reincarnation of a type of organization found in China in the past under various guises, uniting the finances, charitable energies, status-seeking, and business sense of the wealthy to community service and the preservation of religious traditions (Yang 1961:334–5). The Taoist saint Wong Tai Sin has became a figurehead for an organization bent on securing a major position for itself and its directors in the world of Hong Kong temples and temple-sponsored social service and philanthropy.

Yet the increasing divorce of the Sik Sik Yuen from Taoist theology and alchemy has apparently not affected the reputation of the god. His temple is still the largest and most striking urban temple in Hong Kong, and overlooks Kowloon from within a region even more densely populated than during the squatter era. After the building of the subway in the mid–1970s, the temple acquired a new distinction — a subway stop named after the god. Access to the temple from anywhere in the colony has never been easier.

The god's rapid rise from obscurity is the supernatural equivalent of the typical Hong Kong success story — the Guangdong immigrant who arrives in the colony as a refugee and becomes rich through hard work, cunning, and luck.[19] The hard work and the cunning, of course, were supplied by the Sik Sik Yuen and the fortune-tellers. The luck derived from the fortunate coincidence that the temple's location was in an area soon to be flooded with squatters and immigrants, and yet was just far enough from the airfield that it survived the war, and just far enough from the major urban redevelopment areas in Kowloon that it was not seriously threatened until the mid-1950s.

The god was also fortunate in his choice of leaders for the Sik Sik Yuen. They were all deeply religious, but also deeply pragmatic. Leung Yan Ngam had the Taoist-entrepreneurial wisdom and vision to attract wealthy backers for his new shrine in Kowloon, and he chose the site brilliantly; his son, Leung Gwan Jyun, enhanced the temple's reputation through his dealings with the Japanese and with local villagers during the war; and Wong Wan Tin had just the right combination of character, ability, and connections to save the temple from expropriation in 1956, and to remake the Sik Sik Yuen into a charitable and educational foundation acceptable to the government, and increasingly prominent in the community.

5 Believers

WE have described the history of the Kowloon temple, and the growth in worship of Wong Tai Sin. We have also attempted to explain the great success of this god by referring to the historical changes in the region. We have argued that the temple benefited from these events because of its location and because of the astute decisions of its managers. However, we have not yet looked closely at the people who now believe in Wong Tai Sin. Anyone who observes these worshippers on any typical, busy day at the temple cannot fail to be struck by the diversity of people who come to ask the god for help and advice. Male and female, old, middle-aged, and young, they climb the steps to the temple courtyard, light incense sticks, and bow toward the central shrine containing the god's image. Most of them then kneel on the ground to lay out offerings and petition the god. Why do these people come to the temple? What do they believe about this god? What are his special interests? How do they think he helps them?

In this chapter we will present what we have been able to learn about these people, about their beliefs and expectations regarding Wong Tai Sin, and about their experiences of his power.

Sources of Data on Believers

The best way to get a general profile of people who worship Wong Tai Sin would be to get a complete list of current worshippers, draw a random sample from the list, and interview the people in the sample. This would allow generalizations to the total population of worshippers. Several problems make such a study impossible. First, there is no list of worshippers. Most people come to the temple, make their offerings of food to the god, pray or consult a fortune-teller, and leave. They do not register with the Sik Sik Yuen, and their names are never recorded. Hence there is no easy way to draw a proper sample.

If one still wished to make statistical generalizations about the characteristics of worshippers, the next best alternative would be to conduct a large number of interviews with a sample of the population in Hong Kong, and then extract a sub-sample using those who have reported that they occasionally go to the temple to worship the god. However, a recent survey suggests that only about 30 per cent of the adult population of Hong Kong will admit going to temples such as the Wong Tai Sin temple (although in some districts the proportion may be higher).[1] The proportion who acknowledge going to the Wong Tai Sin temple will be some sub-group of these people. Further, while most of the people who visit the Wong Tai Sin temple live in Kowloon, this would not allow us to exclude other areas in designing a survey; any sample would have to cover Hong Kong Island and the New Territories even though relatively few people visit the temple from those areas. Hence, a survey based on a random sample of the Hong Kong population would be a very expensive way of trying to interview believers in Wong Tai Sin.

The third alternative is to interview people at the temple. This is far from ideal, for several reasons. Any such survey would probably be restricted to only a few interviewing days during the year, and it cannot be assumed that a selection of worshippers on these days would be typical of the total population of believers. If housewives usually go on weekday mornings, young people on weekends, businessmen at Chinese New Year, and fervent believers on the first and fifteenth of the month, a proper survey at the temple would require many days of interviewing over several months.

There is an additional problem: some people visiting the temple are not willing to be interviewed, or are willing to answer only a few questions before quitting the interview. The 'refusal rate' varies with the characteristics of the interviewee and the demeanour and interpersonal skills of the interviewer, who must entice busy and absorbed worshippers to stop, quite unexpectedly, and answer questions from a stranger. Despite these problems, approaching and interviewing worshippers at the temple is the most economical method for researchers and has been used in all surveys of believers of which we are aware. Data from four such surveys will provide most of the information in this chapter.

For a general profile of worshippers at the temple, we will use four surveys carried out by university students in Hong Kong:

(a) interviews with 34 worshippers by eight students in the Sociology Department at the University of Hong Kong (Chin, et al., 1977);

(b) interviews with about 90 worshippers by two students in the Department of Religion at Chung Chi College, Chinese University of Hong Kong (Fong and Luk 1989);

(c) interviews with 60 worshippers by a student also in the Department of Religion at Chung Chi College (Shum 1990);

(d) interviews with 24 worshippers by three students in the Sociology Department at the University of Hong Kong (Chan, Chow, and Hung 1990).

All of these student surveys were well-done, and included interesting and thoughtful analysis of the results.[2] Since the first two surveys asked essentially the same questions, and often used similar or identical categories to classify the answers, while the last two surveys focused primarily on fortune-telling at the temple and thus had a somewhat different focus, we will rely most heavily on the data from the 1977 and 1989 surveys, supplemented whenever possible by data from the 1990 surveys.

For an account of how worshippers perceive Wong Tai Sin — their general knowledge about this god, their beliefs about his teachings, and their 'miracle stories' showing the god's effectiveness in predicting the future or in helping worshippers — we will use:

(a) material collected by six students recruited by Lang from the Chinese University of Hong Kong who interviewed about 70 worshippers at the temple in November and December, 1989;[3]

(b) information from interviews in November 1983, with about 14 worshippers at the temple carried out by students in the Anthropology Department at the Chinese University of Hong Kong (Chan, et al., 1984); and

(c) results of several other pre-arranged interviews with selected believers.

We will begin with a general profile of worshippers using data from the student surveys; then we proceed to examine the beliefs of worshippers about Wong Tai Sin and his powers; and finally, we attempt to explain the appeal of this god in terms of the problems and life experiences of worshippers.

Believers: A Profile

Residence

In both the 1977 and 1989 surveys, the majority of respondents lived in Kowloon (1977: 81 per cent; 1989: 56 per cent), that is, in the residential districts within about 8 kilometres to the east, west, and south of the temple. A smaller proportion came from Kong Kong Island and the New Territories.

Fig. 1 Residential Districts of Worshippers (1977 and 1989)

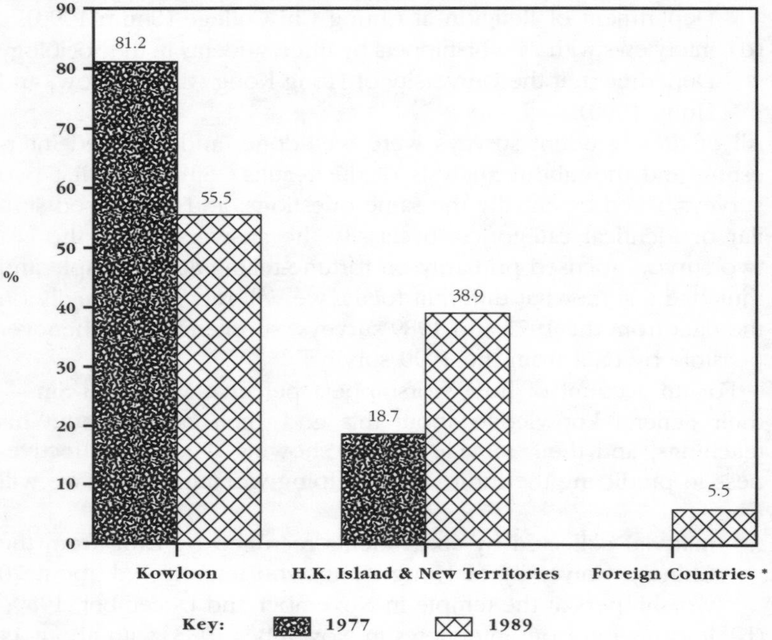

Key: 1977   1989

Sources: 1977: Chin, et al., 1977: Table 2
1989: Fong and Luk 1989: Table 4

The 1989 survey, however, showed an increase in the proportion of worshippers coming from these latter districts, compared to 1977 (see Fig. 1). This difference between the residential distribution of worshippers in 1977 and in 1989 may be due only to the small size of the two surveys, particularly the 1977 survey. However, the expansion of rapid transit between 1977 and 1989, in the form of new electric trains and a new subway system,[4] made travel to the temple from Hong Kong Island and the New Territories much easier and quicker. Hence the greater number of worshippers from these areas in the 1989 survey may reflect a real change.

Many people from Kowloon have moved to the New Territories during the last fifteen years, and those who worshipped at the temple before relocating can now continue to visit from their new location. Potential worshippers in these areas who were in the past deterred by the long and tiring journey can also now visit the temple with ease. Hence, we are inclined to believe that a substantially larger proportion of worshippers now come to the temple from outside Kowloon than was the case in 1977. The temple has never been the focus of worship for any single community. It has always drawn worshippers from outside the villages in its immediate neighbourhood. With the dispersal of population into the new towns, and the tremendous increase in the speed and efficiency of public transportation, the residential distribution of worshippers is probably even wider now than it was in the past.

All three surveys also detected worshippers from foreign countries. In the 1977 survey, only one such person is mentioned: a 40 year old woman working as an amah in Thailand who came to the temple to worship whenever she visited Hong Kong. In the 1989 survey, 5 of the 90 respondents were living in other countries — one from each of England, Canada, Malaysia, Japan, and Indonesia. In the 1990 survey, the interviewer encountered worshippers from North America and from Thailand. These are all Hong Kong-born Chinese who have emigrated or are living abroad for business reasons but visit the temple on return visits to Hong Kong. We had heard of such visitors anecdotally, and had met a few of them in Canada and in Sweden, but were interested to discover that they show up as a significant group in a sample as small as 90 worshippers. This suggests that Chinese living abroad are now a significant part of the temple's clientelle.

An interesting question, which we will raise without giving a clear answer, is whether Wong Tai Sin's power and influence are perceived by worshippers to be primarily local, or whether he is a truly transnational god. Where does he live? How far does his knowledge and influence extend? It is clear that worshippers abroad still feel that he can help them with their problems. However, they do not seem willing to pray to him from abroad. Either they return to Hong Kong to ask for his advice and benevolent attention, or they ask relatives to go to the temple on their behalf. The god's power, his 'presence', seem to be focused around the temple. It is also interesting that the Wong Tai Sin police station is the only one in the territory (as far as we know) which includes a shrine to Wong Tai Sin along with the typical police station shrine to Guandi. Wong Tai Sin is the presiding deity of the district which has been named after him, and they decided they could not ignore his power.[5]

Socio-economic Status

In the 1977 survey, nearly half of the respondents were skilled or unskilled workers (mostly factory workers), while 12 per cent were white-collar workers; 12 per cent were housewives, and 23 per cent were retired; there were also two students among those interviewed (Chin, et al., 1977:21).

Excluding the retired, the housewives, and the two students, the skilled and unskilled workers comprised 80 per cent of the employed worshippers. In the Hong Kong labour force in 1976, there was a higher proportion of white-collar workers and a lower proportion of skilled and unskilled workers.[6] Thus, the skilled and unskilled workers appear to be over-represented in this sample of worshippers. The numbers in the 1977 survey were small, but these data are at least consistent with Lee's conclusion (Lee 1985:208) that it is people in the lower socio-economic strata who are more likely to worship the Chinese gods.

The 1989 survey did not include a question about occupation, but did include a question about respondents' total family income in 1988 (Fong and Luk 1989: Table 5). Income data are also available for Hong Kong, as well as for the Wong Tai Sin district comprising several dozen square kilometres surrounding the temple, for 1986. We can roughly compare the income distribution of the worshippers' families with those of Hong Kong in general, and with the district surrounding the temple: At the low end of the income scale, 22 per cent of worshippers at the temple came from families with gross incomes of less than HK$4,000 (HK$78 to US$1) per month. By contrast, in 1986, 35 per cent of families in Hong Kong, and 37 per cent of families in the Wong Tai Sin district, had incomes of less than HK$4,000 per month.[7] The next income category, HK$4,000–6,000, accounted for 36 per cent of worshippers' families, compared to 23 per cent for Hong Kong and 25 per cent for the Wong Tai Sin district. The two categories, taken together, might be considered to define the lower income strata in Hong Kong. They comprised 58 per cent of worshippers and of Hong Kong residents, and 62 per cent of people living around the temple. We could conclude, tentatively, that the distribution of people from low-income families among the worshippers appears to be not very different from the proportions of such families in the general population, and if anything, the poorest families are under-represented among the worshippers.

However, upper-income earners were not found in the 1989 survey. In 1986, about 18 per cent of families in Hong Kong, and about 12 per cent of families in the area around the temple, had incomes above HK$10,000 per month, while none were reported in the sample of worshippers. This finding, however, is mislead-ing. The members of the Sik Sik Yuen include many wealthy men who are believers. They will never appear in a survey conducted in the temple courtyard, since they worship inside the temple (one of the privileges of membership). Also, anecdotal evidence and observation suggest that many businessmen come to the temple to thank the god during the Chinese New Year period, and none of the surveys were conducted at Chinese New Year.

To summarize: the socio-economic data suggest that worship-pers include approximately the same proportions of lower-income families as are found in the general population, and that these lower-income families constitute the majority of the temple's clients. Upper-income families are not usually found among ordinary wor-shippers in the temple courtyard. However, people from very poor families may also be under-represented.

Sex

Despite the fact that the 1977 and 1989 surveys were separated by twelve years, their findings were identical: 74 per cent of the inter-viewees in each survey were female, while 26 per cent were male. The ratio in the 1990 survey was very similar: 70 per cent female and 30 per cent male. It is possible that student interviewers find it easier to approach female worshippers, or that female worship-pers are more willing to be interviewed than male worshippers,[8] but since these findings match our own casual observations of the proportions of males and females at the temple, we will tentatively accept them as probably accurate during most of the year (with the qualification that during the Chinese New Year period, a larger proportion of men visit the temple, as clearly indicated in photo-graphs of the crowds during this period. Some men evidently come to the temple only during the New Year period, probably to offer thanks for the year's business or career successes).

There are several reasons why more females than males go to the temple. Firstly, many women in Hong Kong work only part-time, or are primarily housewives, and consequently they have time to visit the temple during the day. In 1988, about 48 per cent of women 15 years or older were in the labour force, while about 80 per cent of men were in the labour force (Ng 1989:122).

Secondly, many Hong Kong women serve as the religious spe-cialists for their families (in part because many of them are not working outside the home and have more time). They service the household altars to ancestors and to other figures such as the stove god (burning incense, setting out offerings, and so on), and also see themselves — and are often seen by their husbands — as responsible for visiting temples to solicit the help of the appropriate gods to protect and advance the family. Other studies report a similar finding.[9] In the 1977 survey, asked whether they were petitioning the god only for themselves, or also for other people, a number of the women said that they were asking the god to help others, which invariably meant their families.[10]

Thirdly, women have more potential health problems than men as a result of child-bearing. Their longer average lifespans also mean that there are more elderly women than elderly men. (In 1986, among Hong Kong people 65 years or older, females outnumbered males by 33 per cent [Kwong 1989:370].) Elderly people are frequently beset with medical problems. Thus, the god's reputation as a healer and purveyor of medical prescriptions could be expected to produce a higher proportion of women than of men at the temple.

Fourthly, it is possible that many women feel less powerful than men. In mate choice, most women do not feel they can be as aggressive as the men. With less freedom to pursue preferred options, they must find more subtle means of getting what they want. In their careers, their sense of control may also be lower than that of men,[11] and of course, many women do not work outside the home, or work part-time, or have relatively low incomes, and hence they are more dependent on the income provided by other family members. To the extent that women feel more powerless for any of these reasons, the prospect of help by a god may be appealing. The temple offers access to a source of power which they can use to gain more control over their fate.

Age

All ages are represented in the 1977 and 1989 surveys (Fig. 2). Those over 50 were especially noticeable: 35 per cent of the 1977 interviewees, and 28 per cent of the 1989 interviewees. Those aged 20 or below were only a small proportion of each group: 9 per cent in 1977 and 4 per cent in 1989. The biggest difference between the surveys in 1977 and in 1989 was in the proportions of people in the age group 20–30: they comprised 21 per cent of the 1977

Fig. 2 Age of Worshippers (1977 and 1989)

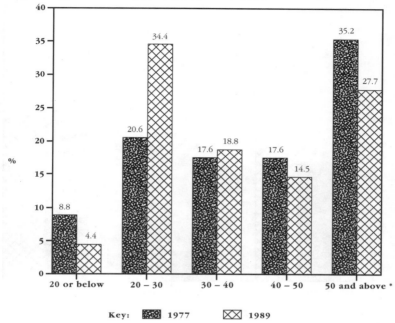

Key: ■ 1977   ⊠ 1989

Sources: 1977: Chin, et al., 1977: Table 1
1989: Fong and Luk 1989: Table 3
Note: 1989: 50–60: 11.1%; 60 and above: 16.6%

group, but 34 per cent of the 1989 group.[12] With such small numbers in each group, it is not possible to draw any conclusions from
this difference. We merely note that young people are clearly well-
represented, and their numbers roughly match the numbers of worshippers above the age of 50.

Indeed, it is striking that in both surveys, roughly two-thirds or
more of worshippers are *not* over the age of 50, and between 30
per cent and 40 per cent of each group were under the age of
30.[13] Since most of these younger worshippers grew up in Hong
Kong, not in China, it is clear that the temple has attracted a
second and third generation of worshippers who will replace the
people who began worshipping at the temple as refugee squatters
in the 1950s. This fact also stands out sharply in the data on
duration of worship.

Fig. 3 Duration of Worship (1977 and 1989)

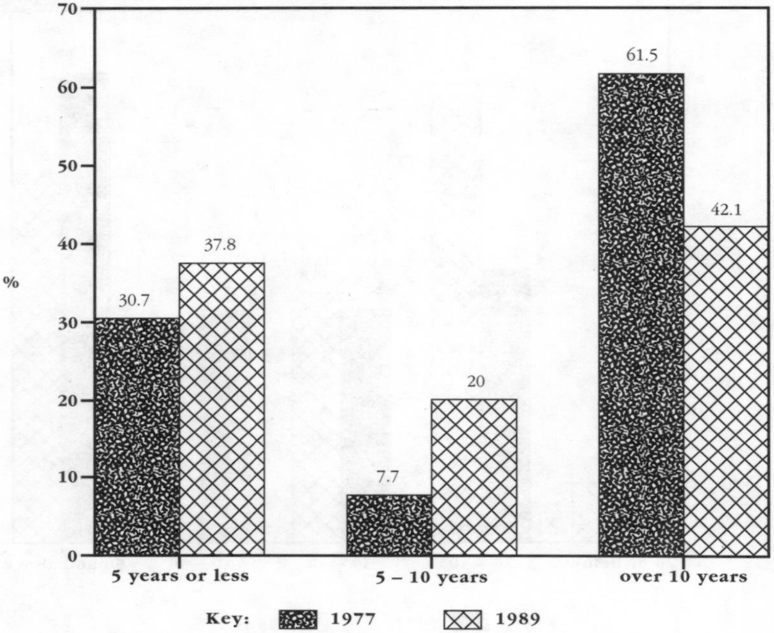

Key: ▓ 1977   ⧅ 1989

Sources: 1977: Chin, et al., 1977: Table 5
1989: Fong and Luk 1989: Table 6
Note: 1989: 10–15 years: 11.1%; 15–20 years: 5.5%;
20 years or more: 25.5%

Duration of Worship

Both the 1977 and 1989 surveys asked respondents how long they had been going to the temple, and the results again show the success of the temple in attracting new worshippers (Fig. 3). A large proportion of the respondents in both surveys had been going to the temple for five years or less (31 per cent of the 1977 respondents, 38 per cent of the 1989 respondents).

At the same time, the temple had clearly retained the allegiance of other worshippers over long periods of time. About 60 per cent of the 1977 group and 42 per cent of the 1989 group had been visiting the temple for more than 10 years. In the 1989 group, 26 per cent of those interviewed had been visiting the temple for 20 years or more.

To summarize: while continuing to attract many people who began worshipping at the temple in the 1950s and 1960s, the temple has also been able to attract large numbers of new worshippers in the recent past.

Frequency of Visiting the Temple

The three surveys show that only a small proportion of worshippers go to the temple as often as four or more times a year: the actual figure is probably in the general range defined by the surveys: 17 per cent (1977); 21 per cent (1990); 24 per cent (1989). A very small number of these worshippers attend almost weekly. But the vast majority — 76 per cent to 83 per cent in the surveys — go three times per year or less. Indeed, in the 1989 survey, 40 per cent of those interviewed reported going to the temple only once in the past year. In the 1990 survey, 53 per cent reported going only once or twice during the year.

There is some possibility of under-reporting of temple visits. Younger respondents may be aware that some university students consider such temple visits to be 'superstition', and may be embarrassed to be apprehended at the temple by a student interviewer. One such embarrassed response is described in the 1977 study. Given such reactions, some of the younger respondents may be admitting only their current visit, which of course they can hardly deny.

However, we believe that the data are probably accurate. Interviews by Graeme Lang's student interviewers in 1989 also showed that most people went to the temple only once or twice a year.

Reported Reasons for Going to the Temple

Most people in the 1989 survey reported going to the temple to ask for something from the god: help, advice, or predictions. The two most common questions or petitions to the god were about health (23 per cent) and career prospects (22 per cent). There was some difference in emphasis between males and females: the females asked more often about health (25 per cent) than about careers (20 per cent), while the men asked more about careers (26 per cent) than about health (17 per cent). Much smaller proportions asked about family matters or about fate in regard to love and marriage, and a few asked about their studies.

There was also a more general type of petition, for a 'peaceful life (*ping an*)' (14 per cent of respondents). These people are basically asking for freedom from anxiety. For most people, to desire *ping an* is to desire a life without tensions or crises. The god provides this sense of peacefulness by offering a kind of blanket protection from crisis and discord. The visit to the temple helps to produce this feeling, since people have the experience of communing with a powerful and benevolent supernatural patron who pays some special attention to them during their visits to the temple. This feeling of peace and enhanced security may even contribute to their physical health.[14]

A much smaller number went only to thank the god (7.7 per cent) or only to worship (7.7 per cent). The number of people who go to thank the god will vary enormously depending on the time of the year. Around the end of the year (just before Chinese New Year) and during the New Year period, many people go to the temple to show their gratitude for the peace and good fortune of the previous year.[15] During this period, one sees a large number of roast pigs among the offerings brought to the temple: these worshippers are both thanking the god for a good year, and asking for another one just as good.

During most days of the year, however, worshippers go to the temple because they have a problem or a question, or are seeking peace of mind in the face of the potential problems which threaten them.

Are Worshippers Monotheists or Polytheists?

Traditionally, Chinese popular religion has been polytheistic. The practice of deifying historical persons has led to a large number of 'gods', some of whom were first promoted to godhood by the State for their extraordinary abilities as warriors, sages, or bureaucrats (Yang 1961), or were co-opted into the State-supported pantheon from among the saints worshipped by the common people (see, for example, Watson 1985).

Most of the temples in Hong Kong and the New Territories include shrines to several gods or goddesses besides the central shrine to the temple's main god. The reason is simply that many worshippers bow to more than one god, and like to be able to do this while visiting a temple. (Altars to other gods also increase the 'drawing power' of a temple by broadening its appeal). Polytheistic beliefs and the presence of statues of several different gods in the same temple appear to be quite typical of Chinese popular religion as practised in Hong Kong. The Wong Tai Sin temple is no exception. Smaller buildings on the grounds of the temple contain icons representing Guanyin, the Buddhist goddess of mercy, and Lu Dongbin, another Taoist immortal. It would not be surprising, then, to find that worshippers at Wong Tai Sin also worship other gods, and go to other temples when their main business is with one of these other gods. Many of them do go to other temples. In the 1989 interviews, worshippers mentioned the Chegong temple near Shatin most often, and several others mentioned going to a Guanyin temple. One woman said she also went to a temple to the goddess Tianhou — who is worshipped primarily among people who make their living from the sea — because she said her family included several sailors. Given the typical polytheism of popular religion, such visits to other temples are not unusual.

What is truly surprising, however, is that some worshippers of Wong Tai Sin do not worship other gods. In the 1977 survey, 20 of 27 respondents said that they do not go to other temples. Some of them no doubt worship other gods, either at the Wong Tai Sin temple or in their homes (some of which, for instance, will have small statues of Guanyin on the family altar), but many of them apparently worship only Wong Tai Sin. In the 1989 survey, 44.5 per cent of those interviewed said they do not worship other gods (Fong and Luk 1989: Table 11). Most of them evidently believe that only Wong Tai Sin is powerful and efficacious for the kinds of problems that they face.

It is not easy to explain this finding of 'quasi-monotheism' among believers in Wong Tai Sin. Very tentatively, we suggest that some people who would not go to any other temples, and are otherwise not particularly religious, are willing to go to the Wong Tai Sin temple because going there is much more pleasant. Most other urban temples in Hong Kong are inconveniently located on back streets, usually some distance from a subway stop and requiring ten or fifteen minutes walk. Access to the Wong Tai Sin temple, by contrast, is easy and convenient (right on the subway line). As other commentators reflecting on the worship of Wong Tai Sin have observed (for example, Cheung 1975; Chin, et al., 1977; Fong and Luk 1989), the temple draws people in part because worship and petitions to this god are very easy and convenient. Visits to the temple require little time, and produce quick results in terms of the god's 'answers' to their questions. It is the ideal type of religion for busy urbanites who have little interest in complex doctrines or frequent rituals and ceremonies. Most other urban temples in Hong Kong are also quite old by the standards of Hong Kong buildings, with few of them built later than the early twentieth century. Their exteriors are usually dirty and discoloured, and over many decades of use their interiors have been blackened with the smoke of burning incense. The Wong Tai Sin temple, by contrast, is large, beautiful, and spacious, and because ordinary worshippers are not allowed to burn incense inside any of the buildings, the interiors are still immaculate. Finally, in most other urban temples, if one wishes to worship the god, one must enter the building, where one inevitably encounters the resident fortune-teller and temple-keeper. For devotees, the personal attention they receive from the fortune-teller and the temple-keeper may be appealing. If they donate regularly, they will be greeted by the temple-keeper and given special treatment. For others who want to avoid being singled out for attention, the Wong Tai Sin temple, with its large courtyard and its thousands of worshippers, affords a welcome anonymity.

The temple has also benefited from a large amount of publicity in the Hong Kong media, including regular annual news reports on television about the huge crowds at the temple during Chinese New Year. Media interest in the temple eventually also led to a TV drama series about the life of Wong Cho Ping, which was broadcast on the most popular of the Hong Kong Chinese TV stations (TVB) in 1986. The details of the life of Cho Ping in the series were largely fictional (that is, not based on literary sources). The plot drew themes from the popular Hong Kong movie genre in which the supernatural errant knight (in this case, Wong Cho Ping) battles evil forces, and there was even some borrowing from the Judeo-Christian mythic tradition to add spice to the plot.[16] This coverage of the temple and of Wong Tai Sin by the media is only partly due to the temple's popularity with the masses. It also results in part from another fortunate coincidence for Wong Tai Sin: one of the principal 'nodes' of the Hong Kong media world is located on Broadcast Drive in Kowloon Tong, about one kilometre west of the temple. Apparently, some of the movie and television people who work at the studios go to the temple to ask for Wong Tai Sin's help or predictions for their projects, and when their productions succeed, they return to the temple to thank him. The good-humoured and favourable coverage of the temple in the Hong Kong media is thus due in part to their proximity to the temple and their own interest in this god. The occasional picture in Hong Kong tabloid newspapers showing comely local actresses posing at the temple while performing their religious duties also help to make the temple a fashionable place to visit, especially for young people.[17]

For all of these reasons, many who might otherwise avoid going to temples are thus willing to try a visit to Wong Tai Sin, to ask the god a question and see what happens. Some of them, inevitably, will receive an answer which impresses them — they will recover from an illness, a family or business problem will be resolved, or a prediction will turn out to have been accurate (after reflection about its meaning) — and they will return to thank the god and perhaps to ask another question the next time they have a problem.

Another source of appeal which may make Wong Tai Sin more attractive than some other gods is that while most of the others are specialized, he has become a generalist. For example, Tianhou, the 'Queen of Heaven', was originally worshipped by fishermen for her power to protect them from disasters at sea. She is still worshipped mainly by fishing communities (or communities with a strong historical link to the sea), and by sailors. Some coastal villages now engaged in agriculture also worship her (see Watson 1985), but she is still mainly associated with the ocean, with those who work in boats, and has little to offer to ambitious and hyperactive urbanites. Guandi, the so-called 'god of war', was reknowned during his lifetime as a fierce and loyal warrior, and was canonized for these qualities. His statue is now found in small shrines in many shops, protecting the establishment from harmful forces. His qualities have also endeared him to the police, who maintain shrines to him in the police stations, and evidently also to the triads, for much the same reasons, but he is not worshipped as one who has an interest in the ordinary problems of ordinary people. Guanyin, the Buddhist 'goddess of mercy', is widely worshipped by women for her special interest in problems of the family: pregnancy, the health of mothers and children, and protection from amorphous dangers which threaten them, but she is too specialized to appeal very much to business people, factory workers, or students. Wong Tai Sin, by contrast, is not confined within any traditions which closely identify him with some particular type of activity (most worshippers know little or nothing of Wong Cho Ping). He has become available for all of the kinds of problems which face ambitious but insecure urbanites in the rapidly changing capitalist industrial society which Hong Kong has become since World War II. Because he is unspecialized, he is able to respond to most of these problems, and so in the eyes of some believers worship of this god makes it unnecessary to worship other gods.

Differences Among Worshippers: Qualitative Data

The survey data suggest that there are a number of different reasons why people go to the temple. Considering the range in age, and the differences between those who grew up in China and those who grew up in Hong Kong, we might also expect a variety of different perceptions of the god. We now proceed to a more nuanced account of the kinds of beliefs, perceptions, and forms of behaviour which can be found among the worshippers at the temple.

Young Worshippers Under 20

Among the young people interviewed at the temple in the various surveys, some had come with their parents and a few others had gone at the instigation of parents. However, there were also a number of teenagers who came to the temple in groups. These groups are interesting for what they reveal about the motivations of young worshippers.

In 1983, for instance, five girls, 15 to 16 years old, were interviewed at the temple (Chan, et al., 1984). They were all attending the same school. All five claimed that this was their first visit to the temple. They bought incense and then proceeded into the temple courtyard, where they knelt and bowed to the god. Unlike most older worshippers, they did not bring any food offerings such as meat or fruit. (When asked why they had not brought food offerings, one of them said: 'We don't know what Wong Tai Sin likes to eat'). After performing the customary bows, they asked the god various questions using the fortune sticks (*qiu qian*). It is not easy to shake one of the sticks out of the container, and they were not skilled in the procedure. When the first girl managed to shake out one of the sticks, the others all cried out in delight. Eventually, each girl got two or three answers using the fortune sticks.

The questions they asked the god were about their studies, about their personal lives and prospects, and about their families. They also asked a few questions on behalf of classmates who were too busy to accompany them to the temple. When they had finished, they took several of their questions to a fortune-teller outside the gates, and used the small book which explains the fortune-poems to try to determine the god's answers to their other questions.

When asked whether the god had predicted good or bad outcomes in regard to their prospects, they replied that it was unimportant; they didn't care whether the answers were good or bad. They evidently wanted to give the impression that they didn't take the proceedings very seriously. They had come to the temple, they seemed to be saying, for fun, or for an interesting experience. (Jordan and Overmyer [1986:158] have noted similar behaviour among Chinese schoolgirls in Taiwan). Indeed, they claimed that they had no particular religious beliefs.

However, they also said they had come to this temple because they had heard other people say that the god Wong Tai Sin is very 'efficacious' (Cantonese: *lihng-yihm*) in his predictions and advice. They also acknowledged going to the Chegong Temple near Shatin. Thus, while the visit to the temple with a group of friends was indeed a 'fun' experience for them, and while they didn't treat the divination very seriously, they were clearly 'playing' at religion to see if they liked it, and to see what would be the outcome of their questions. Going as a group made this easy and pleasant for them.

Another group of three females, about 18 years old, were interviewed at the temple in 1989. They said they came to the temple several times a year, and also during the New Year period. One of them began going to the temple with her mother, and was now continuing to visit with her two friends. One of them also acknowledged visits to the Chegong Temple when having bad luck (the Chegong Temple is widely seen as a place to petition for a change from bad fortune to good fortune). They were accustomed to using the fortune sticks and consulting fortune-tellers. They had no knowledge of the historical figure Wong Cho Ping, or of his miracle of turning the stones into sheep. They were mainly conscious of the god as a source of supernatural aid and advice for a variety of situations which they faced in their lives, but they also believed that there was a moral dimension to worship of Wong Tai Sin: in response to a question about what Wong Tai Sin teaches, one answered that one must behave well and do good things, and good fortune will follow.

These two groups of teenage girls illustrate the variety of attitudes among worshippers in this age group. Some, like the younger group, are trying out these religious activities to see how they feel, and asking the god questions to see whether the answers are interesting. Others, like the older group of girls, are more serious in their devotions and in their petitions to the god. They have already encountered the ethical dimension stressed by both Buddhism and Taoism, and realize that the god's response to their petitions may be influenced by their own behaviour as well as by the quantity of their offerings.

Both groups show that a visit to the temple with friends is a congenial form of worship for young people who have not yet set up their own families, and are still enmeshed in their adolescent peer groups. We may assume that many young people who would not go to the temple on their own are carried along on temple visits by a group of their friends. As the peer group begins to dissolve as its members drift off into careers, marriage, and child-raising, some of these people will return to the temple on their own, or with members of their own family, in the pattern more typical of adult worshippers.

Adult Worshippers

What do adult worshippers know about the life and miracles of Wong Cho Ping? What do they believe Wong Cho Ping expects of them, if anything, besides worship and offerings of food and incense? How do they think Wong Cho Ping intervenes in their lives? What stories do they tell about the exercise of his power in their world? We will consider these questions in turn.

In 1989, Graeme Lang instructed his student interviewers to ask worshippers about the life and miracles of Wong Tai Sin by asking them the following questions: 'Do you know in which part of China Wong Tai Sin lived before he became an immortal?'; and, 'Did Wong Tai Sin perform any miracles before he became an immortal? Which miracles?'. Very soon, however, it became apparent that asking these questions was largely a waste of time.

Very few of the worshippers knew the answers to either question. Most of the worshippers seemed to have no knowledge at all of the life of Wong Cho Ping. The few who had an opinion about the life of Wong before he became an immortal gave responses such as the following: 'he was a teacher'; 'he healed so many people he became a god'; 'he always helped people on earth, so he became a god', and so on. A few people knew that he had looked after sheep — several had learned this from a television drama broadcast on local television several years earlier. A few more people were also aware of the miracle of turning the rocks into sheep. One man had read about this miracle in the book of fortune poems. A fifteen year old boy visiting the temple with his mother had learned about the miracle of rocks into sheep from his religion class at one of the schools sponsored by the Sik Sik Yuen (in which the mandatory religion classes include some coverage of the life of Wong Cho Ping). All of his classmates, he said, also knew about this miracle, but very few adult worshippers at the temple seem to be aware of this story.

Nobody seemed to know where Wong Tai Sin lived in China before he became a god, even though 'Jinhua', the mountain where he lived and became an immortal, is written in large characters on a stone façade above the entrance to the temple courtyard. As might be expected, this general lack of detailed knowledge leaves gaps which people will sometimes fill with their own constructions, borrowing details from other local stories. A few examples will illustrate the process.

Oral Accounts Containing Novel Details

Occasionally, people will recount stories about Wong Tai Sin which did not originally refer to Wong Tai Sin, but to some other figure.[18] For instance, in a paper on temples on Hong Kong Island, Marjorie Topley related the account given her by a Cantonese lady of the life of Wong Tai Sin. Her informant claimed that he was found dead, sitting in a Buddhist [sic] meditation position at the base of a cliff, and covered with earth from a landslide. When his body was removed, it was found to be sweet-smelling and uncorrupted. (Topley and Hayes 1966:129). There is no such story in the written sources about the life of Wong Cho Ping. Topley's informant obviously had not had access to these sources. Such unusual details as she related are unlikely to have been fabricated on the spot by the informant herself. Where then did she get her version of the story?

The story of a saint whose body remains uncorrupted long after death is a common motif in Christian legends (Loomis [1948:54] cites about 200 instances) but we discovered a probable local source for her story about the body of Wong Tai Sin: a similar story would have been circulating in Hong Kong in 1966 concerning the monk Yue Xi. This monk had died in 1965 at the age of 87 after presiding over a Buddhist temple and pagoda in the hills above Shatin, New Territories, since the early 1950s. After he died:

His body was placed in a sitting position in a square box. It was then buried in the hillside behind his temples, and after eight months, the body was exhumed. People who were there have recorded that there was hardly any sign of decay, and that the body had a phosphorescent glow (Savidge 1977:107).

The coincidence of details between the two cases — in both, the individual was buried in a sitting position on (or at the base of) a hillside, and when exhumed the body had not decayed — suggests that Topley's informant was transferring a miracle story she had heard about an obscure monk who lived in the mountains to explain the origins of a famous god who was once an equally obscure hermit.

Although stories about Wong Tai Sin which draw elements from local stories about other gods or temples are only a small fraction of the responses which greet the interviewer's questions to worshippers, they are nevertheless interesting because they illustrate the kind of mixing and mingling of traditions which must have characterized the early history of many religions prior to the establishment of canonical literature. As noted above, most worshippers know little or nothing about Wong Tai Sin's life on earth as Wong Cho Ping, and given his reputation for efficacy, they probably do not care about his origins. (Elliott [1955:78–9], who studied Chinese cults in Singapore, also observed that worshippers did not know, and did not much care, about the biographies of some of the gods whom they worshipped.) By contrast, most worshippers readily answer a question about what Wong Tai Sin expects of worshippers.

What Does Wong Tai Sin Teach?

Student interviewers from the two universities in Hong Kong have been struck by the individualistic and utilitarian character of worship at the temple (Chin, et al., 1977); people go to the temple to get some personal benefit from a few simple acts of worship and from petitions and offerings to the god, but their relationship with this god is unburdened by complicated doctrines or requirements, or by any strict morality (Fong and Luk 1989). This kind of analysis probably contains an implied comparison with the major 'ethical' religions of Buddhism and Christianity, in which adherence to some ethical system is required, along with some sense that religion induces a concern for the welfare of others, in addition to whatever gratifications are sought from the religion for oneself. In other words, for some educated observers, the worship of Wong Tai Sin is based on the pursuit of self-interest, and lacks a commitment to ethics, doctrines, or any transcendent goal.

We do not reject this depiction; it contains a large measure of truth. Most worshippers do go to the temple to ask for something: help and advice about medical problems, family, career, future prospects, and so on. A few worshippers also state that Wong Tai Sin is only concerned with such matters. One said, for instance, that Wong Tai Sin has no teachings except 'ask and it shall be granted'. Another said that Wong Tai Sin tells you what to do in the numbered fortune poems: in other words, his answers to particular questions from worshippers through these poems are his only messages to the world.

Our own interviews however, have established that most worshippers believe that a god such as Wong Tai Sin advocates certain moral principles. We will sketch the most typical responses below, along with several minority opinions from the interviews.

The most common response to a question about Wong Tai Sin's teachings is *xiang shan* (Cantonese: *heung sihn*), which means something like 'pursuing goodness', with goodness having the implication of kindness or benevolence. Men and women of all ages used this phrase spontaneously. The Sik Sik Yuen does stress *xiang shan* as a teaching of Wong Tai Sin in its various pamphlets and brochures, some of which contain the slogan *pu ji quan shan* (Cantonese: *pou jai hyun sihn*), which the Sik Sik Yuen translates as 'to act benevolently and to teach benevolence'. The first Wong Tai Sin temple in Guangzhou, set up by Leung Yan Ngam in 1897, adopted the title Pujitan, literally, the 'temple/altar [dedicated to] providing all embracing help to those in need', and the Sik Sik Yuen has incorporated this concept in its rhetoric (*pu ji quan shan*) since 1921. While many worshippers seem to be unaware of the Sik Sik Yuen's role in managing the temple, they are nonetheless aware of the emphasis on 'benevolence'. There were a few variations on this general theme of 'goodness': for instance, some people used the alternative phrase *xing shan* (Cantonese: *hahng sihn*), which means to act benevolently (and may be somewhat stronger than *xiang shan*); others said Wong Tai Sin teaches people to have a good heart; to have a good mind or intentions; or to be honest and frank. But most worshippers readily and comfortably used 'pursuing goodness' to summarize Wong Tai Sin's moral injunction to worshippers.

Most of the respondents did not elaborate on the meaning of 'pursuing goodness', but a few explained further. One woman said it means if you have money, it's wise to donate to charity. Another explained that one must not harm people. A third person, who had seen the television drama about Wong Tai Sin, commented that Wong Tai Sin was 'good' because he helped poor people. Probing for the meaning of 'pursuing goodness' among other respondents would likely elicit similar explanations.

Some respondents believed there was a pragmatic pay-off for worshippers who obeyed Wong Tai Sin's moral injunctions. One 30-year-old woman said that if a worshipper 'pursues goodness/benevolence', it will surely result in peace and harmony for the whole family. An 18-year-old girl said that if a worshipper acts benevolently, it will lead to good fortune. It is difficult to tell how many people hold such a belief. The question of rewards for pursuing goodness was not raised in the interviews. However, only two people volunteered this view, and it appears to be the opinion of only a minority of worshippers.

Most worshippers, by contrast, seem to believe that being a good person and not doing bad deeds is simply a general moral principle which does not need to be analyzed or interpreted, and which everyone should follow. They assume that this principle is taught by their god because he also is 'benevolent'. However, there is no record of any such teachings by Wong Cho Ping in the original source (Ge Hong). According to Ge Hong, Cho Ping was a hermit preoccupied with Taoist alchemy. Perhaps, then, Wong Tai Sin has simply soaked up the prevailing moral standards among religious Chinese, and reflected them back to worshippers as 'teachings'.

It also appears that for most worshippers, 'pursuing goodness' does not imply self-sacrifice or a great deal of altruism. It is quite compatible with their main motive in going to the temple: their desire to achieve some benefit from the god for themselves or their families. 'Pursuing goodness' does not require abandoning the quest for money and success, or any great devotion to the welfare of others outside one's family. The minimum requirement is only that worshippers avoid doing bad things to others. Many worshippers still go to the temple to get more, or to protect what they already have.

A small minority of worshippers have a different view: they believe Wong Tai Sin's role is not to help everyone succeed, but rather, to give people peace of mind. One 35-year-old man, for instance, said he did not believe in the slogan 'ask and it shall be granted' because many requests from worshippers would be incompatible: for instance, he explained, if one person sells umbrellas, he will pray for rain, while another person selling salt fish will pray for sunshine. The god cannot satisfy contradictory requests. Instead, worshippers should learn to accept fate, and concentrate on practising the virtues of pursuing goodness and being loyal and filial. Another man, about 30 years of age, stated that Wong Tai Sin's teaching is that people should not be greedy and over-eager for advantage. A 27-year-old woman said that Wong Tai Sin teaches people to be good, but also to be content with what you get in life. A 25-year-old woman said that for people who have problems which they can't solve, what Wong Tai Sin has to offer is advice and the feeling that someone is sharing their burden, which will make them feel better. A 65-year-old woman asserted that Wong Tai Sin is compassionate, but teaches people not to be greedy; requests for money, or for help in betting, will not be granted.

To summarize: Only a few worshippers go to the temple solely for practical advantage without any awareness of an ethical dimension in the cult of Wong Tai Sin. Most worshippers, by contrast, believe that Wong Tai Sin teaches 'goodness' or 'benevolence'. The Sik Sik Yuen has been quite successful in propagating this view. Some worshippers are also aware of the Sik Sik Yuen's charitable activities using funds donated to the temple, and this awareness may help to add the moral dimension to the god's image.[19] But only a few worshippers see the god's ethical injunctions as his most important legacy, or revere him mainly for his benevolence. Most worshippers visit the temple to solicit help and advice with particular problems or aspirations, and they also hope that Wong Tai Sin will protect and advance their general well-being, their families, and their businesses. They go to the temple because of the god's reputed power to offer such help, not because of his ethical teachings. Laying one's problems before the god can clearly alleviate anxiety, and give worshippers greater peace of mind. However, only a few worshippers believe that the god's function is to help them learn to accept fate with calmness. They are engaged in a continual struggle for personal, financial, and familial well-being, and they want help and advice from the great saint who will listen to their problems no matter how many other worshippers are simultaneously seeking his ear.

Degrees of Belief

Before leaving the topic of the characteristics of worshippers, we must acknowledge that there is a spectrum of faith among those who come to make offerings to the god. At one end of the spectrum are people who fervently believe in Wong Tai Sin. Some of these people believe the god has helped them with specific problems, and are truly grateful. There are others, apparently also fervent believers, who are not able to describe any particular incident in which they have received help from Wong Tai Sin, but they also derive gratification from going to the temple to make offerings and praying to the god: they usually say that it gives them psychological benefits, such as peace of mind and relief from anxiety.

At the other end of the spectrum are people who seem to have the attitude that 'worshipping' the god is not a very serious business, and there may be nothing to be gained by it, and it may be superstition as some people allege. However, they believe there is no harm in going once, or occasionally, since the cost in time and money is minimal, and there is always the chance that something can be gained by it. This attitude is probably common in the motivation of many people who engage in the various kinds of traditional religious practices in Hong Kong (Lee 1985:208).

It should also be noted that some Christians go to the Wong Tai Sin temple. There were two or three Christians among the 70 people interviewed in 1989, and there are probably a few Christians among any 100 worshippers at the temple.[20] Most of them come with friends, and are skeptical but curious. Others are lapsed or inactive Christians. One attraction in visiting the temple may be that it gives those involved a greater feeling of participating in Chinese culture.[21] In any case, these Christians fall into the category of people who have no strong belief in Wong Tai Sin, at least at first, but go to the temple to see what will happen. If their friends are believers, and if Wong Tai Sin seems to give them an accurate prediction, they may become more regular visitors to the temple.

Somewhere in the middle of the spectrum of belief is a partially skeptical, partially believing approach, which can probably move either toward fervent belief or toward complete skepticism depending on the outcome of petitions to the god. For example, one man interviewed at the temple in 1989, related that many years ago, when he lived near the temple as a boy, he didn't yet believe in Wong Tai Sin. Nevertheless, he went to the temple and asked the god a question, then shook out a fortune stick representing the god's answer. He then repeated the procedure, asking the same question again, to see if he got the same stick. It was a clever test of the procedure, if one accepts the assumption that the god should continue to give the same answer to the same question. (This test does not seem to have occurred to the great majority of worshippers, although most would no doubt consider it highly irreverent or sacrilegious.) The first time he tried this test, the god 'failed': two different sticks fell out. However, he tried the test again later, and managed to get the same fortune stick when he repeated his question. After that, he said, he began to believe. The god, he claimed, made a number of accurate predictions about his life: that he would have two wives, that he would go to many places, and that he would have 'women trouble'. But he said that he still does not completely believe. He recently asked the god a question and took the god's answer — the number from the fortune stick — to eight different fortune-tellers to see whether their explanations of the god's answer in the fortune poem were similar. He is interested in seeing what the god has to say, but is still testing the procedures, still not completely convinced, still 'experimenting' with this kind of religion. His quasi-experimentalist approach to the alleged powers of Wong Tai Sin is probably rare, but we suspect that many other 'worshippers' go to the temple to test the accuracy of the god's predictions and advice, and that the outcome of these tests determine whether some of them return.

Others worship and believe in the god's powers, while simultaneously aware that it may be superstition, and that the 'benefits' they derive may have non-supernatural explanations. They continue to worship as long as it seems to work, and as long as they are not actually harmed by it. This curious state of provisional belief may be very common. Even apparently fervent believers may on some level be aware that their own actions produce some of the outcomes which they attribute to the actions of the gods, and yet they manage to keep this awareness from interfering with belief.[22]

We now turn to some examples of the kinds of stories worshippers tell about the god's help with their problems.

How the God Helps Worshippers

Medical Help

If Wong Tai Sin has a speciality, it is in helping people with medical problems, curing some and keeping others in reasonably good health. This has been his particular art since the time of the plagues in the 1890s. In the absence of plagues, his greatest appeal as a preserver of health and as a healer is now to women, perhaps especially to older women. The belief that religious worship can bring medical benefits is evidently stronger among women in Hong Kong than among men (Lee 1980:350). But men also have medical problems, and both men and women ask Wong Tai Sin for medical help and advice.

Wong Tai Sin's role as a healer has probably declined over the last 50 years as modern medicine has become much more widely available to Chinese in Hong Kong, and as their faith in modern medicine has grown.[23] However, modern medicine often fails to heal people's ailments, and some of these people then resort to traditional Chinese medicine.[24] Much of traditional Chinese medical lore is essentially 'secular' — gods and spirits are not required for its effectiveness — and most people in Hong Kong use these medicines as tonics and for recovery from mild medical problems (Lee 1980). But a minority of the population believe that supernatural forces can also be invoked with the proper use of ceremonies and potions, and may produce healings where Western-style medicine or Chinese 'secular' medicines have failed. Even if only about 20 per cent of ordinary people in Hong Kong believe in the efficacy of magical-religious remedies, or in the possibility of medical benefits from worship at temples, as Lee (1980) concludes, this still provides a very large number of potential worshippers for a god who offers the prospect of healing. Hundreds of thousands of people in Hong Kong believe that the gods sometimes restore health to the sincere worshipper (a belief also prevalent among some religious groups in Europe and North America), and the reputation of Wong Tai Sin as a healer and prescriber of medicines continues to draw many of these people to his temple.

Wong Tai Sin's formula for success has always included the offering of limited quantities of free Chinese herbal medicines, along
with the prospect of dramatic cures through the medicines prescribed by the god. The stone façade above the temple courtyard
includes large characters announcing that this god perfected medicines which can produce a 'return of Spring': that is, a return of
youth and vigour. In China, and for much of the twentieth century in Hong Kong, many medicines were too expensive for most
people, and the possibility of getting free medicine prescribed by
a god drew many people to the temples in Fangcun, Rengang, and
Kowloon.

Some worshippers still go to the Kowloon temple to get such
medicines.[25] Some worshippers tell stories of going to get medicine from the clinic — the choice of medication dictated by the
number obtained through shaking out a fortune stick — and subsequently recovering from their medical problems. Most of these
stories describe cures for what seem to be relatively mild afflictions,
but the cures are none the less much appreciated. One woman
interviewed in 1989, who had obtained medicine from the clinic
in the past and received some benefit from it, now donates money
to the clinic whenever she goes there, so other people who are
poor can be provided with medicine.

The most dramatic accounts of healings seem to be told about
others. For instance, a 65-year-old woman who had lived near the
temple for many years told of a man who went to the temple in
desperation about 30 years ago, seriously ill, without money, and
near death. He asked Wong Tai Sin for help, and got a prescription number using the fortune sticks, but it turned out to be a medicine which is considered to be a strong poison. He took it anyway,
to show obedience to Wong Tai Sin, then slept that night at the
gate of the temple. The next morning, he was well again.

Other worshippers, however, show some lack of confidence in
the free medicines available at the clinic. A 40-year-old man said
that one can go to the clinic for medicine if the illness is not serious, but for a serious illness one should not go to the temple, one
should go to see a doctor. Another man indicated that he had been
cured of a disease by medicine from the clinic in the past (with
the god providing the prescription through the fortune sticks) but
he also commented that the medicine from the clinic is not so
effective. The woman who recounted the story of the man who
took the poisonous medicine and was cured, also mentioned that
she herself was suffering an illness, but uses the services of the

temple only to petition the god for a prescription. She goes to the clinic to learn the names of the medicines specified by the god's prescription, but if you have the money, she advised, it's best to go to a shop and buy the medicine rather than trying to get it free from the clinic. In short, only a small number of worshippers at the temple go to the clinic for medicine.

A larger number of worshippers ask the god for help with medical problems: in the 1989 survey, 25 per cent of the women, and 17 per cent of the men (Fong and Luk 1989). Many of them believe there are other ways to be cured, besides the medicines and prescriptions available at the clinic. For instance, some believe that the ash from the incense burnt at the temple may have curative properties, so they collect the ash in small containers and drink it later mixed into cups of tea. Some miracle stories about this ash are quite dramatic. For instance, one woman told a story about another woman who had cancer, drank ash tea, and recovered. Another woman reported that she was healed of headaches by incense ash.

Some people also attribute magical efficacy to sources of water at the temple. The water from the well next to the temple in Fangcun was thought to have curative properties, and similar beliefs have been held by worshippers at the Kowloon temple. For instance, the *fuji* master who performed at the temple until the early 1970s used to write with his *fuji* stick in a tub of water, after which worshippers would collect the water in small bottles for use as medicine. There are some dramatic stories of healings achieved with this water. For example, a wife of one of the directors of the Sik Sik Yuen recovered from tumours after this treatment. After the *fuji* master died, *fuji* was no longer performed, but some worshippers believe that the water now provided in a series of taps in the temple courtyard has healing properties; some of them wash their hands or face in this water, or fill small bottles with it so they can drink it slowly at home. Such beliefs are still common (and of course are also found in other religious traditions).[26] One woman interviewed at the Wong Tai Sin temple said that illness is due to fate, and not to Wong Tai Sin's lack of power to heal, but such fatalism appears to be rare among worshippers. When they have medical problems, they hope the god will help; when they are relatively healthy, they ask the god to give them continued health, and are grateful when this wish seems to have been granted. This is not to say that Wong Tai Sin is always a friendly healer. Like other gods who offer healing, his medical oracles sometimes tell the worshipper to show more diligence in religious duties, or else a healing cannot be expected. Most worshippers who seek a prescription, however, will eventually get one. But Wong Tai Sin has also become a generalist. In the eyes of worshippers, he is able to help them with most of the problems which they face in urban Hong Kong.

Careers

As noted above, the second most common request to the god in the 1989 survey was for career advice. Some of the stories of worshippers describe the god's perspicacity in giving such advice. For instance, a 60-year-old woman recalled asking Wong Tai Sin if she should apply for a job in Mongkok (a densely crowded area of Kowloon) and was told she should not. She went anyway, but shortly afterward she damaged her neck at work. This, she said, proved she should have followed the god's advice. A 35-year-old man said that the god helped him get his singing career off the ground by giving him guidelines for finding a good singing teacher, and by giving him the confidence to work hard toward his goals as a singer. He also recalled that his sister, years ago, had just started a new job, and asked the god if she would have good prospects for advancement in this job. The fortune poem to which the god directed her attention, by way of the fortune sticks, contained an allusion to a famous poet who saw a reflection of the moon in the water and tried to scoop it up: a useless endeavour, and an indication that it would also be useless to wait for advancement in her job. Sure enough, he said, his sister found after some months that she was still stuck in the same low position in the company, proving the accuracy of the god's prediction. A 20-year-old woman said she had asked Wong Tai Sin about her prospects in a new job several years earlier, and was advised that she should stay with the company for an extended period, since there would be good opportunities for promotion. She took the advice and remained in the company, and was soon promoted by the manager.

Help With Housing

The greatest changes in housing for many worshippers occurred in the late 1950s and early 1960s, during the move from squatter housing into resettlement huts, and into government-subsidized apartment blocks. Subsequently, many of these early, primitive apartment blocks were replaced with much more modern apartment buildings, as described in the previous chapter. Many families would have experienced considerable anxiety both during the early phase of rehousing, and during the later moves of many people into better apartments, but we did not expect to find many stories about the god's help with housing. It would be the older worshippers who had moved into the area as refugee squatters in the 1950s who would be most likely to have solicited the god's help in getting their families into better quarters, and who would remember their gratitude when they succeeded. However, several stories about housing were mentioned in the 1989 interviews.

For example, one elderly woman who was born in China and later moved to Hong Kong described how she and her son had lived in a squatter hut and were very poor, but they prayed to Wong Tai Sin and worked very hard and were finally able to move into an apartment. She gave this example (along with instances where the god had cured them both of illness) when asked how the god had helped her.

Another woman, about 40 years of age, related that she had hoped to get a government flat in a public housing estate and finally, with the god's help, succeeded. This woman said that she went to the temple two or three times a year. She must have asked the god for help or advice with many things, but this was the example she gave when asked how the god had helped her.

Another woman, about 25 years old, had come to the temple on behalf of her family to thank the god for his help with a much more ambitious goal: her parents had hoped to buy an apartment, and asked Wong Tai Sin for his blessing on their quest for the very large amount of money required. They received the god's encouragement. Three or four months previously it had become apparent that they would succeed, and just the day before the interview, they had finally paid off the entire amount. She had come to the temple to thank the god for his help. This young woman had commented at the beginning of the interview that she didn't know much about Wong Tai Sin, but came to the temple because her parents were believers and their belief had a strong influence on her. We were interested to discover that the god's help with a housing problem of the parents could produce greater belief among their children.

1. Wong Tai Sin, as depicted at the main temple (Sik Sik Yuen).

2. The Wong Tai Sin statue in the new shrine at Mt. Jinhua (courtesy of Peter W. K. Lo).

3. The main temple in Kowloon. Once sitting among empty fields, it is now surrounded by high-rise apartments.

4. Fortune-tellers and clients.

5. Worshippers in the courtyard (Chinese New Year 1993).

6. Young worshippers try a question to the god in the courtyard of the Wong Tai Sin temple.

7. Some of the last remaining squatter shacks near the temple, surrounding the last old houses in the village of Chuk Yuen (1993).

8. Lars Ragvald and Rengang villagers discuss the gatestone of the temple which was torn down during the Cultural Revolution (1987).

9. A Hong Kong pilgrim places a stick of incense on the gatestone of the Rengang Wong Tai Sin temple (1992). The gatestone had been moved indoors when it became apparent to villagers that Hong Kong people were interested in visiting the site.

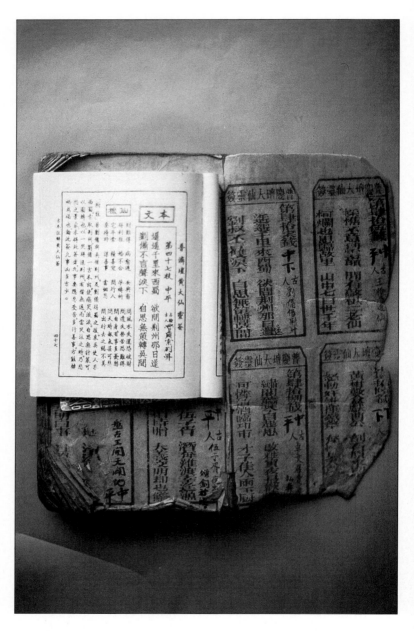

10. The original book of fortune-poems brought to Hong Kong by Leung Yan Ngam in 1915, with the modern book with glosses and interpretations added for each poem.

Help For Immigrants From China

Despite the fact that the major waves of immigration from China into Hong Kong had already ended several decades before our interviews in 1989 (most entered Hong Kong between the late 1940s and the early 1960s), a few worshippers interviewed at the temple still tell stories about how the god helped them, or some-one they knew, to get established in Hong Kong.

A 45-year-old woman, for instance, recalled vividly how one of her relatives had managed to sneak across the border some years ago. At that time, Hong Kong sent refugees back to China if they were caught in the countryside, but if the refugees could manage to get to the city, they were safe and could apply for residency (this was sometimes called the 'touch base' policy). Not knowing the way into the city and fearing arrest on the roads, he sent a message to her asking for help. She was afraid she would be arrested herself if she was caught helping him, but went to the temple to ask Wong Tai Sin for advice. The god's advice was to help the man. So she went out to the countryside, found him, and they began walking back to the road. On the way, they became lost. She covered her face with her hands and asked Wong Tai Sin for help. Immediately, they came out on the main road, and at that very moment a mini-bus came along, and they boarded. There were no police roadblocks on the way back to the city, and they arrived safely. She attributes this fortunate sequence of events to the god's protection.

Another woman, about 50 years in age, related that she and her husband, who was an editor in China, had left for Hong Kong many years ago because they were poor and because there had been political trouble for him in his job as an editor. After their arrival in Hong Kong, a friend of her husband had brought him to the temple to ask for help and advice. The god advised him to go into business. He did, and prospered. She herself, she said, has not been helped by Wong Tai Sin, but after the god's help for her husband she believes in the efficacy of Wong Tai Sin and comes to the temple occasionally for advice.

In rare cases, a refugee from China becomes very rich after solic-iting the god's help, and thanks the god with generous gifts of money. For example, a young man fled from Shanghai to Hong Kong in the 1950s, and asked Wong Tai Sin to help him succeed in business, promising to give some of his money back to the god if he succeeded. He eventually became wealthy in the garment industry, and after his emigration to the United States he used some of his wealth to help set up a shrine to Wong Tai Sin in New York city.

It is possible that Wong Tai Sin still helps immigrants to Hong Kong. In 1989 one woman who came to the temple with her two daughters related that she had a friend in China who had applied to come to Hong Kong. This friend asked her to petition Wong Tai Sin about whether her application would be successful. The god answered that she would succeed in coming to Hong Kong, and this prediction turned out to be correct.

Gambling Tips

There is a persistent story, repeated in a number of books and articles which discuss temples in Hong Kong (for example, Chamberlain 1983:161; Topley 1974:243), that Wong Tai Sin helps gamblers by giving tips about winning numbers at the races. Worshippers apparently ask the fortune-tellers for these tips (the fortune-teller interviewed by Wan [1988], for example, acknowledged receiving such requests). However, accounts of the god actually providing the winning numbers in a race are quite rare; we only encountered two such stories. One of the interviewees in 1989 had heard a story that a man had become rich after betting on the numbers he got from the fortune sticks, and mentioned this story in response to a question about how Wong Tai Sin has helped people. At the private Wong Tai Sin temple, several people also told a story about how they had asked the god for the winning numbers at the dog races in Macau, and how they had lost their money because they bet the numbers in reverse order to the winning sequence. They felt they had simply misunderstood the god's message. Another person interviewed at the Kowloon temple reported that several people whom she knew had asked the god for advice about betting on horse races, and they had been scolded by the god (through the fortune-teller) for asking such a question.

No doubt some people still try to get gambling advice from the god using the fortune sticks, but most worshippers would probably say that Wong Tai Sin does not give people gambling tips. The rationalist might observe that if hundreds of people use the fortune sticks to get gambling numbers every week, eventually some of the numbers are bound to be winners, and so the random selection of fortune sticks would inevitably lead to some stories about the god's ability to pick winners at the races. People who dismiss the possibility that the god gives racing tips do so for other reasons: the god is not concerned with such trivial matters; or his purpose is to help people deal with problems, not to help them find easy wealth. One man, for instance, said that people who come to ask the god for money will always be unsuccessful: the god can help people who are suffering, but does not help people who merely want to get rich.

Travel

Several young women reported asking the god to keep them safe during their travels abroad, and because they had returned safely, they felt the god had kept them from harm.

Children

Some women also seek the god's help in regard to children. One woman, asked if she had heard of any stories about Wong Tai Sin helping people, said she had heard of other women who asked Wong Tai Sin to help them have a son, and their wish had been granted. The degree of anxiety which women experience about the need to have a son will vary with their upbringing and with the attitudes of their husbands, but for many women, having a son is virtually a marital imperative. Since the burden of this imperative falls entirely on the woman, and since she can do nothing else to influence the outcome of a pregnancy, an appeal to the god is understandable.

Some women also dedicate a child to Wong Tai Sin by formally declaring that the child is the godson (Cantonese: *kai jai*) or goddaughter of the god. Becoming the godfather to a child was, in the past, a solemn and important undertaking for the Chinese. It signified that the godfather or godmother would look after the child if anything happened to the parents, and would also give help to the child whenever it was needed. Wise parents would choose a godfather or godmother carefully from among their closest friends. By adopting Wong Tai Sin as the child's godfather, the parent was asking the god to help the child throughout life, and also imposing upon the child the obligation of honouring and worshipping the god. Apparently, some women promise Wong Tai

Sin that if he helps them to conceive a son, they will formally adopt Wong Tai Sin as the child's godfather, binding the boy to the god for life.

Finding a Mate

Some people also go to the temple to ask for the god's help in finding a husband or a wife. Many young people are unwilling to allow parents to arrange their marriages (see, for example Salaff 1981:268), but their peer groups often do not include enough potential mates, especially after they have left school. The god's help is enlisted to search out the right person, and bring them together. One woman, about 30 years old, said that she went to the temple before her marriage for this reason, and Wong Tai Sin had helped her find a husband. She had come to the temple with her husband and child, whom she embraced during the interview. She now visits the temple two or three times a year, and at New Year, to thank the god and seek his further blessings on the family. In the 1989 survey, 6.7 per cent of those interviewed had asked Wong Tai Sin about their prospects regarding love or finding a mate.

To fully understand the behaviour and attitudes of worshippers, we also need to understand the role of the fortune-tellers. Nearly every worshipper will have taken a question or problem to a fortune-teller after getting the god's answer through the fortune-sticks, and the fortune-teller then becomes the god's mouthpiece, using the fortune-poems to explain what the god is saying to the petitioner. The next chapter will examine this interaction between believers and fortune-tellers.

6 Divination and the Fortune-tellers

WONG TAI SIN does not speak to his worshippers through sacred texts, as in some religions. Nor does he speak to them in dreams and visions. He can no longer be consulted (at least at the main temple) through spirit-writing. No priests publicly teach and explain his doctrines, and no prophets proclaim his judgments. His only means of communicating with ordinary worshippers at the main temple is through a set of printed oracles or fortune-poems.

The god expresses his answer to the worshipper's questions or petitions by selecting a number, corresponding to the number of one of the poems, through a procedure called *qiu qian* (Cantonese: *kauh chim*)[1]. First, the worshipper[1] kneels in the courtyard facing the main altar, lays out appropriate offerings (which may range from a few oranges to a feast of an entire roast pig), and formulates a question to the god. For some worshippers this is a fervent moment — they seek the god's attention, and must give great concentration to framing the question in their minds and transmitting it to the god with all the intensity they can muster. The next step is to shake a bamboo container holding 100 numbered bamboo sticks. While they are shaking the container, the god causes one of these sticks to rise slightly above the level of the other sticks, and the worshipper must continue carefully shaking the container until this stick finally falls out onto the ground. Some worshippers ask the god to confirm that the correct stick has fallen out by dropping 'moon-blocks' — semicircular wooden blocks with one flat and one convex surface. When dropped on the floor, their position indicates the god's answer: 'yes' (one flat side and one convex side down); a mild 'no', (both convex sides down, in which position the blocks may briefly rock back and forth, sometimes interpreted as the god's amusement at the question (Jordan, 1972:61–2); and a more emphatic 'no' (both flat sides down). Some people consider that it is unnecessary to require the god to confirm his selection of the fortune-stick by using moon-blocks. Once a numbered stick has fallen out of the container, the next step is to consult the poem with the same number.

This method of consulting a god is used in Chinese temples throughout Asia, and there are many such sets of fortune-poems (see Pas 1984; Banck 1985), ranging from small sets with only 24 poems to very large sets, with 365 poems. Temples to the same god often use the same set of poems.[2] There are 100 of these poems in the set used at the Wong Tai Sin temple. We do not know the author of Wong Tai Sin's set, but it was probably compiled in connection with the rise of the Wong Tai Sin cult in Guangdong at the end of the ninteenth century, since no one has found an older example of the set.[3]

The method of selecting a stick from a container of sticks is very old, and may have historical links with similar divination systems which have existed elsewhere in Asia.[4] The use of numbered sticks to select fortune-poems, however, may date from not much earlier than the Song dynasty, when the use of printing blocks allowed the rapid dissemination of sets of poems.

In some temples, the fortune-poems are printed on small rectangular pieces of paper and kept in numbered pigeon-holes. The worshipper can take one of these and ponder its meaning later. More commonly, these papers are kept in a tray at the fortune-teller's table. The worshipper at the Wong Tai Sin temple can also buy a booklet containing the complete set of poems, which is available in stalls outside the temple.

The booklet is designed to be somewhat 'user friendly'. While the poem which the god has selected may be obscure, and on the surface may have nothing to say about the worshipper's problem, several items have been added to make it a little easier for the worshipper to understand its meaning.

Firstly, the poems in many sets include titles, written beside the poem, which refer, not to the content of the poem, but to some famous person or event from Chinese cultural history (Pas 1984; Eberhard 1970; Morgan 1987). Many worshippers would know about these events or persons from legends and popular dramas. The stories were often used, in fact, to teach moral lessons (about filial piety, loyalty, and so on), and hence adding these titles also adds a moral element to the set of poems. This helps the worshipper to understand the poem's message. For example, the twelfth poem in the set includes the title *Li Po Attempts to Seize the Moon*, referring to a famous incident in which a poet fell overboard and drowned while leaning over the side of the boat attempting to embrace the reflection of the moon in the water. The incident showed the disastrous consequences of striving foolishly for what cannot be achieved, and tells worshippers that they should rethink their plans (see also Morgan 1987).[5] Worshippers may remember the title of the poem and its message when they have forgotten the poem itself.[6]

Secondly, the poems in the booklet are graded, using a six-step scale which runs from *shangshang* (literally 'upper-upper', or excellent prospects) to *xiaxia* (literally 'lower-lower', indicating difficult times ahead).[7] Worshippers can thus get a kind of quick answer to whether the god thinks their plans and hopes are likely to be realized, or are likely to be dashed. The 100 poems in the Wong Tai Sin set are distributed over this six-step scale as follows:

Best: great good fortune (*shangshang*):	3
Second best: auspicious (*shangji*):	10
Middle best: fair prospects (*zhongji*):	32
Middle ordinary: mediocre prospects (*zhongping*):	36
Middle low: poor prospects (*zhongxia*):	1
Lowest: very inauspicious (*xiaxia*):	18

We will call these grades attached to each poem 'tags'. Several observations about this distribution of tags might be made. The fortune-poems which predict very bad prospects (18) outnumber those which predict very good prospects (only 3), with most of the other poems promising only something between very good and very bad. There is a certain sociological cunning in this distribution. We could also observe that, as Shum (1990) points out, the fortune poems which are positive and offer at least moderately good prospects (45) outnumber those which predict bad prospects (19). Thus, while the fortune poems do not commit the god to highly optimistic predictions for more than 3 per cent of worshippers, they promise 45 per cent of worshippers that they have reasonable to good prospects of realizing their hopes.[8] As many worshippers readily admit, they come to the temple in part for peace of mind and reassurance, and based on the distribution of the tags between auspicious and inauspicious, many of them will indeed be reassured by the god's answers to their questions. Combining the 'middle best' and 'middle ordinary' categories of fortune-poems, we might further observe that 68 per cent of worshippers will receive answers that do not commit the god to predicting either a very good or a very bad outcome, and hence allow worshippers and fortune-tellers great flexibility in matching eventual outcomes to the obscure messages of the poems.

The booklet of fortune poems also includes, for each poem, an explanation of the poem's meaning and a set of standard answers to various questions, which outlines what the poem is saying about the worshipper's prospects in business, marriage, travel, the search for lost articles, and so on. To give an example, one of the three *shangshang* poems in the Wong Tai Sin set, poem number 73, bears the title *Sunlin Achieves the Top Mark in the Imperial Examinations*. The imperial examinations provided an opportunity for studious and diligent commoners to become officials, and success in these examinations conferred prestige and honour not only on the candidate, but also on the candidate's family and village. For this reason, successful candidates were remembered and honoured by their families and their villages for generations. The poem describes the scene of what might be Sunlin's triumphant return to his home town (here paraphrased):

> Crowds line the streets, flowers and the hooves of the horses in
>   the procession add colour and excitement,
> He left dressed in a commoner's blue clothes, but returns wearing
>   embroidered silk robes,
> Along the whole street, pretty girls are eager to see (and be seen
>   by) the returning hero,
> Some day all will look up and see his name on the pagoda.[9]

The explanation appended to this poem in the book of fortune poems runs as follows (using the translation by Sham 1988):

> Fame and wealth will be in plenty.
> Recovery from sickness takes no time.
> Visitors will soon arrive.
> The pregnant will give birth to a promising son.
> The family will be blessed with prosperity and prestige.
> Business and farming will be accorded with great success.
> Plans and desires are happily realized.

However, the worshipper is about six times more likely to get a fortune poem such as poem number 43, which carries the title *Hanyu is Demoted [by the emperor]*. Hanyu was a famous high official of the Tang dynasty, who became renowned for his courage in delivering to the emperor a criticism of the state of his regime.

The furious emperor is reported to have demoted Hanyu and sent him away from the capital. The poem describes the travels and travails of someone who could be Hanyu:

His straightforward advice made the emperor furious,
[Exiled,] he travelled day and night, hardly leaving the saddle,
Both the master and his servant were exhausted,
Worse still: heavy snow blocked their way to [or through] Languan.[10]

To this sombre poem is appended the following gloomy forecast (Sham 1988):

Riches will be difficult to come by.
Fame is impossible to gain.
Illness is hard to heal.
Plans look ominous.
Business and farming are unrewarding.
Travellers will have obstacles on the way.
Marriage will be disagreeable.
Pregnancy will experience uncomfortable symptoms.
The family will experience difficulties.
Care is necessary in time of ill luck.

(If the fortune poems teach lessons to worshippers, the lesson of this poem is clear.) In the explanation next to the poem, the editor of the booklet adds the advice that those who receive this fortune-poem ought to be very careful, and that they must be sure to perform good deeds (to help them avoid or mitigate the predicted difficulties).

However, as noted, only a minority of the poems are very good or very bad. Most of them are somewhere between good and bad, and hence the answer to the worshipper's question, or the prospects for one's marriage or pregnancy or business, are often not very clear. Further, the standard answers appended to each poem often do not precisely match the worshipper's question. Hence, most people consult a fortune-teller[11] to find out what the god is saying.

The huge popularity of the Wong Tai Sin temple requires legions of these professional fortune-tellers, and has led to what must be the largest single cluster of such people in Asia. There are now more than 150 stalls near the gates of the temple, and during the Chinese New Year period, most of these stalls contain fortune-tellers. This extraordinary concentration of professional diviners is

completely without precedent in Hong Kong, where one or two
such persons in a temple is typical, and may not have a parallel
in the history of religion in China.[12]

The Growth of Fortune-telling Around the Wong Tai Sin Temple[13]

As far as we know, the first fortune-teller to set up a stall outside
the Wong Tai Sin temple was a minor employee of the Sik Sik
Yuen who had previously been engaged in doing odd jobs at the
temple. He apparently set up his stall around 1931 or 1932.[14] By
1936 or 1937, there were four fortune-tellers outside the temple.[15]
There was plenty of room for fortune-tellers' stalls inside the
temple compound, but the Sik Sik Yuen had been forced to close
the main gates because of the threat of expropriation under the
Chinese Temples Ordinance of 1928. Since worshippers still wished
to come to the temple, some enterprising individuals saw an opportunity to take a share of the business. They set up small icons of
the god in their stalls, and evidently also sold incense, as well as
offering their services as fortune-tellers. As large numbers of
people fleeing the Japanese armies moved into Kowloon in 1938
and 1939, there was apparently another increase in the number of
fortune-tellers at the temple.[16] After the war, some of these fortune-
tellers still operated outside the gates of the temple, and when
the area was flooded with refugees in 1949 and 1950, many more
fortune-tellers set up stalls next to the existing ones.

In 1956, the government threatened to expropriate the temple
and use the land for public housing, and the temple was saved
only after the new chairman of the Sik Sik Yuen arranged to have
admission fees collected at the temple and passed on to the Tung
Wah Group of Hospitals. As part of this deal, Tung Wah would
also collect rent from the fortune-tellers. As the landlord for the
stalls, Tung Wah required the fortune-tellers to sign leases, which
not only specified rents but also contained regulations about what
the fortune-tellers could and could not do in their stalls, and provided some limits on what they were allowed to charge clients.[17]
Tung Wah thus gained some control over the activities of the
fortune-tellers.

However, the fortune-tellers also had some power, at least in so
far as they could act collectively, in their dealings with Tung
Wah: the financial gain to Tung Wah from renting these stalls to

the fortune-tellers was sufficiently great that when they boycotted new stalls built for them at about this time,[18] they were able to force Tung Wah to rebuild the stalls around the temple gates so that worshippers were funnelled past most of the stalls when entering the temple (Lee 1971:213). These stalls still surrounded the gates of the temple in 1984, and worshippers had to walk through a kind of bazaar consisting of corridors lined with booths selling fortune-telling services, incense sticks, paper offerings, and religious icons before they could get to the temple.

This clustering of stalls around the gates was obviously beneficial to the fortune-tellers and the sellers of incense and icons, since they could solicit each worshipper coming to the temple, but it was not necessarily beneficial to the Sik Sik Yuen. In the late 1980s, Tung Wah built a new set of stalls for the fortune-tellers which preserved some of the character of the original bazaar, but also left a paved path running alongside the bazaar and connecting the gates of the temple to the nearby street and the subway exits. Thus, worshippers were able to bypass the bazaar and walk directly to the temple. The stalls were separated from the path by a barrier consisting partly of chicken wire, and the more aggressive of the stall-owners still solicited worshippers through the chicken wire as they walked along the path to the gates of the temple. Later, permanent quarters for the bazaar were constructed, in a building to the left of the entrance, and the stall-owners must now wait for customers who voluntarily enter the bazaar. They can no longer proposition everyone who passes by on the way into the temple courtyard. However, there is still plenty of business. There were (as of 1990) about 160 stalls around the temple. The rent for these stalls, before the move into the permanent quarters, ranged from HK$800 (US$1 = HK$7.8) to HK$1,200 per month (in 1990), and thus it can be estimated that the income obtained by Tung Wah from renting these stalls to fortune-tellers and purveyors of religious materials, assuming full occupancy, amounted to at least HK$128,000 per month (Shum 1990).

As noted, the fees for interpreting the fortune-poems are regulated by the lease which the fortune-tellers sign with Tung Wah. In 1989, the fee was about HK$6 per question, and by 1990 it had risen to about HK$8. No doubt competition among the fortune-tellers would keep the fee relatively low in any case. Since many worshippers ask only a couple of questions, the fortune-tellers do not make much money from interpreting these fortune-poems. One fortune-teller told a newspaper reporter in 1988 that during the low season (June and July) he got no more than about 15 clients per day (Wan 1988), which would have produced a monthly income, after paying rent on his stall, of no more than HK$3,000.[19] However, the much higher income during the New Year period made the business more profitable. The same fortune-teller related that during the New Year month he received up to 50 customers per day (Wan 1988). On one reasonably good day during this period, he took home about HK$450 — approximately the daily wage of a construction worker.

The key to high earnings for the fortune-tellers, especially during slack periods, is to perform other services for which the fees are not regulated by the lease. By far the most lucrative is geomancy, for which the fortune-tellers charged a minimum of HK$1,000 in 1987. For face-reading and palm-reading, the fortune-tellers charge less because of the pressure of price competition with other fortune-tellers nearby, but these services are also very lucrative. While able to charge only about HK$5 for interpreting a fortune-poem, for instance, the fortune-teller mentioned above charged HK$50 for palm-reading and HK$50 for face-reading (on which, see Greenblatt 1979). He might have as many as 300 customers for this type of fortune-telling during the New Year month, and clearly earned much of his yearly income during this period. The fortune-tellers are not all so successful, and some barely eke out a living at the trade, but others earn amounts comparable to the incomes of clerical workers or small merchants.

The Fortune-tellers

The people who become fortune-tellers seem to fall into several categories. Some of them had a parent who was also a fortune-teller. For example, one man interviewed in his stall at the temple claimed that his father had been among the first four fortune-tellers at the temple in the 1930s, and that his grandfather had been a palm-reader. He and his mother had taken up the business when his father died several years earlier. Some fortune-tellers are retired individuals who take up fortune-telling as a relatively unstressful way for an older person to make some additional money. For example, one dignified gentleman who had evidently worked for years in the Hong Kong civil service took up fortune-telling at the age of 61 after leaving the post he had occupied during most of his working years. His father had been a fortune-teller who had retired at about the same time, at the age of 90.[20] Other fortune-tellers are immigrants who had white-collar occupations in China and were unable to find comparable work in Hong Kong. One fortune-teller interviewed by one of Graeme Lang's student interviewers in 1989 said that he had been a teacher in a police academy in China before his arrival in Hong Kong.

The fortune-tellers, as noted above, do not need to have any formal qualifications. However, they must be more literate than most worshippers, since many of the Chinese characters used in the poems are in a type of language seldom encountered in local newspapers or popular media. For many worshippers, reading some of the poems would present problems similar to those of an English-speaking person, with little formal education, attempting to read a poem written in Chaucerian English. The fortune-tellers will also be familiar with the classical stories and legends alluded to in the poems, so that they can draw on these stories as they interpret the messages which the god is encoding for the worshipper in the poem. The fortune-tellers do not even have to claim belief in Wong Tai Sin;[21] some clearly consider themselves to be offering a kind of professional service which makes use of their knowledge of classical language and literature and their ability to relate subtle elements of the fortune-poems to the daily lives of their clients. In this sense, they are not at all like the blind men in pre-modern China who offered their services as fortune-tellers on the basis of an alleged mystical 'second sight' somehow connected to their blindness. Many of the current fortune-tellers at the temple are much more like educated, fee-for-service professionals, at least in their own eyes. In this sense they are like the geomancers, who sell their services to clients on the basis of professional knowledge about how to identify and manipulate the latent forces in nature. Because the fortune-tellers typically value literacy and formal education, their children may turn out to be well-educated.[22]

The fortune-tellers' interpersonal skills are also obviously important. The Macau fortune-teller described by Bloomfield (1980), for instance, was reknowned locally for his wit and humour in explaining the poems, and attracted many people to the Macau temple in which he carried out his work. The success of the fortune-teller also depends on his or her ability to 'read' the client through the cues of dress, expression, and body language, and through the client's responses to the fortune-teller's calculated probes (Greenblatt 1979:86–7).

The most important characteristics of the successful fortune-tellers, however, are their skills in carefully relating the fortune-poems to the problems and concerns of their clients. Observing the Chinese fortune-tellers in Malaysia, one writer compared them to therapists: 'Many of the [fortune-tellers], described as "streetside psychiatrists" by one informant, are good listeners who provide sympathetic advice to those who consult them. The "fortune" that the bird, cards, sticks, or palm-reading produces may, in many instances, be less significant than the 'therapeutic conversation'. (Dunn 1975:314). The same point could be made about some of the fortune-tellers at the Wong Tai Sin temple.

Some worshippers 'shop' for the right kind of fortune-teller. One woman interviewed at the temple by one of Graeme Lang's students said that when choosing a fortune-teller, she would sometimes stand nearby while a fortune-teller talked to one of his clients, to see if the fortune-teller gave a clear and detailed explanation. Another man said that after getting the number of a fortune-poem using the divination sticks, he had gone to eight or ten of the fortune-tellers to see how each one interpreted the poem, and to see whether their answers were consistent. No doubt other worshippers also try different fortune-tellers deliberately, and will not return to one whose explanations are too vague or general. While it is rather difficult to document, it appears that successful fortune-tellers build up a regular clientele who consult them when faced with problems or important decisions.[23] Satisfied clients will often recommend a fortune-teller to friends or relatives.

Many worshippers go to the temple too seldom to build up a relationship with one fortune-teller. More than half of the people interviewed by Lang's students indicated that they did not go to the same fortune-teller each time they came to the temple. They simply pick one 'at random' — although they sometimes explain that this 'random' decision is based on an intuition or subjective impression of a fortune-teller as they are strolling past the stalls. The fortune-tellers, of course, are quite aware of the importance of these impressions, and try to decorate their stalls to attract the attention of worshippers.[24]

Some worshippers are quite cynical about most of the fortune-tellers. Several worshippers who said they always go to the same fortune-teller explained to the interviewer that they have confidence their preferred fortune-teller will not cheat or deceive them (as other fortune-tellers might). Several other people interviewed at the temple said that after getting the fortune-stick selected by the god, they preferred to read the poem from the booklet and search out their own understanding of the god's message, avoiding the fortune-tellers, in whom they had little confidence. These people are not only exceptionally literate, but also possess the confidence that they can understand the allusions and subtle messages in the poems just as well as the fortune-tellers.

Most worshippers, however, are not confident that they can understand what the god is saying to them without some help. Shum (1990) interviewed 60 people at the temple who had used the fortune-sticks, and found that 75 per cent of them subsequently went to a fortune-teller to have the designated fortune-poems explained to them in relation to their particular problems or requests.

How Fortune-tellers Deal with their Clients

To give the reader some idea of what happens when a client consults a fortune-teller, several examples follow:

1. A student walked along past the stalls, and was called over by a fortune-teller. He agreed to consult the man, and sat down. The fortune-teller told him to select a fortune-stick, and to be honest and sincere in his petition to the god. He was instructed to tell the god his age, address, and name. The student did as he was told, mumbling this information to the god as he obtained his fortune stick. He had asked about studying abroad, and drew number 92, a poem about Confucius travelling to another State in the sixth century BCE. The fortune-teller first asked the student's age, then consulted a book listing the names of the years and found that the student had been born in the Year of the Rabbit. His prognosis: 'You were born in the Year of the Rabbit. The rabbit has long ears, and so you can receive information and news very well and very fast. [He then checked the student's eyes and confirmed that he was indeed favoured.] Your fortune was good when you were born, and your health is quite good also, but luck will change every year, so interpretation is needed [presumably, regular consultations]. The poem is about Confucius, and you yourself are clever, and can become as good as Confucius. You should go abroad to further your studies. You will be welcomed, because you have good relations with others. But, you are not very good in your studies now. . . . You should communicate with important people'. The student then asked whether he should return to Hong

Kong after completing his studies, but the fortune-teller replied that the answer to this question required the use of a different method — the study of the face. As this method is much more expensive than interpreting the fortune-sticks, the student declined. In a brief conversation which followed, the fortune-teller held forth on several themes, including the opinion that people in the world are always unsatisfied, and always want more; and the opinion that it's a scientific age, and so study and education are very important, otherwise you will be left behind. The student listened to these remarks, then thanked the fortune-teller and left.

In analyzing this interaction, we can note that the fortune-teller used the student's year of birth to begin his analysis, temporarily ignoring the fortune-poem, and also did a very cursory face-reading, focusing on the eyes. He evidently prefers face-reading (it is much more lucrative), and he eventually tried to get the student to accept a face-reading for the answer to his next question. When he turned to the fortune-poem, he used the poem and the brief explanation attached to it in a very straightforward manner to answer the student's question about studying abroad. The poem and the explanation ('travel will be rewarding') are both easily interpreted to mean that the student should indeed go abroad to study. However, the fortune-teller also went considerably beyond the poem, adding additional diagnosis ('you are clever'; 'you are not very good in your studies right now') and advice ('you should communicate with important people'). Thus the fortune-teller clearly provided a more detailed counsel than the student could have obtained from the poem alone, and also used additional methods (year of birth, appearance of the eyes) to add further angles to his diagnosis. Worshippers seem to value this additional detail, and it is what prompts them to go to a fortune-teller rather than to try to read and interpret the poem on their own.

2. A female student went to one of the fortune-tellers (a woman) and asked four questions. Her first question was about 'self'. She drew number 47, which the fortune-teller indicated is 'just below average'. The advice: 'Deal carefully, because you are too simple, too honest. Be careful not to be treated badly, because there are many bad people in the world. However, it will be safe to travel abroad'. Regarding 'study', she drew number 85, one of the best. The advice: 'You have a good relation to books, and will graduate from this year of study with excellent results. You will do especially

well if instructed by a male professor. You have to study hard. You will have a chance to travel abroad'. Next, she asked about 'love', and drew number 98, characterized as above average. The advice: 'Love will just happen naturally: you don't have to do anything in particular to achieve it. You will find true love next March. Nothing will happen before then, but be patient and wait.' [At this point, the fortune-teller asked her if she was already in a love relationship]. Finally, in regard to 'future', she drew number 99, which is 'average'. The advice: 'You will meet some difficulties and stumbling blocks. Be patient, you will meet someone who can help you. In regard to your future work, it is best to be a professional, and best to study arts rather than sciences. In general, your future will be good, and you will overcome the difficulties'.

When we review this fortune-teller's advice, it is clear that she has been guided by the tags associated with each poem. Her words of caution and warning in response to the question about 'self', for instance, were related to the somewhat inauspicious tag attached to the poem and its general negative tone, not to any specific content. A few of her prognostications are related to the content of the poems. For instance, the prediction that the student would do well in the current year was strongly constrained by the fortune-poem itself, which is one of the most auspicious of the poems in the set and refers explicity to a scholar who studied hard and became very successful. Similarly, the prediction that the student would ultimately overcome difficulties in the future was related to the final line of the poem (number 99), which says: 'In youth, set yourself goals; [then] nothing will deter you'.

However, the fortune-teller also went beyond the poems and their tags and added additional advice and predictions. Most of the advice and predictions were general enough that they were free of risk for the fortune-teller. Several of the 'predictions' had a high probability of coming true for any student. For instance, 'You will do especially well if instructed by a male professor' (most of them are male), and 'you will meet some difficulties and stumbling blocks'. However, the fortune-teller added that it is necessary to study hard, and if the student did not do well, this qualifier could be recalled to prove that all the conditions for the fulfilment of the prediction had not been met.

The most striking prediction, however, was the one about love. Here, the fortune-teller departed completely from the poem and ventured the prediction that the student would find love several months hence, in March. In making such a prediction, the fortune-teller was taking the risk of being proved wrong in the very near future. Why would she take such a risk? One possible reason is that with a new client, the fortune-teller may be aware of the need to capture the client's attention with a bold prediction. Then the client feels s/he is getting good value for money: specific and even riveting predictions, rather than bland generalities. The value of the fortune-teller's contribution to the exchange is increased, and the client is less likely to begrudge the fee. The fortune-teller may also expect to receive more respectful attention after such a specific prediction. The similar prediction of the Macau fortune-teller visited by Bloomfield (1980:52–3) may have been prompted, in part, by this kind of motive.

However, the fortune-teller also gains more from such predictions than the temporary attention and respect of the client: making a specific prediction is also a good way to convert some of the new clients into regular visitors who will patronize the same fortune-teller again in the future. Why would a fortune-teller risk specific predictions, knowing that most of them will fail? Why is it good business to make such predictions? We suggest that the fortune-tellers may be aware, at some level, of the following rationale: given the casual approach of many young people to fortune-telling, and the small probability that the client will return soon, the fortune-teller knows that she must take some risks. If she sprinkles one or two specific and falsifiable predictions among the general and unfalsifiable predictions which comprise most of her consultation, and if these specific predictions are carefully crafted to match the probabilities facing her clients, she is bound to have some successes. Some of the specific predictions will be fulfilled. Whenever this occurs, it is very likely that the client will be amazed and impressed, and will return in the future for more predictions and advice. Equally important, this client will tell some of her friends and family about what happened, and the fortune-teller may gain further clients. Of course, the god gets the credit for the accuracy of the prediction, but the client will probably also be impressed with the fortune-teller's ability to draw this successful prediction from a poem which, on the surface, contains no such information. Meanwhile, the other specific predictions which were not confirmed may be forgotten or rationalized by the clients, and in any case these clients will find something which was fulfiled among the more general predictions ('difficulties will be overcome', 'you will do especially well if taught by a male professor', and so on). In short, it is highly *rational* for the fortune-teller to take one or two risks in making a series of predictions to new clients, because the pay-off for the fulfilment of a fraction of these predictions greatly outweighs the costs of the failure of the rest of the predictions. (This could no doubt be modelled mathematically.)

The fortune-tellers, however, do not have complete freedom in their interpretations, since they must take account of the tag attached to each fortune-poem, as well as its content. The fortune-teller must be particularly skillful in dealing with clients who have selected fortune-poems which are tagged as highly unlucky. The fortune-teller can hardly deny that the prospects for the worshipper are not good, since the tag for each poem ('upper-upper', 'lower-lower', and so on) is easily understood even by illiterate worshippers. However, to predict that the worshipper's hopes will be dashed is not likely to produce a happy customer, or lead to any repeat visits. The fortune-tellers rely on the concept that while the bad outcome is inevitable under current conditions, it can perhaps be avoided by various means.[25] In other words, some immediate action can be taken to bend the flow of fate in one's favour and prevent the onset of misfortune.

There are various remedies. Some fortune-tellers, drawing on Buddho-Taoist conceptions, advise good deeds. It is not usually made clear how good deeds will influence one's fate. Perhaps the god will be more sympathetic and intervene to prevent misfortune. (Most worshippers are of course aware that the god advises '*heung sihn*', or charity and benevolence, as noted in the previous chapter; perhaps such action might induce the god to intervene on one's behalf.) Or perhaps the weight of one's virtue provides some quasi-mechanical protection against misfortune. In any case, the 18 per cent of worshippers who will draw unlucky fortune-poems probably contribute something to the pool of charitable activity and donations in Hong Kong as a result of this kind of advice.

Other fortune-tellers are not above trying to make a little extra money from these unlucky clients. One client from overseas, for instance, asked a question about her brother's future, and drew a poem which predicted quite bad prospects. The fortune-teller advised her to buy a booklet of prayers and burn them (to send the prayers to the god) and the alarmed worshipper bought the booklet immediately for a substantial sum — from the fortune-teller, who just happened to have a supply of these booklets. It appears that the more common advice, however, is to do good deeds.

Some worshippers ignore bad predictions and only pay attention to the good or interesting predictions, but for those who firmly believe in the procedure, drawing an unlucky poem is serious and disturbing, and we could expect that the advice of the fortune-teller about how to avoid the misfortune will usually be heeded.

The tags do not always completely control the fortune-tellers' options in explaining the fortune-poems, since many of the poems contain complex allusions, and as noted above, the tag is not always entirely consistent with the content of the poem. Sometimes the fortune-tellers may develop quite complex explanations based on relations which they perceive between the poem and the worshippers' particular questions, and it is in these complex explanations that the fortune-tellers doubtless find the greatest challenge and pleasure in their work. For instance, fortune-teller Mr Mak On-sang related the following incident, told to him by the fortune-teller in the next stall:

Once a customer of my counterpart next door had a prediction slip indicating very bad luck. He asked whether he should start buying gold for investment. It would be very obvious to most people that if he bought gold, he would lose money. But that wasn't the case as the story on his prediction slip was about General Yue Fei in the Sung Dynasty. Yue was our national hero but the Sung emperor used 12 gold medals, a symbol indicating the highest authority, to order him back from the border and subsequently sentenced him to death. When a worshipper gets a slip like this, most fortune-tellers will relate his luck to that of Yue. But the prediction at this stage should be considered a good sign to buy gold, as there are 12 gold medals in this story. As it later turned out, the customer made a good profit with his gold investment. He offered HK$10,000 to the lady fortune-teller. (Wan 1988).

Of course, this fortune-teller was taking a great risk if indeed she advised the man to buy gold, especially since the fortune-poem was, on the surface, very unlucky and would normally indicate terrible prospects. Mr Mak himself indicated that he is very conscious of the risks: 'I should be very careful with my predictions or interpretations. For one thing I am not ready to damage my own reputation. For another, I do not want customers storming my stall and asking for their money back' (Wan 1988). This caution leads many fortune-tellers to add qualifiers to predictions in which the stakes are high. The fortune-tellers are most comfortable making specific predictions when the stakes for the client are low, as in the prediction that the female student would meet her loved one in March.

Sometimes, however, the client insists on having the fortune-teller determine the correct course of action, and the fortune-teller, assessing the risks, may decide to comply. Mr Mak, related the case of a teenage girl who pressed him to make such a choice: 'She gave me names of three guys and asked me which one could be her steady boyfriend. I was bound to decide for her but I did sympathise with the two unlucky ones, who would lose her for no good reason.' (Wan 1988). It is quite possible that Mr Mak need not have worried about the other two prospective boyfriends, since we know that many teenage girls treat these consultations as a kind of amusing, intriguing entertainment (see the previous chapter, and Jordan and Overmyer 1986:158), and Mr Mak's young client no doubt ultimately made her own choice among the three suitors. However, among older and more serious clients, the fortune-teller must occasionally take some risks with potentially more serious consequences. The stories about the great accuracy of Wong Tai Sin's predictions are common, while it is difficult to find stories about the spectacular failures which must have occurred.[26] The scarcity of such stories can be attributed, in part, to the great skill of most fortune-tellers in providing specific and highly falsifiable predictions only on matters which carry low risks to worshippers, and in carefully qualifying those predictions which carry more fateful consequences. The fortune-teller may also refuse to be specific, however urgently he or she is pressed for specific advice.

There are other reasons why the researcher will not hear stories about the failures of Wong Tai Sin's predictions: Firstly, worshippers can quite easily rationalize or forget the failures of prediction. Rationalizations include the interesting belief, expressed by one of the worshippers interviewed at the temple, that the god is never wrong in his predictions and hence any mistakes are due to errors by the fortune-teller in interpreting the fortune-poems. Given the obvious caution of the fortune-tellers in making specific and falsifiable predictions, such a belief would protect a worshipper indefinitely from any crisis of faith.

Fortune-tellers also have ways of explaining 'errors' in their analysis. For example, when his assessments of the client's life, based
on date and hour of birth, turn out to be incorrect, the fortune-
teller may claim that the time of birth was given incorrectly. Few
worshippers are sure of the exact time, and the blame for a failure of diagnosis is shifted from the fortune-teller to his client
(Greenblatt 1979:27).

Secondly, worshippers whose expectations are unsatisfied by
their visit to the temple — including worshippers who are given
a prediction on which they place great hope which is not fulfilled
— may not return to the temple. (They may try other temples until
they finally get a prediction which comes true.) Since all studies
of worshippers to date have been carried out at the temple, it is
unlikely that the researcher will hear about failures of predictions.

Thirdly, most worshippers keep mental note only of the striking cases which confirm their faith in the god. These are intrinsic-
ally interesting to the worshipper because they are extraordinary,
and because they help to justify the time and money spent on
visits to the temple. They are 'filed', while any failures of prediction are rationalized and then forgotten. There are cases where a
failure of prediction is not minor, and is not easily forgettable, but
some worshippers seem quite able to deal with these also without any loss of faith. For example, during an interview with an
elderly woman whose husband had died of cancer, the woman
recalled that during his illness, she had asked Wong Tai Sin whether
he would recover, and had received a positive answer (an auspicious fortune-poem), but since he died soon after, the prediction
was obviously incorrect. When questioned about this, she offered
the opinion that perhaps Wong Tai Sin was 'not at home' when
she asked the question, and hence cannot be blamed for the incorrect answer. (Perhaps the idea that the god was 'not at home'
should not be taken as her firm belief, but merely as an *ad hoc*
response which indicates her willingess to forgive the god for this
'mistake'.) An extensive study of how worshippers accommodate
the god's predictions would no doubt turn up a number of other
ways of handling major failures of prediction which protect the
worshipper from any loss of faith.

The fortune-tellers are a key link between worshippers and Wong
Tai Sin. They are free to improvise with their own predictions and
advice. At their best, they function as counsellors with whom Hong
Kong's anxious urbanites can discuss their hopes and anxieties,

and for such clients they provide reassurance, or (if the fortune-poem is inauspicious) advice about how to avoid misfortune. The fortune-tellers are thus one of the reasons why many people report that a visit to the temple brings them psychological benefits such as release from anxiety. With the frenetic pace of change in modern Hong Kong, its people cannot easily find peace and security in the embrace of tradition. Worshippers of Wong Tai Sin believe that the god watches over them and tries to show them what lies ahead, and the fortune-tellers help them to understand what the god is saying.

7 Offshoots

MOST religious movements eventually splinter or produce offshoots, sometimes because of doctrinal quarrels, sometimes because of ethnic, social, cultural, or regional divisions (which often underlie the doctrinal quarrels), and sometimes simply because members migrate elsewhere and set up their own version of the cult in their new location. The cult of Wong Tai Sin has also generated offshoots. In this chapter we will consider seven cases. There are others which we will not discuss here;[1] each of the seven described below illustrates something different about the origin and fate of such offshoots.

The first three sprang up outside China: in Macau (in 1906), in Kowloon (in the 1940s), and in New York City (in 1983). All were started by believers, but none of them have attracted large numbers of worshippers. Study of these cases increases our conviction that Wong Tai Sin could not have achieved fame without the unique conditions surrounding the main temple in Kowloon.

The last four offshoots, and the most recent, are within China: three in Guangdong province (1987–90), and the fourth in the Jinhua area of Zhejiang province (1991). Two of these offshoots were funded by Hong Kong believers; the other two were established by organizations inside China with the intention of attracting Hong Kong believers to come as tourists. The popularity of Wong Tai Sin in Hong Kong is helping the god to achieve a foothold, once again, in the country of his birth.

A Defunct Wong Tai Sin Temple in Macau

Macau is a 400-year-old Portuguese colony on a peninsula about 65 kilometres south-west of Hong Kong. Most of the population of about half a million is Chinese. Like Hong Kong, Macau has attracted migrants fleeing the political and economic turmoil in China during the twentieth century. However, for a variety of reasons Macau has not experienced the rapid industrial development and economic growth of Hong Kong. Consequently, it has never had the kind of magnetic appeal for migrants and refugees which

Hong Kong has had. Nevertheless, Macau was an alternative destination for people from Guangdong province who wished to find a safer or more profitable place to live.

Early this century, a few of these migrants established a shrine to Wong Tai Sin in Macau.[2] We have found this shrine especially interesting because it seems to have been an offshoot from one of the now destroyed temples in Guangdong, and to display features of the cult which have long since disappeared in Guangdong, and which are no longer remembered in Hong Kong. It is therefore a kind of religious fossil which gives us a glimpse of a past otherwise lost.

The Macau temple lies in a residential quarter of the city behind the ruins of the old Sao Paulo cathedral, in a small two-story building next to one of Macau's larger public Taoist temples. The larger temple is still patronized by local people, but the smaller building containing the Wong Tai Sin shrine is no longer used as a temple. The ground floor of the building, when visited by Graeme Lang in 1990, contained a workshop where two craftsmen produced etched soapstone carvings for sale. The upper floor contained three rooms, two of which were used as a residence by one of the craftsmen. One of the rooms was separated by a makeshift barrier from the main room on the second floor, which was once an active shrine to Wong Tai Sin. This room had not been accessible to worshippers from outside the building for about 20 years, and was seldom entered by anyone. The floorboards were broken in places, and anyone who entered was in danger of falling through into the workshop on the ground floor. The altars were covered with dust, and the statues blackened from years of exposure to incense smoke. Only the family living in the next room occasionally entered to light incense.

The side-altars next to the main altar did not sharply distinguish the shrine from the main temple in Kowloon. As in the Kowloon temple, the side-altar to the right of the main altar was devoted to the Monkey God (Chai Tin Dai Sing). We know that the veneration of Monkey is a very early feature of the cult of Wong Tai Sin, since messages from Monkey appear in the Leungs' *fuji* manuscript prior to the founding of the Kowloon temple. The side-altar on the left includes small statues to Tianhou and to Taisui, the god worshipped in the larger temple next to the shrine. This reflects some local influence on the shrine, since Tianhou and Taisui are both important in the area. Neither side-altar is drastically different from what we would expect in a Wong Tai Sin shrine if it were an offshoot of the Kowloon temple.

The main altar, however, was very different from the Wong Tai Sin altars in Hong Kong, and clearly showed that this shrine was not copied from anything in Hong Kong. On the main altar were the statues of three gods sitting in ornate chairs. The statue in the centre was not solid wood, like the other two statues, but had been constructed partly of paper and fabric. The sleeves and hem of the robes of this statue, along with the god's hat, were a bright yellow colour. The head had come away from the neck and hung down onto the chest, held only by a few strands of fabric. The statue was larger than the other two statues, and more ornate. This was Wong Tai Sin, but this Wong Tai Sin was not at all like the one in the Hong Kong temple. The presence of two god-statues flanking Wong Tai Sin also sharply distinguished this shrine from the main altar in the Kowloon temple, where Wong Tai Sin occupies the central altar alone. Where did this version of the Wong Tai Sin cult come from?

While the statues were not like anything to be found in Hong Kong, they were similar to the statues of Wong Tai Sin which once existed in the Fangcun and Rengang temples. Firstly, the gold-coloured clothing on the Wong Tai Sin statue was undoubtedly copied from either the Rengang statue or the Fangcun statue, both of which provided the god with golden or gold-painted robes (see Chapter 2). Secondly, the placement of two statues flanking Wong Tai Sin reproduced the arrangement of statues in the Fangcun temple, in which a statue of Wong Tai Sin was flanked by statues of Lu Dongbin and Wei Zheng. The inscriptions in the Macau shrine show that it was opened in 1906, only two years after the construction of the Fangcun temple and four or five years after the construction of the Rengang temple.[3] We believe that the people who donated money for the Macau shrine had migrated down to Macau from Guangdong, that they knew one or both of the Wong Tai Sin temples which then existed in Guangdong, and that they tried to copy the basic features of the Wong Tai Sin cult as they had encountered it in the Guangdong temples.[4] The reader may recall that in Fangcun, Lars Ragvald was told by elderly residents that during the birthday celebration for Wong Tai Sin, people would come from Hong Kong and from Macau to attend the ceremonies (Chapter 2). It is likely that the Macau people who went up to Guangzhou and crossed over the river to Fangcun for these ceremonies, were the same people who founded or patronized the Macau shrine.

Why was this Wong Tai Sin shrine in Macau allowed to deteriorate to its present decrepit condition? The simple answer is probably that there was no longer an active constituency of worshippers willing to donate money to repair the shrine and to support a temple-keeper, but this shrine survived for 60 years before it finally closed in the 1960s. What caused the shrine to be abandoned? We suggest the following reasons: firstly, the growing fame of the Wong Tai Sin temple in Kowloon from the 1960s onward must have increasingly overshadowed the Macau temple. The Kowloon temple is far more impressive than the one-room Macau shrine, and must have begun to attract Macau worshippers, especially after the destruction of the Guangdong temples.

Secondly, travel between Macau and Hong Kong became easier and quicker as newer and faster boats were added to the Hong Kong–Macau route. Since most worshippers in Macau, as in Hong Kong, probably went to worship only once or twice each year, and since many of them would have found it increasingly convenient to travel to Hong Kong for business or to visit relatives, it was not difficult for ordinary worshippers to visit the Wong Tai Sin temple in Kowloon on one of these visits. This would greatly reduce their patronage of the Macau shrine.

Thirdly, the Macau shrine, located next to a much larger and more impressive Taoist temple, was poorly placed to attract and hold worshippers. The shrine may have been built at that location to try and induce worshippers to visit the shrine on their way to or from the larger temple. If this was the intention, it was an unwise choice. The larger temple building offers everything which the smaller shrine offers (except a statue of Wong Tai Sin), and in a much more impressive setting. Even if some worshippers did indeed visit the smaller shrine during visits to the larger temple, they would be unlikely to attribute whatever good fortune they achieved solely to the intervention of Wong Tai Sin.

Fourthly, there was no large group of refugees or recent migrants living near the shrine. Hence, there was no potential constituency for a new god, no large group of anxious migrants cut off from their favourite temples in China and willing to visit whatever temples and beseech whatever gods they could find nearby in their new environment.

Fifthly, the Macau shrine did not have a special appeal through the provision of medical prescriptions by divination, since the temple next door also apparently provided this service.[5]

Finally as Hong Kong entered its phase of rapid economic development from the 1960s onward, some people from Macau evidently moved to Hong Kong, including the family who had lived in the building which housed the shrine. Hong Kong's success has probably helped to pull away some of the Macau shrine's few remaining patrons.

The custodians of the Macau shrine, at some point before its demise, made an effort to attract more worshippers from the neighbouring temple. Attempting to capitalize on the growing fame of the Wong Tai Sin temple in Kowloon, which would have been well-known to Macau Chinese, they painted a sign on the side of the building, visible to anyone approaching the larger temple, advertising their shrine as the Wong Tai Sin Temple, but this attempt to attract more worshippers apparently failed, so the temple closed permanently.

The room housing the Wong Tai Sin shrine, however, was left largely untouched for the next two decades. The altars and statues collected dust but were not removed. The room was used for storage by the current residents of the building, and for them it is like a dusty attic containing old objects which nobody is interested in anymore. The shrine has survived only because the room was so decrepit that major repairs to the walls and floor would have been required in order to use it for anything other than storage, and because a son of the former temple-keeper still finds it convenient to live in the upper part of the building and use the lower part as his workshop. The survival of this shrine presents an otherwise impossible opportunity to the student of the cult of Wong Tai Sin: to look back in time and see what the earliest altars to Wong Tai Sin might have looked like. This is especially fascinating because it shows how minor offshoots can preserve original features of a cult which were abandoned and lost by the one version which ultimately survived and became highly successful.[6]

We have not managed to answer all of our questions about this shrine. Some puzzling features remain unexplained at the time of writing,[7] but we make the following assertions with some confidence: that this decrepit, untended shrine was the first offshoot from the Guangdong temples; that it preserves some very early features of the Wong Tai Sin cult which were otherwise lost when the Guangdong temples were destroyed; and that it died out because its location and its social context in Macau weighed heavily against its chances for success.

The Private Wong Tai Sin Temple in Kowloon

The next offshoot of the Wong Tai Sin cult was a private temple devoted to Wong Tai Sin founded by Chaozhou people in the 1940s. So far, it has been much more successful than the Macau shrine, although few people in Hong Kong are aware of its existence.[8] It was founded partly because of events during World War II, and partly because of an ethnic cleavage among worshippers.

In the 1930s, some Chaozhou worshippers were attracted to the Wong Tai Sin temple, and some became believers. With the Japanese occupation, the temple's business was interrupted. Chaozhou worshippers wanted to get the god's advice using the *fuji* procedure, and they could not do this at the Kowloon temple. According to one informant, one of them got into the temple and brought back some incense ash. This substance allowed them to draw the god's presence to a new shrine which they set up in private rooms in Kowloon City.[9] Here, they could ask for the god's advice using *fuji*, which was difficult or impossible for them to do at the main temple because of the Japanese occupation.

According to another informant, they also wanted to have a private place for Chaozhou people to worship the god and seek his help. Chaozhou religious traditions are somewhat different from those of the Cantonese-speaking population. The language barrier is also important for many first-generation Chaozhou immigrants to Hong Kong, since the Chaozhou dialect and standard Cantonese are so different that they are mutually unintelligible. For these reasons — language and religious differences, and the resulting Chaozhou desire to worship at temples catering mainly to Chaozhou people — Chaozhou migrants to Hong Kong have tended to develop their own shrines.[10] This motive was evidently present among the people who set up this new private shrine to Wong Tai Sin.

In 1942, not long after the establishment of the new shrine, a charter for the group was formulated which contained the god's instructions about behaviour. The charter told them to carry out good deeds, avoid pride, arrogance, and immorality, and to continue in their faithful devotion to the god.[11] It said that even though the shrine is sacred, it cannot yet be called a real temple and is still only a kind of temporary residence or resting place for the god. Four months later, they received a message from the highest possible authority, the Jade Emperor, in which the god expressed his satisfaction with their benevolence and their devotion, and authorized them to rename their organization the Yun Ching Guk (Yuanqing Ge).[12] The new name means 'Pavilion of the original request/invitation'. It is possible that this title represents a kind of claim to legitimacy: it implies that the Jade Emperor has not only specifically invited them to found their own shrine but has also bestowed some unique favour upon them. Possibly this was intended to counter the potential criticism that they should be worshipping Wong Tai Sin at the main temple like everyone else.

The founder of this shrine was Wong Bat Hung, a Chaozhou rice-importer and wholesaler.[13] Apparently his business was quite profitable during the war. The Japanese had instituted rice rationing after their conquest of Hong Kong, but war conditions and the rice requirements of the army led to shortages of rice. Rice depots in Hong Kong and Kowloon provided these rice rations, but people had to wait in long lines to get their meagre portions of rice. Many people could not afford to wait for hours in queues, and relied on the black market (Hahn 1946:360–61). The price of rationed rice climbed steadily as the scarcity worsened, and the price of black-market rice soared (Endacott 1978:143–4). By mid-April 1944, the shortage of rice was so severe that the rice ration for the general population was cancelled, except for those people directly involved in the war effort.

The shortage of rice was devastating for the poor. Many people were forced to go back to their ancestral villages in China in an often vain attempt to find enough food to survive. During this period, charitable organizations in Hong Kong solicited money to provide emergency food supplies to the elderly, the sick, orphans, and the poor (Endacott 1978:143–4, 158). Wong Bat Hung and some other wealthy persons in Hong Kong donated money or provided some rice at cost to these organizations. In recognition of their good deeds (according to one informant), the god had given Wong's group permission to build a permanent altar.

Just before the end of the war, however, conditions for everyone were very bad. Wong and others asked Wong Tai Sin if they should leave Hong Kong. They were told, through *fuji*, that they should stay. So they did, and a number of these people eventually became very rich. In their minds, this proved the wisdom and foresight of the god.

By 1949, the crowds of poor petitioners at the main temple (many of them recent refugees from China), made these men increasingly determined to establish their own private temple where they could

worship in privacy and in their own idiom. So they acquired a plot
of land in the hills above Sham Shui Po, about a kilometre from
Wong Bat Hung's business premises, and in 1950 they built a substantial temple covering their plot and some adjacent public land,
and hired a temple-keeper from among the Chaozhou refugees
who had recently arrived from China. He remained at his post until
the late 1980s. The temple duplicated the main features of the
Wong Tai Sin cult in the Kowloon temple, including an identical
version of the god's 'autobiography' inscribed on a plaque on the
wall, and the use of a picture rather than a statue.

The decision to use a picture presented them with a problem,
since they could not get an exact copy of the painting hanging in
the main temple. Their solution was to produce their own painting of the god using the *fuji* stick with a brush attached to it. This
fuji painting is thus, in effect, the god's self-portrait. While the
figure in the painting in the Kowloon temple depicts Wong Tai Sin
as supremely confident and all-knowing, the figure in the private
temple wears a quizzical expression: attentive and curious, perhaps even slightly eccentric. But this expression is probably an
artifact of the rather awkward process of painting by *fuji*, and in
other respects the image is clearly modelled on the one in the
Kowloon temple.[14]

Apart from its exclusive and private character, and some minor
differences in ritual,[15] the biggest difference between this temple
and the main Kowloon temple is that *fuji* here is still a central feature of the cult, while it has not been performed in the Kowloon
temple since the early 1970s. The members still solicit the god's
advice individually and collectively, through the *fuji* stick, and keep
a record of all the god's messages. (Here also, as in the Macau offshoot, we can see features of the original cult which have been
abandoned elsewhere, especially the use of *fuji* as a focus for the
group). Since the god's advice that they stay in Hong Kong in 1945
proved to be prescient, and since they are now facing another
potentially fateful decision — whether to emigrate because of 1997
— they have begun in the last few years to ask the god's advice
once again about whether they should leave Hong Kong.

In 1982, the British Government and the Chinese Government
were negotiating the future of Hong Kong, and some of the statements from Peking about recovering sovereignty over the colony
were beginning to cause many residents to think about emigration. Shortly before Prime Minister Margaret Thatcher's visit to

Beijing in September of 1982, some members of the Yun Ching Guk met at the temple and asked Wong Tai Sin what they should do. His answer was expressed in the following oracle:

The wish of the members can be fulfilled. Anyone who has confidence in Hong Kong will stay. Those who do not have confidence in Hong Kong will leave. The ones who leave will return later. 9,9,45. [China] intends to take over, but won't do so. [The powerless British] will leave. The real owners will become masters of their own fate. Members should carefully ponder the meaning of these lines. Then they will understand.[16]

The members of the Yun Ching Guk (Yuanqing Ge) believe that in this oracle Wong Tai Sin has once again shown his power to see the future, just as he did in 1945. They are proud of the oracle, and have had it printed on pink sheets of paper for distribution to interested guests at the temple. Some of the phrases are obscure, but members readily explain the predictions for visitors.

They point out, for instance, that the British did indeed finally agree to leave Hong Kong, despite initial talk of holding on after 1997. They also point to the numbers '9,9,45' as the god's successful prediction of the outcome of the negotiations; obtaining four numbers by divination, and perceiving predictions about political events in various combinations of the numbers, is not uncommon in Chinese divination.[17] In 1984, China and Britain signed the Joint Declaration regarding Hong Kong's future. In this treaty, China agreed to allow Hong Kong to retain its present socio-economic system (including capitalism) for fifty years after 1997: that is, until 2047. Members of the Yun Ching Guk believe that Wong Tai Sin predicted this date, since the sum of '9,9,45' is 63, and 63 years after 1984, the year of the Joint Declaration, is 2047. Of course, other interpretations of the '9,9,45' are possible.[18] However, the members were evidently reassured by the god's confidence in Hong Kong's future.

Shortly after this revelation, another group of Hong Kong businessmen who had already emigrated to the US set up a Wong Tai Sin shrine in New York City. This group very quickly became associated with a much more pessimistic view of the change of sovereignty in 1997.

The Wong Tai Sin Shrine in New York City

In 1983, a group of Chinese businessmen in Manhattan completed their arrangements to set up a shrine to Wong Tai Sin on the second floor of a building on East Broadway, in New York City's Chinatown.[19] They had attempted to get the blessing of the Sik Sik Yuen for this new shrine, and the founder of the group, Mr Ling Gwan Fai (Ling Junhui), had travelled to Hong Kong to try to induce the Sik Sik Yuen's chairman to come to New York for the opening of the shrine, and to bring a Taoist from the Kowloon temple to conduct the ceremony. He was even prepared to send 30 per cent of the money from future donations back to the Sik Sik Yuen (although the chairman of the Sik Sik Yuen, interviewed later, denied receiving any such offer).[20] But Mr Ling was unsuccessful in his attempts to get the Sik Sik Yuen to endorse his shrine. The Sik Sik Yuen people believed (so Mr Ling later commented to a reporter) that he was only opening the shrine in New York for profit. They declined to attend. Nevertheless, the New York group pushed ahead with their plans. A statue of Wong Tai Sin was ordered from Taiwan. Like the painting in the private Chaozhou temple, the statue was modelled closely on the painting in the Kowloon temple but was not identical to it. Other temple objects such as drums and a bronze bell were purchased in Hong Kong. The shrine finally opened in late 1983. This shrine began as the germ of an idea in the mind of Mr Ling when he was a refugee in Hong Kong 30 years earlier, as he prayed for success at the Wong Tai Sin temple in Kowloon.

Ling Gwan Fai had fled Shanghai in 1949 at the age of 19. His next few years in Hong Kong were full of hardship, and like many other refugees, he visited the Kowloon temple frequently and prayed to Wong Tai Sin for help, promising that if the god helped him he would not forget. Eventually, he began to be successful. He found work, married and had eight children, and prospered. After 17 years, he had an opportunity to emigrate to the US, where he became rich in the textile industry. So in recent years he had returned to Hong Kong nearly every year and, while in Hong Kong, had visited the temple to thank Wong Tai Sin for helping him to succeed.

However, as the Sino–British negotiations continued, it became apparent that China would take over Hong Kong in 1997. Ling began to reflect that in 14 years Hong Kong would be lost to the Communists, and that he might not be able to go back to Hong Kong to worship Wong Tai Sin. Perhaps this was a good time to fulfil his promise to the god when he was still a poor immigrant in Hong Kong in the 1950s: that if he prospered with Wong Tai Sin's help, he would remember and would tell people about this god. So he and a group of associates decided to open a Wong Tai Sin shrine in New York.[21] This shrine would allow worship of Wong Tai Sin to continue regardless of what happened in Hong Kong after 1997. In the meantime, it would also allow believers in New York to thánk Wong Tai Sin for his help without having to make the long journey back to Hong Kong.

Mr Ling hoped that the temple would generate enough revenue from donations, so that his group could become a major contributor to Chinese charities in New York. His associates included a man who had once worked in a company owned by a director of the Sik Sik Yuen, and thus the group probably had some knowledge of the operations of the Sik Sik Yuen, and knew of the large revenues which it receives from worshippers. They knew that the Sik Sik Yuen used some of the revenue to sponsor schools and homes for the aged, and saw uses for this kind of revenue in the Chinese community in New York. They were also no doubt aware of the status and influence in the community which comes to those who sit on the board of a temple organization which funnels large contributions to local charities.

The temple opened on a rainy day in December of 1983. The rain was considered a good omen, promising prosperity for the new shrine. Mr Ling made a speech explaining why the shrine had been built, and noted that some its revenue would be directed into local charities. A representative of the local unofficial consulate of the Republic of China, (Taiwan) was also present, along with reporters and cameramen from the local Chinese newspapers. However charitable Mr Ling's intentions in opening the shrine, the political angle of the story did not escape the reporters, and the first weeks of the new shrine were marred by controversy.

Mr Ling had mused in an interview around the time of the opening of the shrine that the prospect of a Communist take-over of Hong Kong in 1997 had been one of the reasons why he decided to open the new shrine in New York. One of the Chinese newspapers in New York ran a story on it with the headline, 'At the mention of the Communist Party, even an immortal [*xian*] has to be afraid', and suggested that the god was himself emigrating to New York because of 1997.[22] This story came to the attention of a left-wing Hong Kong newspaper, which complained about the story and called the chairman of the Sik Sik Yuen for clarification. The chairman was indignant about the story that 'Wong Tai Sin had moved to New York because of 1997'. He said the story was ridiculous, and could only lead people to think that Hong Kong was heading for disaster, and produce panic and turmoil. Such a story was the result of people spreading rumours for their own (political) motives. He denied any link between the Sik Sik Yuen and the New York group, and affirmed that it was impossible to remove Wong Tai Sin to New York, or anywhere else. He expressed his confidence in the outcome of the negotiations between Britain and China, and noted that the negotiations had the clear goal of maintaining Hong Kong's peace and prosperity. The stability of industry and the continuing investment in Hong Kong, he said, showed that there was every reason for optimism, and he expressed his hope that people in Hong Kong and overseas would not be misled by such pernicious rumours as the one about Wong Tai Sin abandoning Hong Kong because of 1997.

In New York, Mr Ling must have regretted his casual comments to reporters. Contacted about the story by a Hong Kong reporter, he completely disavowed any political motives in opening the shrine, and expressed his regret that some people in Hong Kong distrusted the motives of his group. The controversy soon ended. The New York group had wanted to enhance the legitimacy and status of their shrine through an endorsement by the Sik Sik Yuen and through the attendance of Sik Sik Yuen officials at the opening ceremonies, and had failed. Perhaps they had been naïve in expecting such help for what could only be a rival to the Hong Kong temple. Their success or failure as a shrine would depend on other factors anyway: the location of the shrine, the decisions of its managers, and the numbers and the needs of potential worshippers. Mr Ling did his best to ensure maximum publicity for the shrine at every opportunity.

For a time, the shrine attracted large numbers of people. On some weekends during the early months, according to Mr Ling, over 1,000 visitors arrived. Chinese immigrants in neighbouring states chartered buses to visit the shrine. Chinese storefront shrines in New York City attract non-Chinese tourist groups, and evidently some of these visitors also ventured up to the shrine, and even had their fortunes told. Three fortune-tellers and a temple-keeper had been appointed, two of them recent immigrants from Vietnam, and they were provided with small rooms just inside the entrance to the shrine, where they interpreted the god's answers to petitions using the same set of fortune poems as are used in the Kowloon temple. They hoped to be kept profitably busy in this occupation by a steady stream of worshippers from among the tens of thousands of Chinese living in the area.

However, the stream dwindled to a trickle. There was barely enough business to keep two fortune-tellers going. This scarcity of customers sharpened the already notable alacrity with which the fortune-tellers fastened on anyone who climbed the steps to the shrine, but their aggressiveness probably deterred even more people from coming to worship. The number of worshippers visiting the shrine was far fewer than the group which founded the shrine had expected, but they seemed to have no idea how to attract more people. Why has this shrine not succeeded, despite the large number of people from Hong Kong now living in New York City? There are several likely reasons.

Firstly, the journey to the shrine was very inconvenient for most potential worshippers. It required a long walk from the nearest subway stop, or a lengthy and uncertain search for a parking space in the neighbourhood, and hence the shrine was convenient only for those living within a few blocks.

Secondly, the shrine itself was not impressive. It was on the second floor of a nondescript building, sandwiched between the Wah May Press on the first floor and the Cuban Chinese Benevolent Association on the third floor. The worshipper had to climb up a long flight of stairs from the street, and was then confronted with a long room which had little of the ambience of a temple. The statue of the god at the far end of the room was clearly expensive, but the smooth grey face, devoid of expression, offered little to inspire worshippers. The fluorescent lighting, linoleum floor, and clean yellow walls, along with the folding table used for food offerings, undermined the attempt to cultivate a sense of awe and sacredness in the worshipper. Sometimes an elderly person stopped in the street opposite the stairway and briefly bowed in the direction of the shrine, but then continued on her way. This shrine clearly evoked a great deal of interest among Chinese people living in or near New York who had become familiar with Wong Tai Sin before they left Hong Kong to emigrate to the United States. But the shrine was evidently not appealing enough to draw most of them back for return visits.

Thirdly, those worshippers who can afford it still return to Hong Kong, to the grand and famous temple in which they are accustomed to petitioning Wong Tai Sin, to consult the god and to thank him for whatever good fortune they attribute to his powers. Those who cannot afford to return to Hong Kong may ask relatives to worship or petition on their behalf at the Kowloon temple. Thus, a number of people who worshipped Wong Tai Sin in Hong Kong never go the New York shrine.

Fourthly, Chinese-Americans in the New York area do not provide an ideal constituency for a new shrine. Many of those who live in Manhattan's Chinatown came from China earlier this century, and have not previously been worshippers of Wong Tai Sin. If they worship gods at all, they are interested only in the classical figures such as Guan Di or Guan Yin. If they are religious but well-educated, they are likely to be either Christians or Buddhists. Those who lived in Hong Kong and were worshippers of Wong Tai Sin are potential supporters of the new shrine, but unlike in Hong Kong, their children seldom have any interest in such devotions. Many of these families live in the suburbs. Consequently, their children have grown up with American friends and American interests, and so their peer groups very seldom include the children of believers in Wong Tai Sin. Nor would it be a religious adventure for them to go to such an unimpressive shrine. As we saw in the chapter on believers, young worshippers are an important segment of the Kowloon temple's clientele, and the New York shrine has no way of attracting such people.

For these reasons, the Wong Tai Sin cult had not yet been securely transplanted into the New York context. Like the Macau shrine, the New York shrine (as of 1992) simply did not have the right combination of location, a large constituency of potential worshippers with pressing needs living nearby, and an impressive building or impressive ceremonies and services.

Whether there will ever be the funds and the will to establish a major North American temple to Wong Tai Sin depends in part on events in China, and the way in which they affect Hong Kong before and after 1997.[23]

The origin of the next offshoot we will discuss, is similar to the origin of the New York shrine to Wong Tai Sin in one sense — that both were established by wealthy Hong Kong businessmen who wished to thank the god for his favour by donating a temple to him. However, this fourth offshoot was transplanted, not overseas, but back into China.

The Xinhui Temple to Wong Tai Sin at Chishi Yan

Chishi Yan is a resort on the northern slopes of Mt. Guifeng, in Xinhui county, Guangdong. At Chishi Yan there is a guest-house, a memorial hall devoted to Wong Gung Fu, and a Buddhist temple.

As noted in Chapter 2, the Ming dynasty official Wong Gung Fu had returned to his ancestral village near this mountain in the seventeenth century, during the final years of the dynasty. He participated in the battles against the invading Manchus, and became famous as a local patriot — hence the memorial hall to him built by the local Wong clan. After his return, he had written a poem mentioning Wong Cho Ping, and had also renamed the hill 'Chishi Yan', a reference to Cho Ping's act of turning rocks into sheep. Neither Wong Gung Fu nor anyone else in the area ever established a shrine to Wong Tai Sin on the hill.

However, 300 years after the time of Wong Gung Fu, another native of the area established a temple to Wong Tai Sin at Chishi Yan. In 1989, a Hong Kong businessmen, Mr Wong Kwong, decided to provide the funds for a new temple.[24] Mr Wong had been born in the Xinhui area near the Chishi Yan, but had only become a believer in Wong Tai Sin many years later, after his move to Hong Kong. Like some other wealthy businessmen, he felt that as he grew older he should return some of his wealth to the community for worthy causes, and should return something to the gods for their favour to himself and his family. A temple in his home county would be a suitable expression of his gratitude. The authorities in China are often willing to permit such ventures.[25]

Mr Wong had already provided funds for renovation of several local temples near his home town, beginning in 1987. For many years in Hong Kong, he had worshipped the god Chegong, because his father had worshipped Chegong in Xinhui and because he believed that Chegong can help businessmen. However, he was aware of the traditions linking the mountain to Wong Cho Ping, and he perceived Wong Tai Sin to be a god concerned with the ordinary problems and sufferings of people. He had also been influenced by the convictions of a relative from the same village, Mr Wong Shun-wah, now a director of the Sik Sik Yuen, whose wife had been cured of tumours many years earlier by water blessed by Wong Tai Sin through *fuji*. Mr Wong decided that providing funds for a temple to Wong Tai Sin would be appropriate in view of the virtues of benevolence and concern for others shown by Wong Tai Sin. It would also help to attract visitors to the area from Hong Kong.

The villagers applied on Mr Wong's behalf for permission to build two temples on the mountain, one for Wong Tai Sin and one for Chegong. Permission for the two temples was granted by local authorities, on condition that Mr Wong alone would provide the funds.[26] Mr Wong, in turn, specified that if the temple was profitable, revenues should be divided equally between contributions to a local school, to a hospital, to a planned home for the elderly, and to maintenance of the temple. Mr Wong Shun-wah served as financial overseer during the first year of operation, and was regularly sent the accounts by the local operators of the temple.

The two temples were built on the slopes above the Buddhist temple and the memorial hall, in an area not served by a road; evidently all construction material had to be carried up a newly built stone stairway on the mountain. People in Mr Wong's home village supervised the project and helped keep the costs within the budget through careful scrutiny of the work. The formal opening of the new Wong Tai Sin temple occurred on 27 September 1989. Mr Wong had hoped to attract some prominent Hong Kong residents to the ceremony, but many people were unwilling to travel into China after the events of June 4 in Peking several months earlier. Nevertheless, the temple opened as planned, and eventually began to draw tourists from Hong Kong and Macau. Local residents also began to worship at the temple. Unlike in the new Jinhua temple or in the Luofu shrine, the image of Wong Tai Sin in this temple is a picture copied directly from the portrait of the god in the main temple in Hong Kong. As Mr Wong is a member of the Sik Sik Yuen, and his relative Mr Wong Sun Wah is a director, this presented no difficulties.

An interesting feature of the site was the carving of a number of stone statues, further down the slope below the Buddhist temple, showing Wong Cho Ping, his brother Cho Hei, and a number of rocks in the process of turning into sheep, or having just completed the transformation. This tableaux attracts much attention from visitors to the mountain, and in 1992, a pavilion was being planned for people to sit nearby and contemplate the scene.

Thus, two decades after the destruction of the last Wong Tai Sin temple in China, and probably three decades after the end of all overt worship of him, Wong Tai Sin has regained a foothold.

A New Shrine in Rengang Village

The original temple built by Leung Yan Ngam in Rengang in 1901 was totally destroyed during the Cultural Revolution, but pieces of the temple remained in the village, including the original gatestone.

We noticed during a visit to the village in 1987 that the villagers seemed interested in preserving this relic — a revived temple might attract many Hong Kong tourists to the village. Indeed, we learned that villagers subsequently sent requests to members of the Sik Sik Yuen in Hong Kong to see if funds might be available to build a new temple in Rengang. These requests have so far been declined by the Sik Sik Yuen, but we suspected after our visit in 1987, that the temple would one day be rebuilt. Graeme Lang in fact predicted, in a talk on our research at The Chinese University of Hong Kong in early 1990, that the cult would eventually be revived in the village.

The prediction, as it turned out, was fulfilled much more quickly than expected. During a visit to Rengang village by members of the Sik Sik Yuen in late 1990,[27] it was discovered that a small Wong Tai Sin shrine had indeed been recently erected not far from the site of the original temple. The shrine contained a statue of the god with gold-coloured clothing, as in the original statue in the village temple but unlike the Hong Kong temple, which contains only a picture of the god. Apparently the funds were donated by a widow whose deceased husband, once a member of the Puxing Tan in the village, had migrated to Hong Kong. Some of the elderly villagers interviewed by Lars Ragvald in 1991 were quite disappointed with this shrine. It had not attracted many worshippers, and is much less grand than the original temple. The statue of the god is also much smaller and less impressive than the original, they said. To date there is no Hong Kong source of funds for a grander shrine on the site.

Part of the problem with establishing a new temple in Rengang is that it is unlikely that the county authorities would allow a large temple to be built in the village. A new or reconstructed temple on a mountainside, primarily intended for tourists, is much more acceptable to the authorities. The last two offshoots which we discussed fit into this category.

The Pseudo-Wong Tai Sin at Luofu Mountain in China

In 1985, during his quest for traces of the cult of Wong Tai Sin in China, Lars Ragvald discovered that most Guangdong Taoists whom he met, believed that the Hong Kong Wong Tai Sin lived and became an immortal on Mt. Luofu, 100 kilometres north-east of Guangzhou. Mt. Luofu is historically the most important site in the history of Taoist worship and practice in Guangdong province. Like

Xiqiao Mountain, it rises dramatically from the plains around it, with several temples on its slopes to which worshippers have trecked for at least fifteen centuries to seek supernatural solace or to find the secrets of virtue or of immortality.[28] The Guangdong Taoists, who have all learned the lore and legends about this mountain, believed that the Hong Kong Wong Tai Sin is the same figure as a Mt. Luofu 'Wong Tai Sin' known as Wong Ye Yan, literally, 'Wong the wild man', who lived, according to the sources, roughly during the same period as Wong Cho Ping. In August of 1987, we visited Mt. Luofu to find out as much as we could about Wong Ye Yan,[29] and about the worship of Wong Ye Yan on the mountain. We found that Wong Cho Ping and Wong Ye Yan had recently been merged into one figure in the main temple at Mt. Luofu. Evidently this process of the merging of several originally distinct deities into one figure has occurred a number of times in the history of religions,[30] but it is rare that one has the opportunity to witness it firsthand. Before discussing how and why the two figures were merged, we should first describe the character and origins of Wong Ye Yan, as he is known to the Guangdong Taoists.[31]

Wong Ye Yan was by tradition a disciple of Ge Hong, the famous Taoist theorist and writer on Chinese medicine whose capsule biography of Wong Cho Ping formed the basis for the 'autobiography' of Wong Tai Sin used in the Kowloon temple. Ge Hong had retired to Mt. Luofu in about AD 327, after an active career of service to the State, to pursue immortality through the collection of various herbs and the attempt to refine cinnabar into a medicine to produce immortality. Wong Ye Yan is not mentioned in the writings of Ge Hong, but the legend of Ye Yan's relation to Ge Hong is described in a major sixteenth-century reference work on Taoist saints, as follows:

Wong Ye Yan was a disciple of Ge Hong. When Hong lived on the mountain and made cinnabar Ye Yan would always follow him. When Ge Hong was about to ascend to heaven he left a pill between the pillar and the stone at Mt. Luofu. Ye Yan ate the pill, and became an earthbound saint. Even today [this was written in the Ming dynasty] there are those who occasionally meet him in the forest.[32]

The key fact about Ye Yan in this account is that unlike Ge Hong and his wife, who ascended to heaven, according to the legends, after ingesting the cinnabar, Wong Ye Yan somehow failed to achieve this, even with the cinnabar pill left behind for him by Ge Hong.

(According to one account, Ye Yan arrived on the scene too late to ascend with Ge Hong.)[33] Ye Yan still managed to become an immortal but was stuck for some centuries on earth. He seems to have spent his time wandering in the hills, and engaging in the kind of behaviour which gained him the reputation of 'the wild man'. There are no biographical details available which might identify Ye Yan as an actual historical figure, but there are several ways in which such a figure might have evolved. For instance, it is quite plausible that some Taoist hermits in the Mt. Luofu area were recluses, seldom seen, whose odd behaviour could have contributed to the development of a myth such as that of Ye Yan, 'the wild man'. Another possibility has been suggested by Michel Soymie (1954:109–10): that the Ye Yan tradition is based on contacts in ancient times between people of the plains of Guangdong and aborigines living on or near the mountain, or pushed into the mountains by the arrival of migrants from the north. Stories derived from these contacts might have become the basis for the Ye Yan legend. Supporting this interpretation, Soymie notes, is the fact that Ye Yan was thought to be able to appear as a man or a woman, a young person or an old person, and that Ye Yan may be considered a category of 'strange person apparitions' rather than a single person with unique and unvarying features. Clearly, once such a flexible figure had become established in the popular imagination, sightings of almost anything on the mountain could feed into the growing folklore about Ye Yan. In any case, whatever its origins, this figure was seen as benign, even though eccentric, and was eventually credited with several healings.[34]

The veneration of Wong Ye Yan at Mt. Luofu has had a very long history. Poets and writers who visited Luofu from the eleventh to the eighteenth centuries mentioned Ye Yan or described shrines to Ye Yan on the mountain.[35] He has been known in the area, and probably worshipped, since at least the early Song period. There was once a separate shrine to Ye Yan, and when the temple was rebuilt after being destroyed in the early 1800s, Ye Yan was moved into the same room as Ge Hong.

This temple was restored and renovated again in 1985 or 1986.[36] In the process of renovation, the figure of Ye Yan has been transformed. There is now a separate room for Wong 'Tai Sin' at the Luofu Chongxu Guan. He is now no longer identified as Wong Ye Yan, but merely as the Red Pine Wong Tai Sin. The temple keepers and the local Taoists at Luofu claim that this figure is the same as the Hong Kong Wong Tai Sin.

However, the biographies of the two Wongs are clearly irre-concilable. Wong Ye Yan does not bear any resemblance to Wong Cho Ping. Furthermore, there are no literary traditions that Wong Cho Ping went anywhere near Luofu, or anywhere other than Jinhua Mountain in Zhejiang province. We have found no trace of any previous worship of Wong Cho Ping at Luofu. Hence, it is sur-prising that anyone should confuse the two figures. Why has this confusion of the two Wongs occurred?

The Merging of Wong Cho Ping and Wong Ye Yan

As noted, many Guangdong Taoists identify the Hong Kong Wong Tai Sin as Wong Ye Yan of Mt. Luofu. There is a simple explana-tion. They are all aware of Wong Ye Yan because he is a famous figure in the history of Taoism at Luofu; he is a 'Tai Sin', or saint, although not often referred to explicitly as such; and they do not know of the Sik Sik Yuen 'autobiography' of Wong Tai Sin which clearly identifies him as Wong Cho Ping of Zhejiang province (many Hong Kong worshippers are also unaware of these details). The Guangdong Taoists have simply assumed he is the same figure as the Saint Wong whom they know best, Wong Ye Yan.

However, as we discovered when we arrived at Mt. Luofu, attempts have also been made by people with some awareness of the dif-ferences between the two Wongs to merge these two deified Taoist hermit-saints into one person on the basis of similarities and sup-posed historical connections between them. In a pamphlet sold outside the main temple at Luofu, describing the various sites of interest to tourists in the region and providing some background information on the history of the area, there are two short articles on Wong Tai Sin. The first article, titled 'The Legend of Wong Tai Sin', opens with a poem in which the story of Ge Hong's ascent to heaven is retold, taking even his dogs with him, and of Wong Ye Yan's late arrival and subsequent life as an earthbound immor-tal. After relating two stories of healings by Wong Ye Yan (taken from literary sources about the Luofu Wong Ye Yan) the article then asserts that:

According to historical records the Red Pine Wong Tai Sin of the Hong Kong Wong Tai Sin temple was a Jin dynasty man from Danxi. His original surname was Wong and his given name Cho Ping. In his youth when he was tending sheep he was taken by the famous Jin Dynasty refiner of cinnabar, old saint Ge Hong, as an apprentice. Ge Hong jok-ingly named him Wong Ye Yan. After Ge Hong had ascended to heaven

Wong Tai Sin continued to travel all over practising kindness and helping the people. He first went to Mt. Xiqiao, and later to Hong Kong.[37]

The second article, titled 'Ge [Hong] the Holy Man and the Hong
Kong Wong Tai Sin', relates a visit by the author of the article to
the Sik Sik Yuen's Wong Tai Sin temple in Kowloon. After describing the temple, the account begins to describe the life of Wong
Cho Ping, using some of the details from the Sik Sik Yuen's 'autobiography' of Wong Cho Ping. However, the account omits the
miracle of turning the rocks into sheep, and instead claims that Ge
Hong, while passing by Red Pine Mountain, noticed Cho Ping with
his sheep, took him in as an apprentice, and renamed him 'Wong
Ye Yan'. Thereafter, Wong Ye Yan followed Ge Hong to Luofu
where he gathered herbs and refined cinnabar.

These extraordinary attempts to weld the two Wongs into a
single figure are not based, as far as we can tell, on any literary
sources. The pseudonymous authors, who very likely have had
some official connection with Luofu, were engaged in what appears
to us to be the creative reconstruction of myth. Perhaps they expect
that Hong Kong tourists may be willing to visit the site where their
Wong Tai Sin became an immortal. The anticipation of this flow
of tourists and devotees may explain the placing of the statue in
a new 'Red Pine Wong Tai Sin' room. The new statue also makes
the identification with Wong Cho Ping easier because the mute
tiger, evidently represented at the Ye Yan altar before the restoration, has disappeared. (The presence of the tiger, of course, would
strongly distinguish Wong Ye Yan, the wild man, from Wong Cho
Ping the tender of sheep).

Hong Kong tourists are indeed coming to Luofu. We observed
a tourist bus arriving at the temple from Hong Kong and heard
the tour guide, addressing his group by megaphone, refer to the
site as the place of origin of Wong Tai Sin. As of 1990 these tours
were still running from Hong Kong, and the pamphlets from the
travel agency operating the tour identified this stop on the tour as
the place where, according to legend, Wong Tai Sin had lived. One
local Taoist whom we interviewed asserted that 'the masses wish
the two figures [Wong Ye Yan and Wong Cho Ping] to be the same,
and so we'll let them be the same'. Another local Taoist whom we
met at a nearby temple on the plain, dismissed the importance of
the difference in the biographies of the two Wongs with the remark
that the spirit of Wong Cho Ping entered (or could enter) into the

person of the later Wong Ye Yan. These interviews confirmed that some local Taoists were aware of the difference between Wong Cho Ping and Wong Ye Yan, but considered the differences to be unimportant. Considering the amount of revenue which the Hong Kong tourist trade might generate in the area, this position is not surprising.[38] For partly similar reasons, another Wong Tai Sin shrine has recently opened far to the north, on the site where, according to Ge Hong, Wong Tai Sin really did live.

The Return of Wong Tai Sin to Jinhua Mountain

Ordinary believers can be lured to Luofu Mountain to see 'the place where Wong Tai Sin became an immortal' but members of the Sik Sik Yuen have read the 'autobiography' of Wong Tai Sin revealed to them through *fuji*. They know where he lived during his life on earth. They know where he discovered the way to immortality, turned rocks into sheep, and departed for heaven. All of this happened in the Jinhua area, in Zhejiang province, far to the north. That would be the place to visit. It might be expected that, sooner or later, they would begin to explore Jinhua, looking for traces of the origins of their god. If they did go there, what would they find?

Historical records of the Jinhua area suggest that there was a local veneration of Wong (Cho Ping) Tai Sin in the area beginning perhaps as early as the time of Ge Hong in the fourth century (Wong 1985), and that there were shrines to Wong Tai Sin in Jinhua more than a thousand years ago. The shrines to Wong Cho Ping in Jinhua were renovated or rebuilt several times, notably during the eleventh, fifteenth, and sixteenth centuries.[39] We know very little about temples on the site during the Qing dynasty, but as far as we know, the cult was not extinguished in Jinhua until the twentieth century.

In the autumn of 1990 a group of people from the Sik Sik Yuen made a pilgrimage to Jinhua Mountain to see what they could find. They may have been the first Hong Kong tourists to visit the area specifically to look for relics of the worship of Wong Tai Sin. They did indeed find some relics. A temple to Wong Tai Sin had been rebuilt in Jinhua in the 1920s, and although this temple was finally destroyed and submerged under a new reservoir built for irrigation in 1957, the large bell which once hung in the temple had survived (though now badly cracked), and still lay in the grass near the site of the temple.[40]

Local villagers had been aware of the potential value of religious tourism in the area. In fact, during the 1980s they had transmitted several requests to the Sik Sik Yuen to provide funds for a reconstructed temple on the site, promising to split the profits of the proposed new shrine.[41] The Sik Sik Yuen declined. However, the site had by that time attracted the attention of provincial authorities, leading to a striking development. Within a year, the Zhejiang Provincial Government had authorized and built a new temple in Jinhua to Wong Tai Sin, complete with a five-foot high statue of the god which is modelled on the Hong Kong version of the god's image.[42] For the opening ceremonies of the shrine in the autumn of 1991, they invited representatives from the Sik Sik Yuen and the Yun Ching Guk (the group who operate the private Chaozhou temple to Wong Tai Sin in Hong Kong). The Sik Sik Yuen did not participate officially, but a large contingent from the Yun Ching Guk journeyed to Jinhua for the event, treating it as a kind of pilgrimage.[43] Surprisingly, the nearby reservoir had been drained since the 1990 visit by Sik Sik Yuen members, and the foundations of the original temple were now visible. The local villagers had taken the opportunity presented by the draining of the reservoir to carry off several inscribed stones from the site, along with the cracked bell, and had installed these in their village. While there had been a cult of Wong Tai Sin in the area for more than a millennum, the resurrection of this temple at Jinhua, like the opening of the new 'Wong Tai Sin' shrine at Mt. Luofu, seems to be largely due to the great popularity of Wong Tai Sin in Hong Kong, and to the desire to draw Hong Kong pilgrims to the region.

Anyone familiar with the comparative study of religious movements will probably be struck by the fact that the Wong Tai Sin cult is still focused almost entirely on the main temple in Kowloon. The surviving offshoots of the cult have only attracted a few hundred devotees, or are still primarily destinations for tourists rather than for worshippers. With the possible exception of the small new Rengang shrine, they are also offshoots from the main temple in Kowloon, not from the cult's original form in Guangdong. This increases our confidence that it was the location of the Kowloon temple, and its unique relationship to the history of the region around it, that accounts for the cult's success. It is also striking that the god is being reintroduced into his native country by the power of Hong Kong belief and Hong Kong money, after his cult had been effectively extinguished inside China.

8   Conclusions

As we promised in Chapter 1, our explanation for the great success of the god Wong Tai Sin in Hong Kong, has been complex. The diligent reader of the previous chapters will know how many holes the cult could have fallen into along the way, never to reappear, and how many times the history of the cult might have been drastically altered if certain events had turned out differently: if the plagues had not occured in Guangzhou; if a rich man had not been cured; if Mr Leung had not decided to move to Hong Kong; if the Japanese had knocked down the temple during the war, as they intended; if the British Government had knocked it down a decade later, as they also intended; and so on. We would resist any attempt to reduce the explanation for the god's success to any single factor.

Having said that, we will immediately contradict ourselves (partially) and propose one factor as the most important of the many which contributed to the rise of this god. We do this only in part to satisfy those who would demand that we simplify the picture; it is also because one factor does indeed stand out above all the others. This factor would not be sufficient without the contributions of money and organizational skill, and religio-entrepreneurial cunning which were provided by Leung Yan Ngam, his patrons, and several generations of members and officials of the Sik Sik Yuen. But without this one factor, neither their contributions, nor even the best efforts of the god, could have made him what he is today — the pre-eminent god of Hong Kong people.

What might this factor be? If we use the model of a 'religious economy' which has been developed by sociologists of religion to deal with the competition among cults, sects, and mainline religious bodies in a religiously tolerant milieu, several concepts are immediately suggested: most obviously, that the religious entrepreneur will succeed best whose group offers the best 'package' of rewards and compensators, given the current desires and needs of the local population who comprise the 'market' for religion (Stark and Bainbridge 1987:168–9). The package, of course, must also be marketed successfully, and other things being equal, better marketing strategy will prevail. Several features of the Wong Tai Sin 'package' did indeed give the temple an advantage over others: the size of the temple; the offering of some free herbal medicines; and the simplicity of worship (no chanting of liturgies, no regulations about food or behaviour, only the simple slogan, 'ask and it shall be granted').

However, we do not think that the 'package' offered by the Wong Tai Sin temple was so very different from that offered by other temples, several of which have offered free medicines for many years, and some of which are large enough to compete seriously with the Wong Tai Sin temple if size were the main criterion for success. There must be something else from the 'religious economy' model which is important. There is. If an economist were asked about the single most important factor governing the success or failure of efforts by any organization to sell people something from a single fixed outlet, he would give a simple answer: location. The primary importance of this factor is recognized by every successful sales enterprise which sells products on-site (as opposed to travelling to the customer's home, or selling through the media).[1] A temple must sell its product on-site, and hence its location is important, especially if there are other competing temples which are also within travelling distance for potential customers. The Wong Tai Sin temple's location was its single greatest advantage. It was located on land far enough from the urbanized areas of the Kowloon peninsula that its founders were able to build on a large plot of land without great cost; yet it was just close enough to draw visitors from the same urban area. Its location saved it (barely) from Japanese construction work during the war, yet allowed the temple to get the credit for saving the neighbouring villages. Finally, and by far the most important of the advantages conferred on it by its location, it stood squarely in the middle of an area of open fields which was to be covered, within a few years after 1949, by the shacks and huts of thousands of refugees who arrived from China. There was no other major temple in their midst, or even within a convenient distance. The Wong Tai Sin temple was perfectly placed to receive their petitions for help.

However, a perfectly placed building will not sell something that nobody wants. The 'package' offered at the temple was well-suited to the needs of the immigrants and migrants. It was also very important that many of the worshippers of this god-in-their-midst eventually got what they had asked the god to help them achieve:

greater economic security and a better standard of living as they struggled out of poverty. In reviewing these other factors, we will draw some parallels with religious movements elsewhere, with references which are intended to be suggestive rather than exhaustive. First, we must consider the most obvious feature of the Wong Tai Sin 'package': healing.

Healings and Religious Allegiance

In Chapter 5, we noted that the largest single category of requests to Wong Tai Sin in the 1989 survey (Fong and Luk 1989) was for medical help. Not many worshippers go to the clinic at the temple for free medicine, but some still ask the god for a medical prescription. Some of the worshippers tell stories about how Wong Tai Sin has helped them or a family member with an illness. The belief that Wong Tai Sin is capable of healing people is clearly a key element in the god's mystique. Many other religious movements also promise the prospect of healings, and the recovery from illness of new adherents is often an important reason for their continued faith. Helen Hardacre (1982, 1986), for example, has documented how healings produce conversions to religious sects such as Reiyukai and Kurozumikyo in Japan. For worshippers of Wong Tai Sin, belief in his power to heal is based on personal experience of recovery from illness, or on stories heard from others and on the general reputation of the god as a healer and purveyor of medical prescriptions.

The evidence for such healings, as in all such cults, takes the form of anecdotes told by believers. Some of the stories of healings are dramatic; but similar stories are told in virtually every culture, with healings attributed to every conceivable type of supernatural being. A non-miraculous explanation for these stories is possible because of the inevitable recoveries or remissions which occur in any sample of sick persons. Gods get credit, in all cultures, for those recoveries which occur after prayers for recovery.

We are not saying that people are never cured by the intervention of the gods. Social scientists cannot prove that such interventions do not occur. All we are saying is, that because the outcome of some injuries and illnesses are not completely predictable, and because some recoveries are inevitable, any religious movement which claims healings will be able to produce testimonials from some believers that such healings have occurred.

In other cases, stress-related ailments (headaches, indigestion, sleeplessness, depression) may improve as a result of the calming effect of asking the god to share and alleviate one's burdens, and of receiving counselling and reassurance. (At Wong Tai Sin, the counselling and reassurance are provided by the fortune-tellers). Some patients may gain temporary relief from some symptoms as a result of such effects, which may be enough to keep them coming back for more supernatural help. If the worshipper does not recover after praying to the god, there are various ways of rationalizing the lack of improvement: the need for further good deeds or improved behaviour, for more or better herbal medicines of the type prescribed by the god, for greater sincerity and repentance, and so on.

Perhaps Wong Tai Sin's reputation for healing is unusual, compared to other movements, in only one respect: there is virtually no sect-like activity, apart from the inner circle of members of the Sik Sik Yuen, and hence very little social support for worshippers as they wrestle with the course of their maladies and try to relate the outcomes to the actions and obscure messages of the god. Helen Hardacre's study of the Kurozumikyo sect in Japan reveals a more typical pattern: even though a new member has been converted primarily because of a healing, once the member has been socialized into the ceremonies and beliefs of the sect, and has begun to benefit from the social ties and social support available in the group, further personal healings are not essential. Social support for worship of Wong Tai Sin is much more casual, much less intense, and much less frequent. While such support may come in the casual comments of friends and relatives who are believers, and perhaps also from the presence of large numbers of others at the temple whenever the worshipper goes there with a request, it would not be enough to generate recruits to most of the sects and cults which have been studied by sociologists of religion.

However, the Wong Tai Sin temple is, in a way, like a supernatural supermarket of potential benefits for worshippers, and Hong Kong's busy urbanites may prefer to avoid the entanglements of sect-like group activity. At the Wong Tai Sin temple, they can pursue the healing touch or the divine prescriptions of the god without any major investment of time or social energy. The god can be partially comprehended if one imagines him as a supernatural doctor with a general practice and a kindly interest in all of the ailments of his patient-worshippers.

But the god's role as a medical worker cannot explain his great success in Hong Kong. He no longer specializes primarily in medical problems; like some gods in urban Taiwan (Tsai 1979),[2] he is now a generalist who addresses the needs of Hong Kong's driven and anxious urbanites. Evidently, he became a generalist for sociological rather than for supernatural reasons.

Refugees and Religion

We have claimed that Wong Tai Sin had his biggest success among migrants and refugees from China. We have suggested that these people left their traditional temples and ancestral halls behind in China and that on their arrival in Hong Kong they found no easy way of soliciting the supernatural help which ancestors and their traditional gods had once given them. It was impossible to go back to their villages to worship. They turned to Wong Tai Sin because his large and impressive temple was located nearby, and was not already closely connected to any particular territorial or ethnic community, and because the god's reputation for beneficence (free herbal medicines) and power (as demonstrated against the Japanese) suggested that appeals to him would be fruitful. Few studies of religious belief and behaviour among immigrants have described precisely this kind of phenomenon. However, several comparisons with some other studies might be drawn.

We might consider the often noted relation between religion and the maintenance among immigrants of their sense of identity. Scott (1987), for instance, has suggested that the Lao Hmong immigrants in the US held tenaciously to some rituals from the Laotian context because it helped to bolster their sense of identity as Hmong in an alien environment (San Diego, California) which, on many levels, acted to undermine that identity. Similarly, the Chinese refugees who flooded into Hong Kong in the late 1940s came primarily from villages and towns in rural Guangdong province, and in Hong Kong they found themselves cut off from their ancestral villages and from the dense matrix of kin and social life which had once given them elements of their sense of identity. In Hong Kong, many of them had no kin and few opportunities to participate in the communal religious festivals or traditional New Year worship to which they had been accustomed. The biggest festivals in Hong Kong were for the goddess Tianhou, worshipped mainly by the coastal villages and fishing communities for her ability to protect them from disasters associated with the sea, and this goddess was not well suited to the needs of new urbanites. It is possible that some of the gratification which these refugees received from worshipping Wong Tai Sin came from the return to traditional Chinese folk-religious practice as they had experienced it in the villages and towns of their native counties. It made them feel more 'at home', more connected to their roots. Because of its location, the temple was perfectly placed to play this role.

In Hong Kong they also found themselves ruled by a regime which was alien and still, in the 1950s, somewhat racist (though evidently less so than before World War II). As a rapidly and ruthlessly modernizing society which largely disregarded traditional Chinese ways of doing things,[3] Hong Kong society must also have helped to cut them adrift from their traditional conceptions of themselves as Chinese. In Hong Kong, they could make money, and to this end they devoted themselves with passion and energy. But apart from being money-makers, who were they? They were no longer citizens of China, but neither were they true and equal citizens of Britain. It is likely that what some of these people derived from worshipping at the temple was a feeling of grounding themselves in Chinese culture and history. It helped them to feel 'Chinese', despite the otherwise highly Westernized character of capitalist, colonial Hong Kong. This may explain some of the vague references to 'peace of mind' (*ping an*) which some interviewees give when asked about the benefits of going to the Wong Tai Sin temple to worship.

A second type of study of the religious behaviour of immigrants or migrants suggests that under certain conditions they are more susceptible to the appeal of new religious movements than people who have not migrated. Grover (1989), for instance, has shown that the Mormon missionaries in Portugal had very little success in the overwhelmingly Catholic country until Portugese refugees from Angola began to arrive in late 1975, fleeing the violence which marked Angola's transition to independence. Many of these people lost most of their material possessions, and found themselves not only dispossessed, but also rootless and disoriented on their return to Portugal. They were much more open to the preaching of Mormon missionaries than native Portuguese, who were already tied into Portugese economic and social life. For similar reasons, migrants from rural to urban areas in Latin America have proven to be more open to the preaching of various Protestant evangelical churches and sects than long-time urban or rural dwellers.[4] Similarly, it is likely that the migration of refugees from China to Hong Kong produced the same kind of psychological conditions which, in other contexts, have facilitated the joining of novel religious movements: the separation from networks of friends and relatives which had helped to bind them to their former patterns of religious practice, and the need to find something to replace that which they had lost or left behind. The economic dislocation of the refugees in Hong Kong also paralleled the similar deprivation of refugees and migrants in other societies, and this kind of material distress seems also to produce a greater openness to previously unfamiliar religious movements to the extent that these promise material or psychological, supernatural help.

In one respect, however, worship of Wong Tai Sin by refugees in Hong Kong is unlike the conversion of refugees to missionizing religious groups in other countries: Wong Tai Sin's only 'missionaries' were other worshippers telling stories about how he had helped them. Further, the worship of Wong Tai Sin did not include the incorporation of the new believer into a close network of new social relationships, as in most of the missionizing Protestant sects and new religious movements elsewhere. Wong Tai Sin offered help to refugees, but not social bonds. Perhaps the social bonds were not very necessary, because worshippers perceive Wong Tai Sin as just another Chinese god, albeit a powerful one. Hence, where the formation of close social ties with sect members is often necessary in other new or deviant religious movements to lever potential converts into full commitment to the new faith, these social ties are not necessary in Hong Kong in regard to worship of Wong Tai Sin. He was unfamiliar to the refugees, but he was not strange. He was thoroughly Chinese, and the ways in which he ought to be worshipped and consulted were familiar. So the dislocation from their accustomed patterns of worship back in their villages made it easier for them to adopt a new god. Yet his completely Chinese character helped them to retain the comfort of continued immersion in their rich religious tradition in an urban environment which lacked, for them, most of the other anchors of identity.

Adherence and Upward Mobility

In Chapter 3, we suggested that Wong Tai Sin's growing reputation reflected, in part, the upward mobility of the squatters and refugees as they moved up in Hong Kong society and gained better housing and a higher standard of living; Wong Tai Sin received some of the credit for their successes. Thus his fame was really grounded in the hard work and sacrifices of his worshippers, and in the opportunity structure of the dynamic, urban, capitalist economy which developed in Hong Kong from the 1950s onward. A comparable phenomenon has been described by Moroto (1976) in Japan: the case of members of a sect called Myochikai Kyodan in a small village in north-western Japan.[5] Most of the members of this sect whom Moroto interviewed in the early 1970s had joined in the early 1950s, when conditions in the village were very difficult for them. Some, at that time, were also immigrants who had recently moved into the area. Like the worshippers of Wong Tai Sin, many of them had initially joined because they had a problem for which they needed help (Moroto 1976:40:45–7). Like the refugees in Hong Kong, it appears that some of the problems of these Japanese villagers were directly related to their low socio-economic status, their economic insecurity, and the hardships of their lives. However, 20 years later, the members who were still highly active in the sect had experienced greater upward mobility than members who were only moderately active or who had given up any active role in the movement. It appeared that those who had not experienced upward mobility tended to become inactive. The active members, by contrast, evidently gave some of the credit for their upward mobility to their religion.

Thus, as with Wong Tai Sin, early deprivation and economic dislocation were important in impelling people to try a moderately novel religious path, but their subsequent economic success was important in cementing their continuing loyalty and commitment to the sect. We expect that there are many other religious movements, in Asia and elsewhere, which have benefited from a similar process.

At the same time, it should be noted that this process does not repeat itself endlessly. In some societies, economic distress and dislocation are chronic conditions for large numbers of people, and hence a religious movement must offer rewards and compensators which will hold the loyalty of members. In such societies the gods cannot promise, and do not benefit from, the upward social mobility of worshippers. In other social settings, the movement of sect members from economic deprivation to much greater material and social security is a temporary phenomenon associated with unique historical circumstances, such as the period immediately after a war or revolution. During a prolonged period of economic stability and

prosperity, it could be expected that recruitment to a new movement or a new god would decline, in so far as recruitment had
previously benefited from deprivation. The custodians of the movement or the priests of the new god would have to develop additional ways to attract and hold followers.

Fortunately for the gods, stability and prosperity are not typical
of most human societies. Wars, revolutions, and large concentra-
tions of dislocated and distressed migrants continue to occur. Wong
Tai Sin, for instance, must still listen to the problems of anxious
migrants, because of the impending take-over of Hong Kong by
China.

Politics and the Gods: Wong Tai Sin and 1997

In Chapter 5, we reviewed the kinds of requests worshippers make
to Wong Tai Sin, and the ways in which they believe he helps
them. These requests are mostly for personal help for themselves
or their families. We omitted one topic, however: advice about emigrating to other countries. This type of request is strongly related
to people's confidence in the future of Hong Kong.

The Sino–British negotiations about the future of Hong Kong
after 1997, when Britain's lease on the New Territories runs out,
brought this issue onto the front pages of the Hong Kong newspapers in the early 1980s. It quickly became apparent to all Hong
Kong residents that China was in no mood to allow Britain to
remain in control of any part of Hong Kong after 1997, and that
Britain was not prepared to jeopardize trade and diplomatic relations with China by insisting on its right to remain in Hong Kong
after the lease expired. By 1983, it was already clear that the regime
in China would regain complete sovereignty over Hong Kong.

A large proportion of the population in Hong Kong had fled this
regime to pursue a better standard of living and more personal
freedom. Now they faced the prospect of once again being subject to the political system in mainland China. Their nervousness
led many of them to turn to Wong Tai Sin for advice. A Sik Sik
Yuen official told a reporter that donations to the temple by worshippers during Chinese New Year in 1984 had increased by 40 to
50 per cent over the previous year.[6] Many people consulted the
fortune-tellers for advice about emigrating.

Meanwhile, at the private Chaozhou temple to Wong Tai Sin, the
god began to give oracles about the political future of Hong Kong.
As we noted in Chapter 7, they had received an oracle about the

future of Hong Kong in 1984 which reassured them that conditions would remain good in Hong Kong ('anyone who has confidence in Hong Kong's future can stay. . . . the ones who leave Hong Kong will return'). The god was telling them that they did not have to fear the period after 1997.

If they were complacent about the future of Hong Kong after the 1984 revelation, however, their complacency was severely shaken by the events of 4 June 1989, when regiments of the People's Liberation Army killed many civilians in Beijing while assaulting the avenues leading into Tiananmen Square. Again, the god gave this group a revelation about the incident, which they claimed they had received on the morning of 4 June. The revelation, which took the form of a four-line poem, was as follows:

The blood of the ignorant children is running as a river, and even the pine trees and the wind are sympathizing with these events. But they can't help. The government in China is in the dark ages. There are few peaceful days, nothing but chaos. The teacher [the god] says to keep silent, so don't say too much about the incident.

To this poem someone had appended the following explanation:

There is much change, but we should keep our own position, and do our best here. Even though the god wants to help, he can't help right now because the evil is very strong. If we can keep our place, we can protect ourselves.

Several weeks later, they received another revelation:

Hong Kong is a very unusual place. The foundation of this organization, however, is very solid and stable. There are many opinions voiced in this city [about the events of 4 June and about the regime in China], but this causes much fear and disturbs people. You should not be afraid, because your power and the power of the hosts [evidently a reference to Britain and China] are very much the same. Just wait until peace comes.

Some, if not all, of the members were pleased by these revelations. They believed that only trouble could result for Hong Kong people from the furore about the events of 4 June, and they wanted people to keep quiet and wait for a return to more normal conditions in China. The god reassured them that patience and calm, and closed mouths, would be rewarded eventually as the political crisis passed. These revelations, evidently formulated by the *fuji* master with a keen sensitivity to the mentality and values of his patrons, show a deep conservatism and preference for order over turmoil and for silence over dissent — but they also show how disturbed these men were by the military assault on Tiananmen Square.

The wealthy businessmen who sit on the board of directors of the Sik Sik Yuen were also strongly affected by the events of June 4. The Government of China, in fact, invited them up to Beijing in October of 1989, under the auspices of the State Council of Religious Affairs, to reassure them that freedom of religion in Hong Kong was guaranteed by China, and to explain the regime's version of the events of June. The directors attended the banquets and listened to the speeches — though some of them already have relatives overseas, and can move abroad if necessary.

Many ordinary worshippers, of course, were also frightened by the events in Beijing. Some have no chance to emigrate. Others have enough money, or relatives abroad, and they have turned to Wong Tai Sin for advice. One fortune-teller at the temple told a reporter during the Chinese New Year in 1990 that he had seen a 20 per cent increase in business since 4 June. People used to care more about health, wealth, marriage, or luck during the year, but many worshippers wanted to know also their suitability for emigrating and whether they will have the opportunity (Lau 1990). Another fortune-teller observed that some parents had brought their children to the temple to find out whether they should send them abroad to study, and whether, if they went abroad, they would succeed in getting residency rights in a foreign country. One woman came to the temple to pray on behalf of her daughter, who had applied for emigration to Canada. She said, 'I'm worried about her chances of success. . . . I'm also worried about whether she could adapt to the country, where we have no relatives or friends' (Lau 1990). Lau also interviewed a factory owner who had come to the temple to ask the god's advice about whether to set up a factory in Canada or Australia. The fortune poem, as interpreted by the fortune-teller, indicated a cooler place, which seemed to point to Canada. Another worshipper during the 1990 Chinese New Year was a businessman who had flown back to Hong Kong with his wife to thank Wong Tai Sin for his 'timely advice' to emigrate to the US three years ago (Lau 1990). The events of June 4, he felt, had proven the god's foresight in advising him to leave.

The fortune-tellers at the Wong Tai Sin temple are not the only diviners to profit from the emigration anxieties of Hong Kong people. There have been frequent advertisements in the Chinese press for 'emigration *fengshui*' consultations — which include professional advice from a geomancer about which real-estate properties in the emigrant's destination-country have the best *fengshui* and thus take best advantage of the supernatural potencies latent in landscapes. In terms of the sheer numbers of people seeking a diviner's advice about emigration, the Wong Tai Sin temple is probably the choice of the largest number of potential emigrants.

Wong Tai Sin, of course, has quite a good record in regard to advice about emigration. In 1915 he advised Leung Yan Ngam to move from China to Hong Kong, a most fateful choice since it ensured the survival and later growth of the god's cult after it was extinguished inside China. Since at least the late 1940s, Wong Tai Sin has helped refugees from China to succeed in Hong Kong, and a steady trickle of emigrants from Hong Kong to North America have felt they owed the god some gratitude for his help as they became prosperous. Now, the god is once again called upon to give advice about emigration. Other gods have been asked for such advice in the past,[7] but it is unlikely that any god has been consulted through divination by so many potential emigrants. Events in China, of course, will help to determine whether they stay or leave.

The one hundredth anniversary of the founding of the cult of Wong Tai Sin in southern China will be in 1997, and it will be interesting to observe whether that year marks the beginning of hard times, or a new phase of growth, for the cult of this refugee god. As folk religion experiences a cautious revival inside China, it will also be interesting to watch his progress and travels in the land of his birth.

Notes

Notes to Chapter 1

1. References to the great popularity of this temple in articles about religion in Hong Kong include Topley (1974:243), Savidge (1977:30, 33), Myers (1981:282), Law and Ward (1982:28), and Chamberlain (1983:161).

2. We use the term 'god' to include several kinds of supernatural beings which are differentiated from each other in Chinese by terms for which there are no exact equivalents in English. Thus the term *xian* — Cantonese *Sin*, as in 'Wong Tài Sin' — in Chinese, refers (according to the most common understanding of the term) to a supernatural person who was once a human, but found a way to become immortal. The Chinese character for *Sin* uses the 'person' radical, combined with the character for 'mountain', implying a 'mountain-man' — that is, a hermit. Some *Sin* were indeed once holy hermits who pursued 'the Way' through solitary endeavours in the mountains (see Blofeld 1978: Chapter 5). Having achieved immortality, the *Sin* may be venerated for this achievement, and may also be petitioned for help on the grounds that s/he possesses special powers, and may be willing to help humans in distress if properly worshipped. Thus, the *Sin* may be treated very much like a 'god'. The word *shen* (in Cantonese: *sahn*) is a more general term, and refers to a supernatural being who may or may not have been a human at one time, but who is believed to have the power to set rules for humans, and to provide benefits or punishment depending on whether they behave appropriately. *Shen* is closer to the English word 'god', but with the qualification that in a polytheistic culture, a 'god' may not necessarily earn great respect or awe, and in any case is only one among many. Worshippers of Wong Tai Sin use the term *bai shen* (worship god[s]) to refer to their worship of him, in other words, they treat him as a god.

3. *Sin* (*xian*) is sometimes translated as 'immortal' (someone who found the way to achieve immortality). 'Sage' is sometimes added ('immortal sage') because the term *Sin* implies profound knowledge and understanding of the mystical properties of nature and of substances or practices used in becoming immortal. *Sin* has also been translated as 'fairy' on the basis of the magical abilities and powers thought to be possessed by such an individual.

4. The omitted passage runs as follows: 'Jinhua derives its name from the combined brilliance [literally, 'the struggle in brilliance'] of [literally, 'between'] the Golden Star [Jinxing, that is, Venus] and the Wunu Star [Wunuxing]'. Since the phrase would be obscure and puzzling for most readers, and a proper explanation lengthy and tedious, we have omitted it from the translation of the autobiography in the text.

5. It is likely that the writer of this 'autobiography' was aware of attempts to merge the two figures, or of confusions between them. On Immortal Master Red Pine, whose brief biography is found in *Liexian zhuan*, see Max Kaltenmark, *Le Liesien Tchouan* (Paris 1953; revised edition 1987), p.35f and especially p.40, n. 7.

6. Compare Jordan and Overmyer (1986:119).

7. Ge Hong was a native of Jurong in Danyang (present day Jiangsu province). His career included service as assistant to prime minister Sima Rui, and as counsellor

and military staff officer. He was honoured by the State for his services in the suppression of the peasant revolt led by Shi Bing. However, he was also very interested in Taoist alchemy. He was a grandson, on the fraternal line, of the famous necromancer and alchemist Ge Xuan (164–244), and from a disciple of Ge Xuan's he learned the art of refining cinnabar. When word spread that cinnabar sand had been found in Jiaozhi (the ancient name for part of Guangdong and Northern Vietnam) he asked to be relieved of office and left the capital for Guangzhou. In 327 he settled in the Zhuming cave of Mt. Luofu where he busied himself collecting medicinal herbs and refining cinnabar. His extensive writings include several important treatises in Taoism and Chinese medicine. (Source: *Zongjiao Cidian* [*Dictionary of Religion*], Shanghai, Cishu Chubanshe, 1981, pp.997–8; see also *Jin Shu* [*The Book of Jin*], Vol. 72, Zhonghua Shuju). Needham calls Ge Hong 'the greatest alchemist in Chinese history' (*Science and Civilization in China*, Vol. II, Cambridge University Press, 1956, p.437).

8.   This probable origin of the autobiography was pointed out to us by Dr S.H. Wong of the Department of Chinese, University of Hong Kong. The original of Ge Hong's *Shenxian Zhuan* has long since disappeared. Our translation of Ge Hong's account of Wong Cho Ping is from the same version of *Shenxian Zhuan* used by Dr Wong. Another early version is found in the early Song dynasty work (originally printed in 981) titled *Taiping Guangji* (*Extensive Gleanings of the Reign of Great Tranquility*), Chapter 7, p. 1, republished in Beijing in 1961.

9.   Essentially the same story is related in *Huitu Liexian Quanzhuan* (*Illustrated Complete Biographies of Ranked Immortals*), compiled in the sixteenth century by Wang Shizhen (reprinted by Zhongwen Chubanshe in 1971 on Taiwan). This is one of the major reference works on Taoist saints, with capsule biographies on some 500 of them, and covers the entire period from the beginning of Taoism until the last year of the reign of Hongzhi (1506 CE). This source adds only the information that during the Song and Yuan dynasties, both Wong Cho Ping and his brother were awarded honorary titles by the State. The story of Wong Cho Ping also appears in *Jinhua Fuzhi* (the prefectural gazetteer of Jinhua), Vol. 22, in the subsection '*xian shi*' (on immortals). Some of the later accounts of Wong Cho Ping may derive from a short encyclopedia compiled in the tenth century titled the *Shilei fu* (*Rhapsodies on [one hundred] Subjects*), in which Ge Hong's account of Wong Cho Ping is briefly cited and described.

10.   The story about the white boulders turning into sheep at the master's call is one of those miracles which could be explained without much difficulty if one wished to look for such an explanation.

11.   For example, the emperor who first united China in 221 BCE, Shih Huangdi, attracted many magicians to his court, and they convinced him to sponsor maritime expeditions to find the magic islands on which, some believed, one could obtain a drug which prevented death (Welch 1965:98). Expeditions had been sent out to find these islands during the previous century, and the new emperor had the funds and the power to conduct a proper search. Unfortunately (for the emperor and also for his magicians), the magic islands were never found.

12.   Evidently, not only incautious hermits but also some imperial patrons of these hermits' potions died after taking them, leading one Tang-dynasty poet to note that he was much more likely to achieve long life, not caring about longevity, than those who experimented with longevity potions and thus often poisoned themselves in their quest for immortality (Blofeld 1978:123–4).

13.   The slogan 'to act benevolently and to teach benevolence' is the Sik Sik Yuen's translation of the phrase '*pu ji quan shan*' (Cantonese: '*pou jai hyun sihn*').

14.   On the temples to Wong Tai Sin in the Jinhua area, see Chapter 7.

15.   For example, Ragvald interviewed 20 elderly residents of the Lok Fu (Le Fu) area not far from the Wong Tai Sin temple in Kowloon in April, 1984. They

ranged in age from 66 to 81 years old. All were believers in Wong Tai Sin, and all had come from Guangdong, half from Shunde county, and 5 from Nanhai county near Xiqiao Mountain. (We knew that the founder of the Hong Kong temple had come from the Xiqiao area). All of those interviewed had arrived in Hong Kong between 1949 and 1963, most arriving in the 1950s. Thus all of them were at least in their thirties before leaving Guangdong for Hong Kong. None had ever heard of the god Wong Tai Sin until they arrived in Hong Kong. (These interviews were done in connection with our attempts to find out whether immigrant worshippers in Hong Kong had also worshipped the god in Guangdong).

16.   In the Taiwanese village studied by Jordan (1972), the most important deity in terms of protection of the village was the deity Guo Shengwang, patron-ized by the Guo faction in the village, who constituted three-quarters of the village's households. Other villages allied with this village since the period of clan wars in the nineteenth century also came to recognize Guo Shengwang. This is probably an unusual situation, as Jordan points out, but may indicate how a clan god can progress to being the god of a village and eventually of an alliance of vil-lages as a result of warfare and political alliances. Brim's (1974) study of what he calls village-alliance temples in the New Territories shows how worship of such a god functions to cement an alliance among villages.

17.   On this point, see the extended discussion in Yang (1961) on Chinese gods; also Tsai (1979:35) on folk-gods in Taiwan.

18.   See for example Wang (1974:77), on how the timely recovery of a wealthy landlord boosted the fortunes of one temple in Taiwan.

19.   See, for example, Preston (1985), on the growing importance of Chandi temple in Cuttack, India; James Hayes' account of the rise and decline of a Guanyin temple in East Kowloon (Hayes 1983b; see also Hayes 1983a:53–4,58–9); and Myers (1975) on the case of the Tai Wong Ye temple in Kwun Tong.

Notes to Chaper 2

1.   Source: Mr Leung Fuk Chak, letter to Graeme Lang, 11 March 1988.

2.   The Qing regime used foreign employees in the Customs service for sev-eral reasons: (1) It was evidently felt that European customs officials would be better able to deal with European traders, and to induce them to co-operate with customs officials and obey the regulations; (2) The Qing regime evidently also decided that Chinese staff in the high ranks of the Customs Service would be too susceptible to pressures from powerful local officials (Wright 1950:334; see also Kwong 1979:21).

3.   The Qing Government, like governments in some other pre-modern States, had become accustomed to selling degrees and government offices as a source of revenue for the State (March 1961–2; Swart 1940). The people who bought these posts for themselves or for their sons had to recover their investment and then begin to increase their wealth with each opportunity. It would be difficult for other officials to resist such transactions when their colleagues were getting rich at the next desk or at the next pier.

4.   According to Paul King, who served in the Chinese Customs Service dur-ing this period, the recovery rate for plague victims was much higher in Guangzhou. He wrote that while 98 per cent of cases in Hong Kong were fatal, up to 50 per cent of victims recovered in Guangzhou if treated early enough (King 1980 [1924]:215). A favoured remedy was the 'Canton plague plaister'. Whether or not plague vic-tims recovered more frequently in Guangzhou, the belief that they did evidently spurred many sick people to make the trip.

5. See Smith (1991:230); also Hsu (1973), for an account of appeals to the gods and the search for remedies during an epidemic in Yunnan in 1942.

6. Dr Anthony K.K. Siu personal communication; Smith (1991:228).

7. These volumes were lost during the turmoil after the revolution of 1911. The Sik Sik Yuen tracked down some copies in the 1920s and republished them in 1924, but once again, all copies eventually disappeared as a result of war, dispersal, and the death of elderly members; by the 1980s, no one knew where any of these books could be found. However, the volumes were recently rediscovered. A wooden chest belonging to a deceased member of the Sik Sik Yuen had been stored in one of the rooms in the temple for several decades, and during renovations, it was about to be thrown out when an amah found some old manuscripts in the box. She asked a director of the Sik Sik Yuen (Mr Chan Sing Chong) whether the manuscripts were of any value. He discovered that they included the lost *fuji* writings from the 1890s. As a result of their rediscovery, and the kindness of Mr Peter W.K. Lo in supplying copies to Graeme Lang, we are able to supplement our picture of the early followers of Wong Tai Sin, derived from the oral accounts, with *fuji* writings produced by the original circle of believers in the 1890s.

8. Page numbers refer to photocopy pages. Graeme Lang's translators, Laurel Lau, Isabel Lui, and Maggie Lau, worked from a photocopy of the originals, of which, as far as we know, the Sik Sik Yuen holds the only surviving copies.

9. When Taiwanese visitors to Guangdong in the 1890s discovered the efficacy of the Guangdong *fuji*-masters in getting people to give up opium, several *fuji*-masters were invited to Taiwan, and interest in *fuji* increased greatly after they were said to have cured many Taiwanese addicts (Jordan and Overmyer 1986:32–3).

10. For information on several comparable groups, see Tsui (1991:80–2).

11. The god also condemned the exodus of Chinese who travelled overseas looking for some way to become prosperous.

12. Overmyer (1985:230) noted that nineteenth-century *fuji* texts produced by local officials and military men often contained such material.

13. The date (second month of Spring, 1904) is indicated by an inscription on a pillar, one of the few surviving pieces of the temple, lying on the ground on the site.

14. The gods represented in the old temple included the following: in the second building (main hall), the statue of Wong Tai Sin stood in the centre, flanked by Wei Zheng on the left and Lu Dongbin on the right. In the third building stood statues of (from left to right) Mi Le (Maitreya), Ru Lai in the centre (Tathagata), and Wen Shu (Manjusri). There were also statues of Guanyin and Wei Tuo (Skanda, the warrior god, protector of Buddha).

15. According to elderly residents, the rear entrance was close to the river. Those who came by boat entered by the rear gate. Others whose boats were moored farther away or who came by foot would walk up the boardwalk to the front entrance of the temple. These residents were interviewed by Mr Xie Hua of the Fangcun Cultural Affairs Bureau.

16. Li Zhun had been the Commander-in-Chief of the naval forces of Guangdong, as well as supreme commander of the civil defence troops of the province. (source: *Guangdong Jin-Xiandai Renwu Cidian* [*Dictionary of Recent and Contemporary Personages of Guangdong*], Guangdong Keji Chubanshe, 1992).

17. The information about the role of Li Zhun in the reconstruction of the temple was provided to Lars Ragvald by Mr Xie of the Fangcun cultural affairs bureau. An article in the newspaper *Huazi ribao*, 26 December 1903, titled 'Grand Enlargement of Wong Tai Sin Temple of Huadi', refers to the fundraising for this reconstruction. The article also refers to the involvement of a military regiment in worship of the god, and of the regiment's Commander in the fund-raising. David Faure discovered this article and provided us with a copy of it.

18. See, for instance, Day (1969:195).

19. A young resident of the orphanage in the early 1920s later became a famous Cantonese opera actor (perhaps getting his start in the opera troupe of orphans set up by the orphanage). This man, Mr Luo Pinchao, relayed his early memories of the buildings on the site to Lars Ragvald during extensive conversations in Guangzhou in 1985 (Ragvald met him while researching Cantonese opera). Mr Luo entered the orphanage at the age of 12, about 1924, and claimed to have played in the remains of the temple buildings.

20. This information was provided to Lars Ragvald by Mr Xie of the Fangcun Cultural Bureau after his interviews with elderly residents.

21. According to one account which Ragvald heard in Fangcun in 1987 (from a man who had played in the temple as a child), the temple had been torn down by some 'rich' local people for building materials during the Japanese occupation. Apparently, similar actions occurred elsewhere in the region during this period. Helen Siu (1990:784, n. 51) reports that local bosses in one of the towns in the Pearl River Delta tore down many ancestral halls in the area during the Japanese occupation, selling the remains as construction materials. Possibly the Fangcun temple met a similar fate.

22. The main entrance to the factory is on Chong An Jie no.36.

23. After Lars Ragvald's discovery of the site of the original temple, this Wong Tai Sin temple has now been included in the section on temples in Fangcun in the series *Fangcun Wenshi* (*Cultural History [literature and history] of Fangcun*), Vol. 3 (1991), p.35. (This series was published by the political consultative conference of Fangcun district, and is in the Zhongshan library in Guangzhou). The account states that during the Qing dynasty there were two major temples in Fangcun — to Tianhou and Beidi — and at least three other temples to Beidi in the area. After 1921, according to the account, all the temples of Fangcun were (or had been) expropriated by the government.

24. Through interviews in 1985 and 1987 with elderly people living in the area, who were very eager to talk about this temple (one of them was a former novice in the temple), and with the help of the Fangcun Cultural Bureau, Ragvald learned many details about the temple and its operation.

25. See *Nantian Suiyue* [*Years Under the Southern Sky*], published in 1988 by Guangdong Renmin Chubanshe [pp.340–4] for an account of this period).

26. This god is known as Wei Tuo in China, and as Skanda in India.

27. Wei Zheng was a mythical official who slew the dragon king of the Jing River not far from the old Chinese capital of Chang'an, an episode related in Chapter 10 of the well-known Ming dynasty novel *Pilgrimage to the West*. He is reknowned for his loyalty.

28. During the 1930s there was also a herbal medicine clinic outside the Sanyuan Gong, the main Taoist temple in Guangzhou (so Ragvald was told during interviews there in 1987). Chinese herbal doctors would issue prescriptions which could be taken to an ordinary drugstore where one could receive free medicine. The money to cover the cost of the medicine came from donations by rich people.

29. See also Terzani (1985:163–4) on the conversion of temples to factories and dwellings.

30. Gangtou village, near the border between Nanhai and Sanshui counties, is four to five kilometres north of Taiping (the market town near Rengang village), and is not far from the West River. It is likely that the proximity of the West River to Rengang was important to the village economy, and that many worshippers came to the village by river rather than by land.

31. The shrine to Wong Tai Sin's parents was called Zunqin Ci 'temple of honourable [respected] close relatives [parents]'.

32. Hsu (1949:168) describes a case where popular secular icons — a portrait

of Sun Yat-sen, and a tablet for heroes who died in the war against Japan — were set up in a shrine in Yunnan to silence local opposition. (The local opposition was evidently based, in part, on the perception that men and women mingled too freely in the shrine).

33. Some recipes prescribed by the god at the temple in Rengang included 'Puqing Tea', named after the temple.

34. Although the ingredients were ordinary, their supposed efficacy, properly prescribed and prepared, was far broader than most modern medicines. For example, a traditional-medicine shop in Hong Kong visited by Graeme Lang in 1990 advertised the following items: 'Lotus seed: nourish the heart, kidney, and spleen. Treat insomnia, dreamfulness, dysentery, nocturnal emission, vomiting, and indigestion'; 'Chrysanthemum: dispel endogenous wind and heat, improve eyesight . . . treat headache, red eyeball, and dizziness'. See Lee (1980) for a review of the general principles of Chinese traditional medicines.

35. On the secular tradition in Chinese herbal medicine, and the contrast with the 'sacred' methods of pursuing healing, see Lee (1980).

36. The modern Sik Sik Yuen in Hong Kong still follows this practice. During religious ceremonies, a bowl of tea-leaves is placed before the god, and afterward members take some of the tea-leaves home to make tea, which is thought to be especially good for health.

37. Some traditional remedies made from animal products derive their medical properties from their functions for the animal, or from their physical characteristics. For instance, a medicine shop on Hong Kong Island visited in 1990 advertised the following, with accompanying indications: 'Turtle shell: treat strain, overwork, debility, dispel heat from the skeleton'; 'Stag's sexual organ: invigorate function of kidney, increase virility and sexual potency, cure infertility and cold uterus'. These items, of course, are quite expensive. In the early 1950s, Harold Ingrams interviewed a traditional practitioner who described some of his medicines, and noted that the more expensive were for rich men, such as bones-of-a-tiger for rheumatism and tail-of-a-deer (which at the time cost up to £15 [US$ 21] for one-quarter ounce) for kidneys. However he acknowledged, disarmingly, that 'I can prescribe beef or some other cheaper ingredient for a poor man which will be almost as efficacious' (Ingrams 1952:138).

38. This observation relies on the perceptive comments of Graeme Lang's translator, Maggie Lau, after she had read through both *Jing Mimeng* and *Xing Shi Yaoyan*.

39. Some of *Xing Shi Yaoyan* sounds similar to the critiques of urban greed and corruption by Micah and others in the Old Testament, on which, see Lang (1989).

40. In 1913, angered by the policies of the central government of President Yuan Shikai in Peking, the provincial government in Guangdong declared its independence from Peking. Seven other provinces also disavowed the Peking regime. This of course meant war. Yuan sent an army of some 4,000 troops into Guangdong from Guangxi province, and in July of 1913 this army passed down the West River only a short distance from Rengang village (Rhoads 1975:261). It is likely that the passage of this army of hostile 'outsiders' badly frightened people along its invasion route.

41. Government paper money, already losing value as the government printed more to cover its deficits, had declined in value by 53 per cent within weeks after the Guangdong government declared its independence from Peking, and by May of 1914 had lost 67 per cent of its former value (Rhoads 1975:262, 263).

42. A typical document from the period of the campaign against superstition in 1958, outlining the standard Marxist view of religion, is quoted in MacInnis (1972:191). The writing had been on the wall for some years. For instance, in 1953,

Hsu Chein-kuo, Deputy Mayor of the Shanghai Municipal People's Government, broadcast a message on Shanghai radio against Taoist cults (see 'Why Must We Prohibit the Reactionary Taoist Cults', in MacInnis 1972:177–182; for a similar pronouncement from a Nationalist official in Shanghai 30 years earlier, see Day 1969:195). Some of Hsu's charges appear to have been designed to facilitate and justify an attack on the sects ('collaborators, landlords', and so on) but other charges describe practices familiar to any student of folk Taoism. It is evident that some of the charges apply to the kinds of practices associated with the Rengang Wong Tai Sin temple (*fuji*, accepting money in return for supposed medical potions from the gods, and so on). It is not surprising that the Rengang temple did not survive the 1958 campaigns against 'superstition'.

43. The estimate that up to 60 per cent of the temples in Guangdong were sacked or destroyed during the Cultural Revolution was provided to Lars Ragvald in 1985 by a cadre in Xiqiao who had participated in the sacking of temples during that period, and who recalled the Rengang temple as one of those which were destroyed. However, we have no independent evidence about the number of temples which were actually destroyed.

44. The short reference to Wong Cho Ping in *Shilei fu* does not differ in any significant way from Ge Hong's account of Cho Ping's life in *Shenxianzhuan*. One interesting feature of the account of Cho Ping in the *Shilei fu*, however, is that Cho Ping's surname is given as Huang (emperor) rather than Huang/Wong (yellow), as in the modern cult of Wong Tai Sin. The two characters are pronounced identically in both Mandarin and Cantonese. In modern usage, Huang (emperor) is not common as a surname. However, a review of some twenty old texts from Tang and Song, and of some old dictionaries, by Lars Ragvald and two lecturers at the University of Lund, showed that during the Tang and Song period, the two characters were both commonly used as surnames, and were almost interchangeable. The fact that *Shilei fu* uses Huang (emperor) for Cho Ping's surname explains why most later writers who would not have taken the trouble to consult Ge Hong's book also used that character. We assume that Ge Hong used Wong (yellow) rather than Huang (emperor), since most versions of Ge Hong's *Shenxianzhuan*, and most references to Ge Hong's account of Cho Ping, used that character (Wong 1985).

45. Wong (1985) quotes these accounts of the bestowal of imperial favour from *Jinhua Chisongshan zhi*, pp.17–18. The two Southern Song emperors who bestowed titles on Wong Cho Ping and his brother by imperial mandate were Chunxi (in 1189, the last year of his reign), and Jingding (in 1262, two years before his death). Another emperor, Jiaxi (1237–40), reportedly visited the mountain in person to pray for succession. The short-lived Jiaxi lived in the troubled period towards the end of the Southern Song dynasty when the Mongols were over-running the country. According to Wong, the Jinhua gazetteer is the only source for the visits of Song emperors to the mountain.

46. The text of the Mandate of 1189 includes an explicit reference to the desire of local people to have their saint canonized. The mandate is as follows (using the version reprinted in Wong 1985): 'Although Huang Lao teachings have emptiness as their main theme and simplicity as their prime tenet, their original and central purpose lay in the provision of benefit and the care of mankind. Realized Gentlemen [Wong] Cho Hei and [Wong] Cho Ping were both born in the Jin dynasty and lived in seclusion on Mount Jinhua. When [Wong Cho Ping] shouted at rocks and they stood up as sheep, it was taken as proof that [he/they] had obtained the Way. When [he/they] drew water from a well and cured the sick, this spread far and wide [his/their] merit as saviour of men. If a towering palace of the immortals or an awe-inspiring temple is constructed to them, it will remain for a thousand ages. *The people of Dongyang [i.e. Jinhua] gather together and appeal for their*

inclusion among the ranks of the immortals. . . .' (author's emphasis), after which follows the formal conferral of titles. Note that a tradition that Wong Cho Ping offered healing had already become established in the area by the Song dynasty.

47. To give another example: a succession of emperors bestowed titles on a goddess worshipped among coastal peoples in Fujian, beginning in the twelfth century; the first Yuan emperor to do so, Kublai Khan, was actually campaigning in the region at the time when he canonized this local saint. The political motive behind this bestowal of titles has been noted by a number of scholars (for example, Watson 1985). Similar motives for the canonization of local figures can also be perceived in other religions. For example, during the Roman Catholic Pope's journey to Mexico in 1990 he announced the beatification of an Indian peasant who supposedly lived in the sixteenth century and had seen a vision of the now revered 'Virgin of Guadalupe'. The beatification was widely perceived as an attempt to revive the sagging legitimacy and authority of the Catholic church among disillusioned Indians (see 'Pope beatifies Indian peasant as seven-day visit to Mexico begins', by Linda Hossie, *Globe and Mail* [Toronto], 7 May 1990).

48. Leung cites Ge Hong's *Zhenxianzhuan* (the source for all later accounts of Wong Cho Ping), in a preface to one of the *fuji* volumes (*Jing Mimeng* II), and consistently uses the character 'yellow' for Wong's surname, as in most versions of Ge Hong's *Zhenxianzhuan*, rather than the character 'emperor' (pronounced the same as 'yellow') as in the *Shilei fu* and some other sources.

Notes to Chapter 3

1. The concept of a Taoist (or more generally, a religious) 'entrepreneur' is connected to the concept of a 'religious economy' in which religious practitioners compete with each other for clients using some combination of what Stark and Bainbridge (1987) call 'rewards' and 'compensators'. This paradigm for analyzing religious movements is rooted in exchange theory, and has proven to be quite productive in understanding the rise of new religious movements and their differential success. It works best when there is relatively unfettered competition in a milieu of religious pluralism, and is least useful where a monopoly by one religious group is maintained through coercion. Tsui's (1991) account of several Taoists who started temples in both Guangdong and Hong Kong also seems to employ the entrepreneurial metaphor, albeit implicitly.

2. However, with the frequent travel between Guangzhou and Hong Kong by Chinese residents of Hong Kong, it might be expected that some of them would have heard of the new Huadi temple, across the river from Guangzhou. Indeed, a Hong Kong advertisement in the newspaper *Huazi ribao* dated 21 September 1901 announces a proposal to found a new temple in Tai Ping Shan on Hong Kong island, and among the six deities to be 'invited' to the temple was 'Wong Tai Sin Fat Ye' (literally, 'Wong Tai Sin Buddha-Grandfather') of Huadi. While knowledge of this god was weak (as suggested by the use of the honourary term 'Fat Ye'), clearly he had begun to attract some attention. We do not know if an altar to Wong Tai Sin was actually set up in the temple. (We would like to thank David Faure, who found this article while conducting other research, for sending us a photocopy of it).

3. This information was provided to Graeme Lang by Mr Leung's grandson, Mr Leung Fuk Chak.

4. The prescription is described in the first few pages of a *fuji* manuscript, still in the possession of the Leung family, in which messages specifically directed

to Leung Gwan Jyun were recorded. The first entries, and the analysis of and prescriptions for Leung Gwan Jyun's skin problems, were written in 1913.

5. These details are from an account provided by Leung's grandson, Mr Leung
Fuk Chak. Apart from the fact that the site was approximately the specified distance from a pier, we do not know why Leung picked this site, as opposed to
other potential sites. The *Kowloon Rate-Book for 1929–30* shows that lot number
1501 adjacent to the temple was owned by Leung Wai Chuen. Another Leung,
identified as Leung Sa (or Sha) had some connection to this lot, as indicated by a
'surrender deed' dated 1929; he also owned several dwellings and two dye factories in nearby villages. Leung Yan Ngam may have relied on his network of contacts, possibly including kinsmen who had come to Hong Kong from Nanhai, for
the information which led him to the site where the temple now stands. However,
it must be recorded that his grandson denies any such connection, and affirms that
Mr Leung simply followed the god's instructions, and walked north the specified
3,000 paces, whereupon he found the site.

6. The meaning of 'Sik Sik Yuen' can be explained, roughly, as 'leave behind
your earthly desires [when you enter this] garden'. 'Sik Sik' can be interpreted to
mean that people should not dissipate themselves through striving, and should
avoid becoming too entangled in external things; this is the way to pursue life and
'the Way (Tao)'.

7. The Sik Sik Yuen's account lists their names, but does not state that they
were businessmen. However, a summary of the Sik Sik Yuen's history in an official
Tung Wah Group of Hospitals publication (Lee 1971:213) refers to these men as
'reputable merchants'.

8. We were told in an interview with two directors of the Sik Sik Yuen in
1984, Mr Poon Ho-yin and Mr Lo Keng-nin, that most of the deceased members
of the Sik Sik Yuen, whose ancestral tablets are kept in a Memorial Hall near the
temple, were from Nanhai county.

9. In the temple to Lu Dongbin on Mt. Xiqiao, near Rengang, the image of
Lu Dongbin at the main altar is a picture rather than a statue. If such a picture also
hung in that temple prior to 1915, it is possible that this influenced Leung's decision to use a picture of Wong Tai Sin for the altar in Hong Kong. In any case,
when the Hong Kong temple was being renovated, many years later, Wong Tai Sin
was asked whether his followers should set up a gold-covered statue. He refused,
emphatically. His followers interpreted this refusal as a sign of the god's modesty,
befitting a Taoist saint.

10. The story that a *fuji* message confirming Leung Yan Ngam's death in the
village was received at about the same time in Hong Kong is an oral tradition in
the Leung family. The *fuji* manuscript possessed by the Leung family shows that
the severity of Mr Leung's illness was known: the gods were asked for help, and
responded that the illness was difficult to cure.

11. The Sik Sik Yuen's published account notes that due to a slump in the
economy in 1926, caused in part by a strike among boatmen, the Sik Sik Yuen lost
HK$10,000 that year, but the very fact that this loss was considered to be notable
suggests that such financial setbacks were rare.

12. One of these entrepreneurs left his mark in the historical record through
a note in the CSO (Colonial Secretary's Office) files listing land transactions prior
to World War II and stored in the Hong Kong Public Records Office (Alan Smart,
personal communication to Lang). CSO number 2695 records that early in this century, a man who had been a 'doctor and apothecary' in Guangzhou, and was
described by the Assistant Land Officer as 'a sort of half-priest', applied for land to
build a Guanyin temple to serve as a 'residence for pilgrims'. He wanted to build
it on about 10,000 square feet of land on the slope of Kowloon Peak, east of the
site on which the Wong Tai Sin temple was eventually built.

13. See Ordinance No.7, *Hong Kong Government Gazette*, Vol. 74, 1928, p.154.

14. The Bill included a list of temples which were exempted from the Ordinance. These exempted temples 'were originally established by private individuals or particular families, and . . . are still maintained by the descendants of the original founders, and are managed unobjectionably, though, of course, the profits go to the private owners.' (*Hong Kong Hansard*, 1928, p.23).

15. Source: *Administrative Annual General Report*, 1928, p.C–7. The 28 temples which were closed down by the government apparently also contravened Section 4 of the Ordinance, which required that a temple be a detached building. Some of these 'temples' may have been shrines added to already existing buildings.

16. Under 'gods to be discarded', the Zhejiang provincial government committee in 1928 listed the following categories: (1) Stellar or Celestial Gods (Sun, Moon, and so on), (2) Earth gods (Five Mountains, Four Rivers, Sea God, and all City Gods or Gods of City Walls and Moats, along with the tutelary local Earth Gods), (3) Atmospheric Gods (Wind, Clouds, Thunder, Rain), (4) The Eight Gods of Harvest, 'with the exception of the first two, Shen Nung and Hou Chi', and finally, (5) 'All Useless Gods': 'quasi-religious, commercial or money-making, animistic and legendary', gods of plague and smallpox, and so on; the committee recommended that 'all of the above temples and idols should be razed to the ground so that nothing remains' (Day 1969:193).

17. On the history of the Tung Wah Hospital, see especially Sinn (1989); also Lee (1971).

18. For the formal transfer of control to Tung Wah, the reasons for this transfer, and the ways in which Tung Wah was to use income from the temple, see *Ordinances of Hong Kong*, Vol. II, 1901–14 [1937 edition], pp.1053–6. For the history of this temple, and its current state, see Savidge 1977:58.

19. An example of the revenues derived from control of temples by the Chinese Temples Committee is provided in the *Annual General Report of 1928* (p.C–8): 'A noteworthy case is the large and popular Kwun Yam [Guanyin] temple at Hung Hom, the accepted tender for which was HK$3,680 compared with HK$1,850 previously when the temple was under the control of the local kaifong [a committee chosen from among local notables to be responsible for the temple]. The [Chinese Temples] Committee agreed to make a grant of HK$100 per month from the General Chinese Charities Fund to the free school maintained in connection with the temple — an excellent example of how Chinese charities will benefit by the proper control of temple revenues'.

20. The fee for new members included HK$50 for buying medicine (for the shop), HK$50 for the management of temple affairs, and a HK$60 annual fee (Faure, Luk, and Ng 1986:513).

21. There were apparently two large refugee villages in Kowloon in 1938, one at the junction of Jordan Road and Canton Road, on land designated for a park, and another at Tai Kok Tsui (Wong 1970:204). By 1939, there were also hut camps in Ma Tau Chung and Lai Chi Kok.

22. A government report in 1938 asserted that as a result of the influx of refugees, 'the average number of persons to each floor of the typical three storied Chinese houses rose from an average of 18 to 60' (Colonial Secretariat: *Report on the Social and Economic Progress of the People of the Colony of Hong Kong for the Year 1938*, p.184). Those who could not find or could not afford such quarters slept in the streets.

23. The student was writing in 1939 in a special publication of the Kowloon Leshan Tang, a charitable organization in Kowloon City. A copy, one of the few extent, is in the Hong Kong Collection, University of Hong Kong Library.

24. The banana-shaped wooden 'divination blocks' are flat on one side and rounded on the other. They are cast on the ground, after the question is put to the god, and the god's answer is indicated by the position of the blocks: one flat side down means 'yes', two flat sides down is an emphatic 'no'; two flat sides up, in which position the blocks may rock briefly, indicate that the god mocks the question, or alternatively, that he answers equivocally.

25. The fear was realistic: there were guerilla bands operating in the New Territories, and as the military situation deteriorated for the Japanese toward the end of the war, the local garrison had good reason to believe that guerilla bands would become more bold in attacking Japanese units.

26. The first plane evidently landed on the airstrip in 1924. The government took over the airfield in 1927, and it was finally opened as a commercial airport, on reclaimed land, in 1936 (Leeming 1977:145). The Japanese, using POWs for some of the work, cleared additional land of buildings and obstacles — including local shrines — to improve and extend the airfield in 1942. Evidently the Japanese were not solely responsible for all of the destruction of houses which occurred in connection with airport expansion work: James Hayes reports, 'Villagers from east Kowloon told me that the Chinese contractors who did the airport extension work for the Japanese were very unscrupulous. They would demolish more houses, and even small villages, than were strictly needed, so that they could sell the building materials. Nga Tsin Wai [a village near the airport] escaped this fate only because their elders plucked up courage and went to see the Japanese officer in charge of Kowloon to ask him to spare their homes' (James Hayes 'Notes' for Royal Asiatic Society visit to Nga Tsin Wai, 6 April, 1991).

27. A similar loss of faith in the gods apparently occurred in some villages in northern China during a drought and famine in 1942: see Belden (1949:96–8).

28. On population growth in the area, see *Hong Kong Population and Housing Census, Main Report*, 1971, p.22. On the proportion born in China, see *Report of the Census*, 1961, Vol. II, p.66.

29. The post-war housing shortage in Hong Kong was largely a result of the destruction of a large number of dwellings during the war, mostly by bombing (see *Annual Report on Hong Kong for the Year 1946*, p.56–7).

30. A thriving market in huts, and cubicles within huts, soon developed. On this kind of market, see Smart (1985).

31. For example, one of Lang's students interviewed an elderly woman living in one of the huts in Chuk Yuen in 1989 who had moved into the area after the war, and who had heard a version of the story about the two Japanese officers who had fallen, thus saving the villages. (She believed they had fallen off a bridge over a field).

32. The term 'Chaozhou' (Chiu Chow) is used to refer to the people of the Han River valley and coastal areas of north-eastern Guangdong. Culturally and linguistically they are much closer to the people of southern Fujian and Taiwan than to the Cantonese. Many Chaozhou people have migrated to South-East Asia and to Hong Kong.

33. The Chaozhou constituted about 13 per cent of the migrants in the area in 1961 (1961 Census, Vol. II, p.63).

34. By the end of 1952, 34,550 people had been resettled in these hut-resettlement areas (*Hong Kong Annual Report, 1952*, p.94).

35. Aerial photographs of the district taken in 1945, 1949, 1956, 1963, and 1988, were obtained from the Survey and Mapping Office, Hong Kong Government, to assist in analyzing changes in land use in the area around the temple.

36. In 1981, for example, there were about 160,000 households on the waiting list for public housing, with an average waiting time of about seven years (Pryor 1983:95).

37. See *Hong Kong Social and Economic Trends, 1967–1977*, Census and Statistics Department, p.12.

Notes to Chapter 4

1. On selection of officers of a temple by divination, see also Hayes 1983c: 123–4.

2. To sponsor a school, the Sik Sik Yuen evidently raises about 20 per cent of the capital. The rest is contributed by the Hong Kong Government. The Sik Sik Yuen then plays a role in managing the school, and is able to determine the curriculum in the religious studies courses, which (in the Sik Sik Yuen secondary schools) are mandatory for all students. Since these religious studies courses are not part of the government-sanctioned curriculum, however, the Sik Sik Yuen must pay the salaries of the people who teach these courses.

3. The Sik Sik Yuen embarked on a project to produce a red silk scroll with the Chinese character for 'long life' written by 10,000 elderly people in Hong Kong. (Pieces of the 30 square metre cloth were sent to residences and social centres for the elderly, and were later stitched together to make up a single scroll). It was intended to submit the feat to the Guiness Book of World Records.

4. See 'Wong Tai Sin Temple: Brief Introduction', by Peter W.K. Lo, published by Sik Sik Yuen in 1991.

5. Source: Sik Sik Yuen. The contributions for 1989–90, the last year for which we have data, were HK$3,758,848.

6. Leung Gwan Jyun eventually developed ties with the shrine to Wong Tai Sin in Mongkok known as Wah Chung Sin Gun. His shop evidently supplied medicines for patrons of this shrine who had received medical prescriptions from the god by *fuji*.

7. On the use of the term 'flying phoenix' with reference to *fuji*, and for a rich account of the history and dynamics of *fuji* sects in Taiwan, see *The Flying Phoenix: Aspects of Chinese Sectarianism in Taiwan* (1986), by David Jordan and Daniel Overmyer.

8. The Sik Sik Yuen has not published any *fuji* revelations since 1924, when they republished *Jing Mimeng*. Lang has seen only one set of post-World War II *fuji* messages received at the temple. They date from 1962–3, and were copied into a notebook after the sessions by one of the members of the Sik Sik Yuen to whom the messages were directed. In addition to the usual messages about benevolence and virtue, they include messages about his wife's illness from Wong Tai Sin and various gods whom Wong Tai Sin called upon for further help and consultation about the illness, along with encouraging predictions about the member's future prospects in business.

9. Jordan and Overmyer (1986), in their study of *fuji* sects in Taiwan, noted 'the weakness inherent in any sect which subscribes to the proposition that revelations under the control of one or a few people will be taken as divine writ' (p.181). Of course, the most obvious way for the leader of such a group to accommodate *fuji* is to become the *fuji*-master, and to rebuff all attempts by others to take control of the stick. As noted in Chapter 2, Leung Yan Ngam resisted efforts by other disciples of the god in Guangzhou to try the *fuji*.

10. Some disaffected members of the Sik Sik Yuen evidently became associated with a small shrine to the god in Mongkok, where *fuji* continued to be performed long after it was discontinued at the main temple (*see* Chapter 4, n. 6)

11. The elimination of divination in the selection of the Chairman and officers

evidently proceeded in two stages. Until the 1940s, *fuji* was used for this purpose. However, in the late 1940s several new members, holding substantial power in the community and wishing a larger role in the organization, and dissatisfied that they were never chosen by *fuji* to hold important offices, challenged the validity of the method. Perhaps they were suspicious of the individual who performed the *fuji*. According to one account, these new members, emboldened by their growing power in the organization, managed to substitute the use of divination blocks for the *fuji*, thus breaking the control of the older members over appointments. The final stage in the elimination of divination occurred when the Sik Sik Yuen was incorporated, after which it was necessary for legal purposes to select officers by elections.

12. Meyer (1982), for example, describes a group in Taiwan called the Sacred Truth Society dedicated to the propounding of the doctrines and traditional virtues taught by the three religions. Some sects in Taiwan have even attempted to absorb Christianity and Islam into their vision of a sacred unity among the world's religions (Jordan and Overmyer 1986:232, n.21; Seiwart 1981).

13. Of the 131 members (as of 1992), 81 are voting members, and 51 are non-voting members. Only the voting members can be elected to offices in the Sik Sik Yuen.

14. Puns using homonyms for phrases referring to good fortune are quite prevalent at New Year. For instance, many families serve a plate of stringy black vegetables at the New Year meal because the name of the dish is a homonym for the term *faat choih* (gain wealth).

15. Two members of the Sik Sik Yuen in 1984, for instance, were formerly officers in the Criminal Investigation Division of the Hong Kong Police force. Both men were already directors of the Sik Sik Yuen in the 1950s. It is possible that one of them was brought into the Sik Sik Yuen to deal with triads operating in the area around the temple.

16. In the 1960s the average number of free doses given out per year was 158,600; in the 1970s: 156,500; and in the 1980s: 121,250; in the last five years of the 1980s, the average per year dropped to 113,793 (figures supplied by Sik Sik Yuen).

17. See Lee (1980). Many Chinese traditional practitioners also recognize the value of Western-style medical treatment, and will refer patients to medical doctors for some medical problems (Lee 1975:226; Martin 1975:131). Exorcisms to cure disease have declined sharply in the villages around Hong Kong for the same reason; as the village priests readily admit, the success of modern medicine has rendered exorcisms largely obsolete (Faure 1989:260).

18. Figures were supplied by the Sik Sik Yuen.

19. The discussion in this chapter draws on our earlier paper, Lang and Ragvald (1988).

Notes to Chapter 5

1. In a 1988 survey in Hong Kong (see Hui 1991:103), 23 per cent of the 1,644 respondents gave their religion as 'worshipping the gods' (Cantonese: *baih sahn*, literally, 'bowing respectfully to the gods'). In the minds of worshippers, this general phrase can be used to refer to worship of Taoist gods and what the anthropologist might call folk gods, and may also include ancestor worship. In the survey, another 6.6 per cent gave their religion as Buddhism. The rest of the sample claimed to be Protestant (7.2 per cent), Catholic (4.9 per cent), or to have no

religion (58.3 per cent). It is likely that most of the Buddhists and virtually all of those who give their religion as 'worshipping the gods' (that is, about 30 per cent of the sample) will occasionally have visited one of the temples in Hong Kong. It is also likely that some of those who claimed to have 'no religion' also occasionally visit a temple, and even some of the Christians will occasionally be found at a temple such as the Wong Tai Sin temple. However, there is no survey data available on the proportion of Hong Kong residents who have visited local temples for religious purposes.

2. We are indebted to Dr Wong Siu Lun, Sociology Department, University of Hong Kong, and to Dr Kwok Pui Lan, Department of Religion, Chung Chi College, Chinese University of Hong Kong, for kindly providing Graeme Lang with copies of the projects by Chin, et al. (1977), Fong and Luk (1989) and Shum (1990) and to Dr Grant Evans for sending Lang a copy of the paper by Chan, Chow, and Hung (1990). We would also like to thank Mr Fong Pak Tim and Mr Luk Kin Man for permission to use some of their data in this chapter.

3. The students who were recruited from Chinese University of Hong Kong and conducted interviews at the temple included: Ho Keung Sing, Jeung Ho Yin, Ada Jong Pui Ying, Sou Fung Ming, George Lau Yau Leung, and Carla Dou Yun Wan. Gei Yun Ling conducted interviews at the private Wong Tai Sin temple in Sham Shui Po.

4. The new subway system which opened in 1977 made travel to the temple much easier. The temple is on the Kowloon line, at a subway stop named 'Wong Tai Sin'; and between 1982 and 1984 a new electric train system was developed connecting the New Territories to the Kowloon subway line.

5. According to a story which seems to be true, the Wong Tai Sin police station installed the altar to Wong Tai Sin after a series of unexplained accidents and mishaps at the station convinced some officers that they could not afford to ignore this god, and should honour him along with Guandi.

6. In 1976, 54 per cent of the employed population in Hong Kong were 'Production and related workers'. The categories of professional, technical, administrative, managerial, and sales workers — almost all of which would be classified as 'white collar' occupations — together comprised about 28 per cent of employed persons while 14 per cent of the employed were service workers. Some of these service workers would also be classified as 'white collar' workers. (*Hong Kong Social and Economic Trends, 1976–1986*. Hong Kong Census and Statistics Department 1987:12).

7. These and subsequent census data in this section are from *By-Census, District Board Tabulations, Wong Tai Sin*. Hong Kong Census and Statistics Department, 1987:8–9; and *Hong Kong Annual Digest of Statistics*. Hong Kong Government, 1988:15.

8. Chan, Chow, and Hung (1990) assert, on the basis of their experience interviewing 24 worshippers at the temple, that older women are more reluctant to be interviewed than younger women, but men were the most reluctant to be interviewed.

9. Chan, Chow, and Hung (1990) observed that many men who accompanied women to the temple merely stood by while the women knelt to ask the god questions using fortune-sticks (one of the men affirming to the interviewer that 'we men don't believe in this, women do'), but they also noted that the women often asked the god for advice and help on behalf of the men and hence the men indirectly participated in and benefited from the ritual, even if they would not acknowledge this to an interviewer. Elliott (1955:165) made a similar observation regarding the Chinese in Singapore, where women often go to temples on behalf of their families, and with the tacit approval of their supposedly skeptical husbands. Studying a spirit-medium healing cult in Taiwan, Martin (1975:137) noted a similar

phenomenon. In Japan, Hardacre, who studied the religious movement known as *Kurozumikyo*, also concluded that the family's religious observances were typically delegated to the women (Hardacre, 1986:122).

10. A fortune-teller interviewed at the temple noted that in the morning, 'those coming at this time of day are mostly housewives or old ladies, praying for the luck of their families' (Wan 1988).

11. Women in some families were shunted out of school and into temporary and relatively poorly paid occupations because their families viewed major educational investments in a daughter as a waste of money (see for example Salaff, 1981:98). Many Hong Kong families do not have this attitude, but in the 1950s and 1960s, when many current female worshippers were growing up, it was evidently quite common.

12. The age categories were slightly different in the two surveys. Fong and Luk (1989) used the categories '20–30; 30–40' and so on, while Chin, et al. (1977) used the categories '21–30; 31–40', and so on. In Figure 2, we have ignored this difference and used the categories in Fong and Luk's paper.

13. Shum (1990) interviewed 60 worshippers at the temple on a Sunday, 34 of the 60 interviewed (56.7 per cent) were no older than 35 years of age. This compares well with the 1989 survey, in which about 58 per cent were no older than 40 years of age. The 1990 survey, however, found a larger proportion of worshippers in the '20 years old or less' category than were found in the 1977 and 1989 surveys: 15 per cent were 20 years old or less (versus 8.8 per cent and 4.4 per cent in the two earlier surveys). The 1990 survey also found a smaller proportion of older worshippers: 6.7 per cent in the '51 years old or above' category (versus 35.2 per cent and 27.7 per cent in the two earlier surveys). The fact that the 1990 survey was conducted on a Sunday may explain the larger number of teenage worshippers and the smaller number of older worshippers, since the teenagers would be free on a Sunday, but seldom on weekdays, while the older worshippers, especially older women who are not employed outside the home, would probably choose to go to the temple on weekdays when the temple is much less crowded. The 1977 survey was carried out on two successive Tuesdays, and would thus pick up more of these older worshippers.

14. A study by Walsh (1980), comparing immigrants in the US who attend church with those who do not, found that church attendance among immigrants was associated with lower blood pressure. The greater social ties resulting from the congregational nature of worship in American churches may explain the finding. Walsh did not determine how the practice of religion lowers blood pressure among immigrants. However, it is possible that part of the effect is derived from the anxiety-reducing effects of a feeling of supernatural guidance and help. A similar effect could be predicted among immigrant worshippers at the Wong Tai Sin temple in Hong Kong. Certainly many of those interviewed have claimed that worshipping at the temple makes them feel more peaceful and less anxious.

15. The 1977 survey by Chin, et al., was carried out in late December and early January, and the proportion of people who reported giving thanks to the god was much higher: 43 per cent, compared to 7.7 per cent in the 1989 group studied by Fong and Luk.

16. In the movie, Cho Ping is allowed to come down from the Jade Emperor's court in heaven to dwell among mortals, whereupon he narrowly escapes a Herod-type slaughter of male children, since the emperor has had a bad dream which is interpreted by soothsayers to mean that he will be overthrown by a first-born male child. The son of the emperor becomes an evil force with whom Cho Ping must contend. Finally he vanquishes the evil prince in a climactic battle which includes the kind of supernatural-magical martial arts which are typical of this genre in Hong Kong. Traces of Ge Hong's original account survive only in early scenes in which

Cho Ping tends sheep before he finds his true nature, and traces of Wong Tai Sin-the-healer are seen in the incident in which he cures a village plagued by pestilence (caused by evil people). However, the film-maker freely borrowed dramatic motifs from Chinese and Christian legend to build his plot.

17. In the *Tiantian Ribao*, 30 December 1989, for example, a former Miss Hong Kong and another young actress are shown in a series of poses at the temple — praying, casting divination sticks, and so on. The accompanying text related that they prayed for world peace, prosperity, good health for everyone and their families, and for success in their own careers. They also asked that Wong Tai Sin would protect them from any losses in their business ventures. One of them said she always consulted Wong Tai Sin before making investments.

18. This section draws on Lang and Ragvald (1987).

19. In the 1977 survey, 8 of 32 people interviewed at the temple were aware that the temple contributed money toward schools (Chin, et al., 1977:29).

20. Chan, Chow, and Hung (1990) found a Catholic woman among their sample of 24 people interviewed at the temple. She recognized the conflict between her Catholic religion and her visits to the temple to consult a fortune-teller, and speculated that perhaps because of this conflict, the predictions of Wong Tai Sin were more accurate about her family than about herself.

21. Salaff (1981:109) described how one of her female informants 'searched with her companions for the cultural roots that had been overgrown by the industrialist capitalist system in which they were raised'. Sometimes traditional religion can fulfil these needs: in 1984 Lang interviewed a Chinese Catholic lady in New York who had left Catholicism and joined a small private *fuji* sect because, she said, it put her more in touch with her roots. Jordan and Overmyer (1986:237) note that some of the sects in Taiwan which devote time to the study and discussion of classic Chinese moral or philosophical texts have a similar appeal to working class or relatively uneducated Taiwanese.

22. See Jordan (1982) and Jordan and Overmyer (1986:268, 270) for more extensive discussion of this point.

23. A 1972 survey in Kwun Tong, an industrial-residential district east of the temple, found that only 19 per cent of respondents reported that they or members of their family had ever visited a temple for curing disease, and only 22.5 per cent believed that gods or ancestors can help to cure diseases (Lee 1980:350). Such beliefs were strongest among women and also among less-educated respondents. As the educational level of the population continues to increase, and as medical services continue to improve, the natural constituency of Wong Tai Sin as a healer is shrinking. (The Chinese hospitals operated by Tung Wah long ago abandoned the use of herbal medicine and converted to standard modern medical practice).

24. Choa (1967:32) found that many of his Chinese patients in a general ward at a modern hospital had consulted practitioners of traditional Chinese medicine. Some had done so at the beginning of their illness, and then had evidently gone to the modern hospital when the traditional remedies were ineffective. Others had tried modern medical treatment first, and finding no improvement in their condition had resorted to the traditional practitioners. Lee (1980:360) reports on the basis of survey data from Kwun Tong that if initial self-medication does not work, more than 70 per cent of people would consult a Western-style doctor, while only 11 per cent would consult a Chinese-style practitioner. However, if the Western-style medical treatment was not effective, about 20 per cent would resort to a Chinese-style practitioner.

25. In the 1977 survey (Chin, et al., 1977), 5 of 32 worshippers interviewed were at the temple to get medication.

26. See also Preston (1980:78) on belief in the healing properties of sacred ash and holy water at Chandi temple in India.

Notes to Chapter 6

1. As indicated in the previous chapter, some people perform *qiu qian* as an experiment, or out of curiosity, and their veneration of the god is less prominent in their motivation than their petition or question to the god. Hence, the use of the term 'worshipper' requires the qualifier that it is here used loosely, and does not imply that every person who performs *qiu qian* is necessarily a firm or fervent believer.

2. A Wong Tai Sin shrine in New York City, for instance, (described in Chapter 7), uses the same set of poems and the same booklet explaining them as are used at the main Wong Tai Sin temple in Kowloon.

3. A grandson of Leung Yan Ngam maintains that the set was compiled in Rengang village between 1904 and 1909, that is, shortly after the completion of the new temple to Wong Tai Sin in the village.

4. Citing various sources, Pas (1984:14), for instance, notes the practice among the ancient Babylonians, and later among the Arabs, of placing marked arrows or arrow shafts into a container, and drawing one arrow after prayers to a deity, the sign or word on the arrow indicating the god's answer. He claims that the use of sticks, common among the Scythians in Asia, spread from there into China. It is possible that the container full of arrows is the ancestor of the container of fortune-sticks used in Chinese temples. Another method involved the use of dried plant stalks, which may be more directly ancestral. The use of these stalks was probably connected to the origins of the complex system of the *I Ching* (Pas 1984).

5. We would like to thank Carole Morgan for her comments and suggestions on this chapter, and for contributing some ideas from her own work (especially from Morgan 1987), and in personal communications. Of course, any errors in the chapter are entirely our own responsibility.

6. A respondent mentioned in Chapter 5 recalled that the god had given his sister this oracle when she asked whether she could be promoted in her current job; the message was that such a hope was futile, which turned out to be correct. He remembered that the god's answer had referred to the case of the poet who drowned trying to scoop up the moon.

7. W. Banck (1985:264–75) gives both a list of all the tag variations, and the system used in any given set.

8. Other sets of fortune poems have somewhat different statistical properties (*see* Smith 1991:239–41). Pas (1984:17) notes that one of the sets of 100 fortune poems described by Eberhard (1970) had 25 very favourable oracles, 25 which were very unfavourable, and 50 that were average. It might also be noted that in the Wong Tai Sin set, the proportions of poems with various grades has been altered from their distribution in the original set of fortune poems used by Leung Yan Ngam at the Wong Tai Sin temple in Rengang. Most of the original set — the poems from number 41 to number 100 — has survived in a manuscript in the possession of his grandson, Leung Fuk Chak. The poems in the Rengang manuscript are essentially identical to the modern set (with some editing changes to make them easier to understand). The tags were not originally part of the set, but were added to the manuscript later. However, when we compare the tags added to the original set with those used in the modern set in the booklet consulted by worshippers at the temple, it is apparent that many of the tags have been changed, and more poems were revised upward on the scale than downward. Of the 59 readable tags in the Rengang manuscript, 17 have been altered. The number of poems reclassified into a more favourable category outnumbers those reclassified into a more unfavourable category by a margin of 65 per cent to 35 per cent. In effect, the set has become slightly more optimistic.

9. The original poem is of course much more concise, but it is almost impossible to convey the meaning with an equally concise English translation. Lang would like to thank Leung Lai Ching for helping with the translation of this poem.

10. 'Languan' may refer to a town along the route, or it could refer to a mountain pass through which they had to travel.

11. Although they are commonly called 'fortune-tellers' in English, the Chinese term is more apt: they are 'explain-fortune-poem-people' (Cantonese: *gai chim louh*).

12. We would be pleased to hear from any reader who knows of another temple in China which had such a large number of fortune-tellers attached to it.

13. The information in the remainder of the chapter is based on research carried out by Graeme Lang and several of his student interviewers, on papers on fortune-telling at the temple by Shum (1990) and by Chan, Chow, and Hung (1990), and on the interviews carried out by Wan (1988) and Lau (1990).

14. This information was given to Lang by Mr Leung Pun Chak, son of Leung Gwan Jyun and grandson of Leung Yan Ngam.

15. Lang was told that there were four fortune-tellers in 1936–37 by a young fortune-teller whom he and Leung Fuk Chak interviewed in 1987 who claimed to be the son of one of these four original fortune-tellers. (It is possible that some of these individuals were among those who fled from China in 1936 after the downfall of Chen Jitang, when his policies favouring traditional religion were reversed.)

16. According to the elder sons of Leung Gwan Jyun (interviewed by Lang in December 1989), who were in their teens at the time, there were as many as 20 fortune-tellers at the temple immediately before the war.

17. In its 1971 Centenary report, Tung Wah reprinted these regulations from the original leases: 'The lesees of booths must confine themselves to oracle-explaining and the sale of oracle paper only. They must not offer containers of oracle sticks or other oracle equipment for hire [the Sik Sik Yuen provided these containers inside the temple courtyard without charge] or attempt under whatever pretext to exact money from customers. Only the stipulated amount may be collected. . . . Lots will be drawn for the location of the booths for a term of one year, at the end of which another drawing of lots will be held . . .' [a regulation which hints at the disputes which must have arisen over prime locations, especially since the rebuilding and relocating of the stalls in the mid-1950s] (Lee 1971, Book II:182–3). The rent for the ordinary stalls was HK$30 per month (versus about HK$800 in 1990), and the fee for explaining one oracle slip was set at 20 cents (versus HK$6 to HK$8 in 1990).

18. The existing agglomeration of stalls around the gates of the temple had evidently been largely destroyed by a typhoon, and Tung Wah seems to have taken the opportunity, no doubt in consultation with the Sik Sik Yuen, to try to rebuild the stalls in a more orderly fashion which would allow worshippers an easier access to the gates of the temple. The fortune-tellers were not happy with the new plan, and insisted that the stalls be clustered around the entrance as before.

19. Fifteen customers per day (Wan 1988), 25 working days (estimated), average HK$10 (two questions, at an estimated HK$5 per question) per customer, hence a monthly gross income of HK$3,750, minus about HK$750 for rental of the stall for one month. Net income (before paying electricity costs): HK$3,000 for the month.

20. The dignified gentleman, interviewed in his stall at the temple by a reporter from a local newspaper, was Mr Mak On-sang. (Wan 1988). Mr Mak predicted, on the basis of the fortune-poem selected, that Graeme Lang would succeed in getting a teaching post in Hong Kong, and several months later, Mr Mak's prediction proved not to be mistaken.

21. On his personal beliefs, Mr Mak On-sang commented as follows: 'Most fortune-tellers tell people to burn their prediction slips when they go home. As I am a Buddhist I don't believe any of those rituals. As long as one is sincere in

one's prayers the rest is not important. I should confess that I myself am not a true believer of Tai Sin [Wong Tai Sin]. It is true that he is always right with his predictions. But I guess this is the result of *fung shui* [*fengshui*] rather than anything else. The temple is located at one of the best *fung shui* spots in Hong Kong, which goes some way to explaining most of its success stories. I discovered that when I was 15 years old. However, though I don't believe in Tai Sin, I still like to go there for the *chim* predictions whenever I have things that I can't decide myself' (Wan 1988).

22.   One woman (interviewed at the temple by one of Lang's students) who had worked at the temple as a fortune-teller for 25 years had sent her son to university, and he had become a social worker. Mr Mak, the fortune-teller interviewed by Wan (1988), had sent both his children to Britain for a university education. Another fortune-teller, Mr L.H. Cui, interviewed by Carole Morgan, had also sent his sons to college (Morgan: personal communication).

23.   The Cantonese lady who took Bloomfield to the fortune-teller in Macau related that her own family had been going to the same fortune-teller for ten years for advice whenever they faced a family crisis or an important decision (Bloomfield 1980:53). The young fortune-teller interviewed by Lang in 1987 asserted that he had a number of regular clients, some of whom had first consulted him when they were still in school and had continued to consult him for years after leaving school because of his professional skill and imagination in interpreting the fortune-poems to them. Chan, et al. (1984) interviewed a mother and daughter who seemed to have a fortune-teller whom they consulted regularly, and who was especially helpful in advising them how to avoid a bad outcome whenever they got an inauspicious oracle.

24.   During a quiet period when he had no customers, Mr Mak mused that 'as I have nothing to do at the moment, I should be thinking about how I could decorate my stall. I guess this would help with my business when everybody is talking about market image. But I guess I should wait till the low season, round June or July, when I don't get more than 15 customers a day' (Wan 1988).

25.   Mr Mak On-sang described his approach to one such client: 'The guy [his first customer of the day] is quite unlucky as both of his slips indicate that the year ahead won't be an easy one for him. . . . But it won't be too encouraging if I tell him straight away. Instead, I advise him on what he should do to make the best out of his bad luck'.

26.   It is possible that one such case of a failure in the god's prediction or advice led to the incident in which a woman entered the temple and attacked the painting of Wong Tai Sin which hung over the main altar. (According to one account, the painting was damaged, and so the Sik Sik Yuen replaced it with a replica. The original was burnt). Another apparently disaffected worshipper brought a small statue of Wong Tai Sin to the temple, pitched it into one of the large ovens for burning paper offerings, and marched off toward the exit. (Keith Stevens, who witnessed the incident, hastily retrieved the partially burned statue from the oven, and it now sits among his extensive collection of Asian god-statues at his home in England).

Notes to Chapter 7

1.   One of the offshoots not discussed here is the Wah Chung Sin Gun, a shrine located (in 1992) in Mongkok. This shrine was set up after World War II, but can be traced to an earlier pre-war shrine set up in Hung Hom for the convenience of some believers who did not relish the journey to the Sik Sik Yuen.

Evidently, there were several other such small shrines in Hong Kong, all spin-offs from the Sik Sik Yuen, and all using the same portrait and autobiography of the god. The Wah Chung Sin Gun eventually attracted some disaffected older members of the Sik Sik Yuen during the period of change in the organization in the 1950s and 1960s.

2. Professor Graham Johnson of the University of British Columbia informed us of the existence of the Wong Tai Sin shrine in Macau. No one else we met during the course of our research on Wong Tai Sin had heard of this shrine (although Keith Stevens mentions it in his manuscript, in preparation, on Chinese gods). Our information about this shrine comes from a visit to the building by Graeme Lang in 1990, and a second visit the same day accompanied by Dr Choi Chi-Cheung, then at the University of East Asia.

3. Lang is indebted to Dr Choi Chi-cheung, of the University of East Asia in Macau, for dating the shrine from the inscriptions.

4. One of the contributors who donated money for the construction of the shrine in 1906 was an official surnamed Xian. There is evidently a large lineage of Xians living in Nanhai county. Rengang village is located in Nanhai county, and the founders of the Macau shrine may have known of the cult of Wong Tai Sin from visits to the Wong Tai Sin temple in Rengang.

5. We would like to thank Mr Ken Topley, Registrar of the University of East Asia at the time, for providing this information (personal communication, 22 August, 1984).

6. There are other cases of religious movements where offshoots of a cult preserved original features of the cult which were subsequently lost in the main surviving version. This may have occurred, for example, in Christianity (see, for example, Schoeps [1969:133] on the Ebionites).

7. In particular, the inscriptions on the outside of the building housing the shrine advertise two deities: Wong Tai Sin and Chou (Cao) Tai Sin, and refer to these two figures as if they are equal in status. The reference to 'Chou Tai Sin' is very interesting: this figure is included among the saints mentioned in the *fuji* manuscripts produced by the Guangzhou circle of *fuji* devotees in the late 1890s, but all interest in him has disappeared in the modern Hong Kong version of the cult. Hence, his presence at the Macau shrine further indicates that this was a very early offshoot from the Guangdong version of the cult. However, we do not know the significance of the fact that, on the exterior of the shrine, he was given equal prominence with Wong Tai Sin.

8. We would like to thank Dr Patrick Hase for introducing us to this organization, and for taking both of us, at different times, to the temple and to meet members of the Yun Ching Guk. The information in this section is based on a visit by Lars Ragvald, several visits by Graeme Lang (including observation of a *fuji* session at the temple), and translations of inscriptions at the temple.

9. The traditional method for sacralizing a new Taoist shrine is to bring some incense ash from another temple.

10. One difference between Chaozhou and Cantonese religious practice is the Chaozhou interest in performances by male spirit mediums, an interest not shared by most Cantonese (Myers 1981). Myers (1975;1981) describes some of the Chaozhou 'squatter temples' set up in Kowloon by Chaozhou immigrants in the late 1940s and 1950s, especially in Kwun Tong where many Chaozhou immigrants now live.

11. This text, inscribed on a plague on the wall of the temple and dated 15/5/1942, notes that Wong Bat Hung and several others had been worshipping the god faithfully for some time. It counsels against superficial worship, condemns pride and arrogance, and asserts that the true worshipper will be known by good deeds. In a possible reference to the Japanese forces occupying Hong Kong at the time, it also observes that 'there are some evil forces claiming they are the true

god, who will find some women or children to satisfy their desires and need for entertainment; the true god — Wong Tai Sin — will not do this'. It also says that the god will acknowledge and praise 'even those who are unwanted or cast out by others', provided they do good deeds.

12. The private temple now has this message over the doorway, and it reads as follows: 'All the adherents of the *Zhuxi ting* [the name which the group had adopted for themselves] harbour good intentions, which is commendable. Their benevolence is a model [for others to emulate]. Only heaven decides about spiritual matters, and arranges things according to its schedule. It is not for you ordinary people to interfere. However, your honesty and good intentions have been noted. It is to be hoped that you will hereafter carry out benevolent actions to let the will of heaven be fulfilled. I now ordain that the *Zhuxi ting* be granted [the right to call itself] *Yuanqing Ge* (*Yun Ching Guk*), and that it be consecrated to Chisong Xianzi [the Red Pine Master, referring here to Wong Tai Sin]. By imperial order.' The date given is 24 October, 1942. See Jordan and Overmyer (1986:67) for another example of the gods bestowing an exalted name on a recently opened *fuji* shrine.

13. Baker (1983:471) writes that 'the rice trade has been dominated by Chaozhou merchants for many years, largely because of the importance of rice imports from Thailand where Chaozhou people form the majority Chinese community'.

14. The wisk to brush away bad influences, the arrangement of the robes, and the beard are quite similar in the two paintings. The Sik Sik Yuen's painting is more complex, however, and contains elements not replicated in the private temple's image: the pine tree, signifying Wong Tai Sin's title Red Pine Master; the feet arranged in a classic meditational pose; the left hand raised in another classic gesture of piety; and several stones turning into miniature sheep in the lower left corner of the painting. The *fuji*-produced image of Wong Tai Sin could be understood as a rough copy from memory of the Sik Sik Yuen's painting, with any elements which are not strictly necessary left out.

15. Differences in ritual, as noted by a director of the Sik Sik Yuen, include the use of both Buddhist and Taoist prayers in the main temple (reflecting the eclectic views of the Chairman and some directors of the Sik Sik Yuen), whereas the Yun Ching Guk still uses only Taoist prayers and chants; and the use of grey robes by members of the Yun Ching Guk for ceremonies, whereas robes worn by members of the Sik Sik Yuen for ceremonies are blue, and occasionally yellow or red (for the directors and the Chairman, on special occasions).

16. This revelation was dated the 11th day, 7th month (Sunday, 29 August), 1982. The references to China and to Britain in the revelation are implicit, but are readily explained to outsiders by members of the organization. The term 'rice' (*mi*) in the text of the revelation ('the . . . rice will leave') was recognized as a reference to Britain because of the similarity of the character 'rice' to the British flag.

17. A recent example has been reported, for instance, from China. According to the story, which was being told in Kunming and elsewhere in late 1989, Mao had invited some Taoists to lunch during the 1930s, and did not conceal his lack of respect for their beliefs. He jokingly asked one of the old Taoists for a prediction about the future of the country, whereupon the Taoist wrote down the numbers 8,3,4,1 on the table, and then rose and without a word, left the table. Mao, amused, remebered this number, and after he came to power in 1949 he gave the same number to the guard regiment of the People's Liberation Army which protected the top leaders in Peking. However, Mao lived to be 83 — hence the first two numbers in the Taoist's 'prediction'. As for the second number — 41 — if this number is added to the year 1949, when the Communists gained power, the outcome is 1990. The tellers of this story in 1989 were intrigued by the possibility that the old Taoist had successfully predicted the duration of Mao's life, and (with the

events of June 4 still fresh in their minds) that his prediction about the fall of Mao's regime might be fulfilled within a year.

18. The actual numbers in the revelation were '9,9,4,10,5', and the last three numbers could be read as '45', '4,15', or '4,10,5', all equally plausible from the Chinese characters.

19. The information in this section is based on Graeme Lang's visits to the shrine and his interview with Mr Ling in New York in the summer of 1984, and on an interview with Mr Luke Sou, one of the directors of the shrine. Lang would also like to thank Mr Sou for providing him with copies of articles about the new shrine from Chinese newspapers.

20. The story was reported in the Chinese-language newspaper *Dongfang Ribao*, 25 November, 1983. The reporter interviewed both Ling Gwan Fai and the Chairman of the Sik Sik Yuen, Wong Wan Tin.

21. Mr Ling's six associates included a man in the restaurant business, and another involved in investment and banking. One of these men was nominally a Christian, although he acknowledged occasionally going to the fortune-tellers at the New York Wong Tai Sin shrine for advice about business. One of the men who participated in the opening ceremonies was a former Hong Kong police officer who had emigrated to the US and become involved in investment and banking operations. He would probably have known of the operation of the Sik Sik Yuen from the two former Hong Kong policemen of similar rank, also wealthy, who had been on the board of the Sik Sik Yuen since the 1950s. He was given a prominent role in the opening ceremonies.

22. The article on the New York shrine, which appeared in the Chinese newspaper *World Journal* in late 1983, included the following: '1997 has made everyone worry and plan for immigration, and even an immortal [xian] has to escape in advance to another country. If not, when China's Liberation Army arrives in Hong Kong, even the immortal will not be spared'.

23. In 1992, a group in Toronto, Canada, began to plan a large Wong Tai Sin temple in the area, which has a large Chinese population. If the temple is located on a large tract of land in the suburbs, as they intend, the shrine may become successful in attracting first-generation immigrants from Hong Kong.

24. This information was provided by Mr Wong Kwong and Mr Wong Sun Wah in an interview in January of 1992. Lang would like to thank Elaine Liu for helping with translation in this interview. Our information about this shrine is also derived from a visit to the site by Ragvald in 1991, including an interview with the abbott of the Buddhist temple at Chishi Yan.

25. For example, in 1984, the Hong Kong businessman Li Ka-shing provided several million dollars to renovate and rebuild the Kaiyuan Buddhist temple in Chaozhou (his hometown), which had been severely damaged during the Cultural Revolution.

26. The condition that Mr Wong had to provide all of the funds for the project was probably made because the authorities wanted to prevent contributions from villages in the area, which might lead to political difficulties with higher-level authorities.

27. Lang accompanied the members of the Sik Sik Yuen on this visit in December of 1990, and would like to thank Mr F.C. Leung for the invitation. Ragvald also visited the site in December of 1991.

28. According to the *Luofushan Fengwuzhi*, the original temple at Luofu was built in 405 CE, and was called Ge Hong Ci, honouring the great Taoist writer Ge Hong, who pursued immortality on the mountain toward the end of his life. Later in the early Tang, a larger shrine called Ge Xian Ci was built. Another source (*Lignan Gu Jin Lu*, or *Records of Old and Present Lingnan* [Guangdong], edited by Xu Xu, a well-known Guangzhou-based scholar, published in 1984 in Hong

Kong by the Shanghai Book Company) states that a small temple was built at Luofu in 742 CE, called Ge Xian Ci. During the Song dynasty, a Taoist temple was built, called the Duxu Guan, later renamed the Chongxu Guan, the name by which the main temple on the mountain is now known.

29. We will use the form 'Wong Yeren', although the pinyin form is Huang Yeren, because we are using the standard Hong Kong spelling for 'Wong Tai Sin' and 'Wong' Yeren indicates that the two figures shared the same surname.

30. See, for example, from Mexico, the case of the absorption of elements of the Indian goddess Tonantsi into the cult of the Virgin of Guadeloupe (Ena Campbell, 'The Virgin of Guadeloupe and the female self-image: a Mexican case history', in Richard Preston, ed., *Mother Worship: Themes and Variations*, University of North Carolina Press, 1982, pp.5–24). Many other cases of the merging of deities, or of the absorption of one deity by another, could be cited.

31. This section on Luofu Mountain and the merging of Wong Cho Ping and Wong Ye Yan draws from our paper on the subject (Ragvald and Lang 1987).

32. Source: *Huitu Liexian Quanzhuan (Illustrated Complete Biographies of Ranked Immortals)*, compiled in the sixteenth century by Wang Shizhen and reprinted by Zhongwen Chubanshe in Taiwan in 1971. This is one of the major reference works on Taoist saints, with capsule biographies on some 500 of them, and covers the period from the beginning of Taoism until the last year of the reign of Hongzhi (1506 CE).

33. Several different explanations for Yeren's failure to rise to heaven have been proposed by Taoists: see Ragvald and Lang (1987:79).

34. Some stories of healings by Yeren are contained in *Luofushan fengwu zhi [Records of Mt. Luofu Scenery]*, Guangdong Luyou Chubanshe [Tourist Affairs Publishing Co.], 1984.

35. On the writings about Yeren, see Ragvald and Lang (1987).

36. Much of the funds for the renovation were contributed by Hong Kong Taoists.

37. The article, authored by An Shi, is on page 2 of the brochure, which is printed on newsprint-type paper with the heading 'Scenic spots in Luofu, Tangquan, Huizhou'. The brochure, published by the local branch of the provincial tourist agency, was written by journalists and local scholars attached to the local cultural affairs bureau.

38. We learned while in the area that there had been some recent conflict between the proprietors of rival shrines near the mountain in their attempt to get some of the tourist trade. For a time in the spring of 1987, the Beidi temple on the plain several kilometres from the main temple was by-passed by a steady stream of tourists as well as local people making their way up the nearby Wong Sin valley. They were heading for a private shrine, set up recently by an enterprising local peasant, on the site where Wong 'Tai Sin' (that is, Ye Yan) had become an immortal, and where divination (*qiu qian*) was again being performed. The proprietor of the Beidi temple, which had its own *qiu qian* operation, complained to the military authorities (Luofu was still a military region) and they responded by closing the private shrine. The site in the valley may yet become a tourist pilgrimage, however. (We were driven to the valley by Hong Kong tourists.) While there, we met a peasant who had set up a small open-air 'restaurant' in the valley to cater to the tourists, and who told us that the mandarin trees there were growing faster than others in the area due to the power of the god.

39. On the basis of a study of the *Jinhua Chisongshan zhi* (Records of Jinhua Red Pine Mountain), written at the end of Southern Song or at the beginning of the Yuan period by Ni Shouyue, Wong (1985) has concluded that worship of Wong Tai Sin in the area was probably continuous from the Jin dynasty until the Southern Song. The main temple on the mountain, originally called Chisong Gong, was

renamed the Baoji Guan (Temple of Assembled Treasures) in 1008 CE This year marked the beginning of a national Taoist campaign enhancing the status of Taoist temples all over the country. As in modern times, this campaign also was accompanied by central control. Taoist priests were sent out from the central government to be put in charge of the renamed and often reconstructed temples. (In this drive local gods were often replaced by officially sanctioned ones.) A Taoist sent out by the imperial court was put in charge of the renamed (and reconstructed?) temple to Wong Tai Sin (Wong Cho Ping) and his brother. It is this temple, according to the much quoted *Jinhua Fuzhui*, which was for a time the most impressive of the Taoist temples south of the Yangzi river. The temple was evidently rebuilt in 1478 and again in 1584 (ibid.). This northern cult of Wong Tai Sin has a different and much older history than the southern cult, and deserves its own separate treatment. We will discuss the northern cult in a forthcoming paper.

40.   Lang would like to thank Mr Peter W.K. Lo for showing him his photographs of the bell and other features of the site, and for sharing his findings from the trip. Lo has incorporated some of his findings in *Wong Tai Sin Temple: A Brief Introduction* (Sik Sik Yuen 1991), p.11.

41.   This information was provided by a director of the Sik Sik Yuen.

42.   Specifically, the posture, the arrangement of the hands and feet, and the robes of the Jinhua and Hong Kong versions of Wong Tai Sin are almost identical. The main differences are that the Jinhua version is a statue rather than a picture (as in the Hong Kong temple), and that it is much larger than any of the statues or pictures of Wong Tai Sin at the other sites where Wong Tai Sin is worshipped.

43.   Mr Peter W.K. Lo, who attended the opening ceremonies of the new temple, kindly provided Lang with an account of this event and of the new temple. Subsequently, members of the Yun Ching Guk related the further interesting detail that they had gone up to Jinhua prior to the official opening to perform religious rites at the shrine, including a ceremony to 'dot the eyes' of the statue to give it life, as part of the process of calling the god's presence down into it. Local authorities ignored these activities, evidently to accommodate this group of important Hong Kong believers.

Notes to Chapter 8

1.   The importance of location is highlighted in the so-called 'retail gravity' model, which attempts to predict the impact of major new retail outlets such as shopping malls as a function of their size (a measure of the number of stores and diversity of goods, and hence a presumed indicator of their drawing power), and their location relative to other outlets of given sizes, and relative to the density of residential population in the area. This model has been used by planners in some cities to assess the likely impact of new shopping malls on existing malls.

2.   Tsai (1979:29) interviewed worshippers at three temples in the city of Tainan in southern Taiwan, regarding the problems which worshippers had brought to the three gods. He found that of the worshippers at the temple of Baosheng Dadi, known for medical care, 43 per cent of worshippers had brought a medical problem, while the other categories of petitions included 'fate' (23 per cent), 'business' (19 per cent), 'wealth' (5 per cent) and 'marriage' (5 per cent). Thus, Baosheng Dadi still specialized primarily in medical problems, but some worshippers clearly believed that other kinds of help were also available from this god. Since Wong Tai Sin was petitioned for medical help by only 23 per cent of worshippers, while 22 per cent petitioned him about their careers (Fong and Luk 1989; see Chapter

3), it appears that Wong Tai Sin is less specialized for medical problems than Baosheng Dadi. The god Guangong, however, was less specialized than Baosheng Dadi, according to Tsai's data, and hence his appeal to a broad range of people is more like that of Wong Tai Sin. Specifically, Tsai found that worshippers of Guangong, known for 'military and occupational protection' (Fong and Luk 1989), brought problems to him as follows: 'business' (32 per cent), 'other' (25 per cent), 'fate' (19 per cent), 'illness' (13 per cent), and 'marriage' (9 per cent).

3.   When we assert that the modernizing and industrializing processes in Hong Kong 'largely disregarded traditional Chinese ways of doing things', we do not mean to imply that the colonial government attempted to repress Chinese customs and religious practices. Indeed, the government occasionally adjusted its plans for construction of dams and roads in the New Territories to accommodate local beliefs about *feng shui* (geomancy), and even paid for the hiring of geomancers when this proved to be essential to make progress in negotiations with villagers (James Hayes has chronicled some of these incidents in his writings; see for example Hayes, 1983a). Our point, however, is that Hong Kong economic development proceeded largely according to the rules of a relatively unfettered capitalism increasingly linked to international markets and international financial and industrial practices, while Hong Kong urban development proceeded according to calculations which depended on a combination of urban planning and profit. Chinese social and economic life, as most of the immigrants had experienced it in rural China, was either absent or rapidly ploughed under by these forces in urban Hong Kong.

4.   Protestant evangelical missionary groups are quite aware of the sociological conditions which facilitate their missionizing. See, for instance, Sharon E. Mumper, 'Where in the world is the church growing', *Christianity Today*, 11 July, 1986, pp.17–21. Mumper quotes a number of evangelical analysts on the sociological conditions facilitating missions. For instance, Peter Wagner, Professor at Fuller Seminary School of World Missions in Pasadena 'noted that immigrant populations are generally more receptive to the gospel than those that are more stable. "When the Vietnamese came to America in 1976, there was tremendous openness to the gospel", he says. "Now, ten years later, that has largely passed . . ." "When a society is in ferment, the church is ripe for growth", says [President of Dawn Ministries Jim] Montgomery. For 75 years, missionaries working in Cambodia were able to produce only 5,000 to 10,000 converts, he says. Within a few short years, since thousands of Cambodians fled to refugee camps, as many as 20,000 have become Christians. 'Wars, earthquakes, strife, refugees, famines — all can make people more responsive to the gospel"'.

5.   Lang would like to thank Professor Rodney Stark for calling his attention to the fine study by Aiko Moroto.

6.   The article appeared in the Hong Kong newspaper *Ming Bou*, 5 February, 1984.

7.   The Dalai Lama, for instance, consulted the god Dorje Drakden, the protector divinity of Tibet, about whether he should flee Tibet in 1959 as Chinese troops surrounded his palace. The god finally advised him to flee, which he did. He described this consultation with the god through divination in his book *Freedom in Exile: The Autobiography of the Dalai Lama of Tibet* [Hodder and Stoughton 1990]; an excerpt describing the incident was reprinted under the title 'Flight of the God-King' in the *South China Morning Post*, 8 September 1990.

Appendix A

Divination and Spirit-writing by the *Fuji* Method

The Procedure

The *fuji* (Cantonese: *fugei*) method of divination typically uses a stick or a wooden hoop, with a stylus or brush attached, to write the god's messages. In the *fuji* procedure, the god is evidently thought to possess, or communicate through, one of the individuals holding the stick. The message may be written on a tray covered with a thin layer of sand (which is scraped with another stick after each character is written to prepare for the next); it may be written in ink on paper, using a brush attached to the stick; or it may be banged out on a wooden or metal surface. In any case, the procedure requires one or two wielders of the stick, a 'reader' who announces the characters as they are written (although sometimes the writer will call out the characters while writing them), and a scribe who records each character in a book as it is called out by the reader. Other objects besides a stick may also be used. Jordan (1972:57–8) describes a similar procedure in which two men hold a small chair between them, and bang out the god's message on a table. In this case, it appears the god is thought to 'possess' the chair itself, not the men wielding it (see De Groot 1964:1316–18). The characters written by the *fuji* method can sometimes be read by an observer, but sometimes are illegible and apparent only to the writer.

According to Chao (1942), the *fuji* evolved from an earlier form of divination which began as an invitation to a goddess or female spirit named Tzu-ku. Records from the fifth century CE indicate that on this day each year, she was invited back to possess an image of her (either a broom with a skirt attached to it, or a straw image) and to receive offerings. The effigy of the goddess, thus possessed, jumped or danced, indicating by its behaviour the prospects that year for such industries as silkworm breeding and mulberry leaf harvesting.

The writing was evidently done at first with a chopstick added to the goddess's image. Later, the chopstick was stuck in a sieve (used for washing or winnowing rice), and used to write in ashes on a desk, but it was still the lady Tzu-ku who was being invited. The writing was evidently done by girls holding the sieve. The *fuji* eventually began to be used for messages from other gods, goddesses, and spirits of deceased persons (Jordan and Overmyer 1986:39).

This change was related to a change in the social location of *fuji* performances. The *fuji*, initially a rural rite, had spread by the Song dynasty into the educated class. The goddess by this time had learned to write, paint, and compose poems (her image now wielded by educated men). Not surprisingly, spirits of recently deceased men of letters, military heroes, and officials now began to speak through this procedure, reflecting the change in the background of the practitioners. These educated men eventually used the *fuji* to seek advice and help with their immediate concerns: upcoming civil service examinations, for those who had not yet passed them; promotions and prospects for those who had; difficult decisions faced by the literati in their careers as officials; and for everyone, the threat from disease and the inevitable problems of ill-health.

Fuji has also been used with great skill and imagination by religious entrepreneurs in Guangdong, in Taiwan, and in Hong Kong, to preach and to acquire disciples and supporters (see, for example, the cases described by Jordan and Overmyer 1986, and by Tsui 1991).

There is a continuing 'market' for both sectarian and non-sectarian *fuji* services in modern Chinese culture-areas among religious 'seekers' and among those anxious about personal problems or family crises, or faced with crucial decisions. In Hong Kong, some regular *fuji* sessions are held in shrines or private apartments.

Temples and shrines which offer *fuji* are able to attract clients because they offer the prospect of more personal attention from the deity than could be attained by merely shaking out a fortune-stick to get a fortune-poem (*qiu qian*) at a temple. The people who attend these *fuji* sessions also have a keener sense of the supernatural presence, as they watch the god manipulate the stick to write his messages to them.

Glossary

Note: This glossary omits names of most dynasties and emperors, of most cities in China, and of most place-names in Hong Kong, since these are either well-known or easy to find in standard sources. Also omitted are most personal names, except for those who played a historical role in the events described in the book.

baih sahn (*bai shen*) 拜神
Bao Gu 鮑姑
Baoji Guan 寶積觀
Baosheng Dadi 保生大帝
beibu (*bui buk*) 杯卜
Bei Di 北帝
Cangjing Ge 藏經閣
Ch'in (Qin) 秦
Chai Tin Dai Sing (Qitian Dasheng) 齊天大聖
Chang Tao-ling (Zhang Daoling) 張道陵
Chaozhou (Chiu Chow) 潮州
Chegong 車公
Chen Jitang 陳濟棠
Chen Zhengbo 陳征博
Cheung On (Chang'an) 長安
cheung sau (*changshou*) 長壽
chi-bei (*cibei*) 慈悲
Chin (Jin) 晉
Ching Chung Gun (Qingsong Guan) 青松觀
Chishi Yan 叱石巖
Chisong Daxian 赤松大仙
Chisong Xianzi 赤松仙子
Chisong Zi 赤松子
Chisong Gong 赤松宮
Chisong Guan 赤松觀
Chong An Jie (Yong'an Jie) 涌岸街
Chongxu Guan 沖虛觀
Chou Tai Sin (Cao Daxian) 曹大仙
Chuang Tzu (Zhuang Zi) 莊子

Chuk Yuen (Zhu Yuan) 竹園
Ci An Jie 祠岸街
Danxi 丹溪
Daozang 道藏
Datong Si 大通寺
Daxian 大仙
Dazhen 大真
Dongguan 東莞
Duruan 杜阮
Erxian Ci 二仙祠
faat choih (*fa cai*) 發財
Fangcun Wen-shi 芳村文史
Feiluan tai 飛鸞台
fengshui 風水
fengwu zhi 風物誌
Fengying Xian Guan 蓬瀛仙館
fuji 扶乩
Fujian 福建
Fun Ying Sin Gun 蓬瀛仙觀
Gangtou 崗頭
Gaoming 高明
ge (*guk*) 閣
Ge Hong 葛洪
Gexian Ci 葛仙祠
Ge Xuan 葛玄
Guan Di (Guandi) 關帝
Guan Yin (Gunyam) 觀音
Guangdong Fengwu Zhi 廣東風物誌
Guangdong Xinyu 廣東新語
Guangzhou Bainian Dashi Ji 廣州百年大事記

Guanshan 官山
Guifeng 圭峰
Guo Shengwang 郭聖王
hahng sihn (*xing shan*) 行善
Hakka (Kejia) 客家
Han 漢
Hanyu 韓愈
Heshan 鶴山
heung sihn 向善
Hongzhi 弘治
Hsu Chein-kuo (Xu Jianguo)
　許建國
Huadi 花地
Huang Baixiong 黃伯雄
Huangxian 黃仙
Huangxianweng 黃仙翁
Huitu Liexian Quanzhuan
　繪圖列仙全傳
ji 吉
Jianglan Lu 槳欄路
jiaozhi 交趾
jin 晉
jin shu 晉書
Jing Mimeng 驚迷夢
Jinhua Chisong Shanzhi
　金華赤松山誌
Jinhua fenji 金華分跡
Jinhua Fenyuan 金華分院
Jinhua Fuzhi 金華府誌
Jinhua Tang 金華堂
Jinhua Xianzhi 金華縣誌
Jurong 句容
kai jai (*qizai*) 契仔
kauh chim (*qiu qian*) 求簽
Leshan Tong (Leshan Tang)
　樂善堂
Leung Gwan Jyun (Liang
　Junzhuan) 梁鈞轉
Leung Yan Ngam (Liang Ren'an)
　梁仁菴
Liang (*see* Leung) 梁
Li Juesheng 黎覺生
Li Po (Li Bai) 李白
Li Shao-chun (Li Shaojun) 李少君
Li Zhun 李準

lihng-yihm (*lingyan*) 靈驗
Ling Gwan Fai (Ling Junhui)
　凌君輝
Lingnan Gu-Jin Lu 嶺南古今錄
Lingnan Zhanggu 嶺南掌故
Lu Ban 魯班
Lu Dongbin 呂洞賓
Lu Weiqing 蘆維慶
Luo Pinchao 羅品超
Luofu Zhi 羅浮誌
Luofu Fengwu Zhi 羅浮風物誌
Luofusheng Zhi Bubian
　羅浮生誌補編
Man Cheong (*see* Wenchang)
　文昌
Man Mo (Wenwu) 文武
mi 米
Mile 彌勒
Mo Xiuying 莫秀英
nanfang 南方
Nanhai 南海
Ng (Wu) 吳
Panyi 番邑
Panyu 番禺
Pao-sheng Ta Ti (Baosheng Dadi)
　保生大帝
ping an 平安
Po Leung Kuk (Baoliang Ju)
　保良局
pou jai huyn sihn (*pu ji quan
　shan*) 普濟勸善
Puji Tan 普濟壇
Puhua Tan 普化壇
Puqing Tan 普慶壇
Pushan 菩山
Puyi Tan 普宜壇
Pucheng 浦城
qian (*chim*) 簽
Qingsong guan 青松觀
Qingyuan 清遠
qiu qian (*kauh chim*) 求簽
Rengang 稔崗
Sanshui 三水
Sanyuan Gong 三元宮
Shaanxi 陝西

Shancun 山村
shangji 上吉
shangshang 上上
shen 神
Shen Nung (Shen Long) 神龍
Shenliutang 深柳堂
Shenxian Zhuan 神仙傳
Shih Huang Ti (Shi Huang Di)
　始皇帝
Shilei fu 事類賦
Shou-son Chow (Zhou Shouchen)
　周壽臣
sihn (*shan*) 善
Sik Sik Yuen (Sese Yuan)
　嗇色園
Songji zhi jie (Songji
　Zhijie) 松基直街
Taipingshan 太平山
Tai Seui (Taisui) 太歲
Tai Sin (Daxian) 大仙
Tai Wong Ye (Dawangye)
　大王爺
tim ding (*tian ding*) 添丁
Tung Wah (Donghua) 東華
Tzu Ku 紫姑
Wah Chung Sin Gun 華松仙館
Wei Tuo 韋馱
Wei Zheng 魏徵
Wen Chang Ge (Wenchangge)
　文昌閣
Wenshiguan (Wen-shi Guan)
　文史館
Wong Bat Hung (Huang Baixiong)
　黃伯雄
Wong Cho Ping (Huang Chuping)
　黃初平
Wong Cho Hei (Huang Chuqi)
　黃初起

Wong Gung Fu (Huang Gongfu)
　黃公輔
Wong Tai Sin (Huang Daxian)
　黃大仙
Wong Wan Tin (Huang Yuntian)
　黃允畋
Wu Shu 吳淑
Wunuxing 婺女星
xian 仙
Xian shi 仙事
xianji 仙吉
xiaxia 下下
Xing Shi Yaoyan 醒世要言
Xinhui Xianzhi 新會縣誌
Xinhui 新會
Xiqiao Shan 西樵山
Xiyou Ji 西遊記
Xu Xu 徐續
yang 陽
Yangshikeng 羊石坑
yau kauh bit yihng (*you qiu bi
　ying*) 有求必應
Yi Kuan Tao (Yiguandao) 一貫道
Yi Ling 醫靈
yi luk baat 二六八
yi luk faat 易陸發
yin 陰
Yuan Shih-kwai (Yuan Shikai)
　袁世凱
Yuet Kai (Yue Xi) 月溪
Yuhuang Dadi 玉黃大帝
Yun Ching Guk (Yuanqing Ge)
　原請閣
Zhang Liang 張良
Zhong 中
zhongji 中吉
zhongping 中平
zhongxia 中下

References

Baker, Hugh D.R. (1983), 'Life in the cities: the emergence of Hong Kong man'. *The China Quarterly* 9:469–79.

Banck, Werner (1985), *Das Chinesische Temple Oracle*, Vol.II. Otto Harrassowitz.

Belden, Jack (1949), *China Shakes the World* (London, Penguin).

Blofeld, John (1978), *Taoism: The Road To Immortality* (Boston, Shambhala Publications).

Bloomfield, Frena (1980), *The Occult World of Hong Kong* (Hong Kong, Hong Kong Publishing Co.).

Boorman, Howard L., and Richard C. Howard (eds.) (1967), *Biographical Dictionary of Republican China* Vol.1 (NY, Columbia University Press).

Brim, John A. (1974). 'Village alliance temples in Hong Kong'. In Arthur P. Wolf (ed.), *Religion and Ritual in Chinese Society* (Stanford, Stanford University Press), pp. 93–103.

Burkhardt, V.R. (1982), *Chinese Creeds and Customs* (Hong Kong, SCMP Press). [Originally published in three volumes in 1953, 1955, and 1958.]

Chamberlain, Jonathan (1983), *Chinese Gods* (Hong Kong, Long Island Publishers).

Chan, Hau-nung, Wing-hang Chow, and Po-wah Hung (1990), 'A Comparative Study of the Belief in Wong Tai Sin and the Che Mei Tao So'. Department of Sociology, University of Hong Kong. (Unpublished paper prepared for a course taught by Dr Grant Evans.)

Chan, Shuk-hing, Kit-ching Choi, Chun-kwong Lam, Foo-cheung Ng, Tai-yiu Liu, Man-yee So (1984), 'The Chek Chung Huang Daxian Temple' [in Chinese]. Anthropology Department, Chinese University of Hong Kong. (Unpublished.)

Chao, Wei-pang (1942), 'The Origin and Growth of the Fu Chi'. *Folklore Studies* [The Museum of Oriental Ethnology, The Catholic University of Peking] 1:9–27.

Cheng, Joseph Y.S. (ed.) (1986), *Hong Kong in Transition* (Hong Kong, Oxford University Press).

Cheung, Chi-yuen (1975), 'The Religious Phenomenon of Huang Daxian' [in Chinese]. *Ching Feng* (Christian Study Centre on Chinese Religion and Culture, Hong Kong] 45:39–45).

Chin, Margaret, Chiu-ming Lau, Lai-tak Lau, Sarah Leung, Wing-seung Li, Vivien Pau, Stella Poon, Thomas Wong (1977), 'Religion and Organization: A Study of the Temple of Wong Tai Sin'. Sociology Department, University of Hong Kong (Unpublished).

Choa, Gerald (1967), 'Chinese Traditional Medicine and Contemporary Hong Kong'. In Marjorie Topley (ed.), *Some Traditional Chinese Ideas and Conceptions in Hong Kong Social Life Today* [papers from a Weekend Symposium, Oct. 1966] (The Hong Kong Branch of the Royal Asiatic Society), pp. 31–5.

Chow, Steven C. and Gustav F. Papanek (1979), 'Laissez-faire, Growth and Equity: Hong Kong'. Paper prepared for the Ninth Annual Canadian Council of South East Asian Studies Conference, 9–11 November 1979.

Chung, Fung-Chi (1983), 'Changing Occupational Patterns Among Migrants of Rural Chinese Origin in Urban Hong Kong Between 1949 and 1974'. *The Hong Kong Baptist College Academic Journal* 10:135–47.

Day, Clarence Burton (1969), *Chinese Peasant Cults: Being a Study of Chinese Paper Gods* (Second Edition) (Taipei, Ch'eng Wen Publishing Co., revision of original 1924 edition).

De Groot, J.J.M. (1964 [1892–1910]). *The Religious system of China* Vol. 6, Book II (reprinted by Taipei, Literature House).

Duara, Prasenjit (1991), 'Knowledge and Power in the Discourse of Modernity: The Campaigns Against Popular Religion in Early Twentieth-century China'. *The Journal of Asian Studies* 50 (1):67–83.

Dunn, Fred L. (1975), 'Medical Care in the Chinese Communities of Peninsular Malaysia'. In Arthur Kleinman, Peter Kunstadter, E. Russell Alexander, and James L. Gale (eds.), *Medicine in Chinese Cultures: Comparative Studies in Chinese and Other Societies* (Washington, D.C., US Department of Health, Education, and Welfare), pp. 297–326.

Dwyer, D.J. (1976), 'The problem of In-migration and Squatter Settlement in Asian Cities: Two Cases, Manila and Victoria–Kowloon'. In Y.M. Yeung and C.P. Lo (eds.), *Changing South-East Asian Cities: Readings on Urbanization* (Singapore, Oxford University Press), pp. 131–41.

Eberhard, Wolfram (1970), 'Oracle and Theater in China'. In *Studies in Chinese Folklore and Related Essays* (The Hague, Mouton), pp. 191–99.

Elliott, Alan J.A. (1955), *Chinese Spirit-Medium Cults in Singapore* (London, Department of Anthropology, London School of Economics and Political Science, Monographs on Social Anthropology, New Series, No.14).

Endacott, G.B. (1978) *Hong Kong Eclipse* (Hong Kong, Oxford University Press).

Esherick, Joseph W. (1976), *Reform and Revolution in China: the 1911 Revolution in Hunan and Hubei* (Berkeley, University of California Press).

Faure, David (1989), 'Folk Religion in Hong Kong and the New Territories Today'. In Julian F. Pas (ed.), *The Turning of the Tide: Religion in China Today* (Hong Kong, Oxford University Press, in association with the Hong Kong Branch of the Royal Asiatic Society), pp. 259–70.

Faure, David, James Hayes, and Alan Birch (eds.) (1984), *From Village to City: Studies in the Traditional Roots of Hong Kong Society* (Hong Kong, Centre of Asian Studies, University of Hong Kong).

Faure, David, Bernard H.K. Luk, and Alice Ngai-ha Lun Ng (1986), *Historical Inscriptions of Hong Kong* [in Chinese] (Hong Kong, Hong Kong Museum of History).

Fong, Pak Tim, and Luk Kin Man (1989), 'How a Study of the Worship of Wong Tai Sin Illuminates What Hong Kong People are Thinking' [in Chinese]. Department of Religion, Chung Chi College, Chinese University of Hong Kong. [Unpublished paper prepared for a Sociology of Religion course taught by Dr Kwok Pui Lan].

Franck, Harry A. (1925), *Roving Through Southern China* (NY, The Century Co.).

Greenblatt, Sidney L. (1979), 'Individual Values and Attitudes in Chinese Society: An Ethnomethodological Approach'. In Richard Wilson, et al. (eds.), *Value Change in Chinese Society* (NY, Praeger), pp. 65–97.

Grover, Mark (1989), 'Migration, Social Change and the Growth of Alternative Religions: Religion in Portugal Since 1974'. (Paper presented at the Annual Meetings of the Association for the Sociology of Religion, San Francisco, 6–9 August).

Hahn, Emily (1946), *China to Me: A Partial Autobiography* (NY, Garden City Publishing Co.).

Hambro, Edvard (1954), *The Problem of Chinese Refugees in Hong Kong* (Report submitted to the United Nations High Commissioner for Refugees).

Hardacre, Helen (1982), 'The Transformation of Healing in the Japanese New Religions'. *Journal of the History of Religions* 22:305–20.

—— (1986), *Kurozumikyo and the New Religions of Japan* (Princeton, NJ, Princeton University Press).

Hase, P.H. (1983), 'Old Hau Wong Temple, Tai Wai, Sha Tin'. *Journal of the Hong Kong Branch of the Royal Asiatic Society* 23:233–40.

Hayes, James (1966), 'Chinese Temples in the Local Setting'. In *Some Traditional Chinese Ideas and Conceptions in Hong Kong Social Life Today* (Hong Kong: The Hong Kong Branch of the Royal Asiatic Society), pp. 86–95.

—— (1970), 'Old Ways of Life in Kowloon: the Cheung Sha Wan Villages'. *Journal of Oriental Studies* 8:154–88.

—— (1977), 'A Village War'. *Journal of the Hong Kong Branch of the Royal Asiatic Society* 17:185–93.

—— (1983a), *The Rural Communities of Hong Kong: Studies and Themes* (Hong Kong, Oxford University Press).

—— (1983b), 'The Kwun Yam Tung Shan Temple of East Kowloon, 1840–1940'. *Journal of the Hong Kong Branch of the Royal Asiatic Society* 23:212–18.

—— (1983c), 'Secular Non-gentry Leadership of Temple and Shrine Organizations in Urban British Hong Kong'. *Journal of the Hong Kong Branch of the Royal Asiatic Society* 23:113–36.

Hsu, Francis L.K. (1949), *Under the Ancestors' Shadow* (London, Routledge and Kegan Paul).

194   REFERENCES

—— (1973 [1952]), *Religion, Science, and Human Crises* (Westport, Conn.,
Greenwood Press).

Hughes, R.H. (1951), 'Hong Kong: An Urban Study', *The Geographical
Journal* 117:1–23.

Hui, C. Harry (1991), 'Religious and Supernaturalistic Beliefs'. In Lau Siu-
kai, Lee Ming-kwan, Wan Po-san, and Wong Siu-lun (eds.), *Indicators
of Social Development: Hong Kong 1988* (Hong Kong, Hong Kong
Institute of Asia-Pacific Studies, The Chinese University of Hong Kong).

Ingrams, Harold (1952), *Hong Kong* (London, Her Majesty's Stationery
Office).

Jarvie, I.C. and Joseph Agassi (eds.) (1969), *Hong Kong: A Society in
Transition* (London, Routledge and Kegan Paul).

Jordan, David K. (1972), *Gods, Ghosts, and Ancestors: The Folk Religion
of a Taiwanese Village* (Berkeley, University of California Press).

—— (1982), 'Taiwanese Poe Divination: Statistical Awareness and Religious
Belief'. *Journal for the Scientific Study of Religion* 21:114–18.

Jordan, David K., and Daniel L. Overmyer (1986), *The Flying Phoenix:
Aspects of Chinese Sectarianism in Taiwan* (Princeton, NJ, Princeton
University Press).

Kaltenmark, Max (1987), *Le Lie-sien Tchouan* (Paris, Institut des Hautes
Etudes Chinoises, College de France, reprint of 1953 Peking edition).

Kelly, Ian (1987), *Hong Kong: A Political-Geographic Analysis* (Hong Kong,
Macmillan Press).

King, Ambrose Y.C., and Rance P.L. Lee (eds.) (1981), *Social Life and
Development in Hong Kong* (Hong Kong, Chinese University Press).

King, Paul (1980), *In the Chinese Customs Service: A Personal Record of
47 Years* (NY, Garland Publishing Co. [reprint of 1924 edition publ. by
T.F. Unwin, London]).

Kleinman, Arthur (1980), *Patients and Healers in the Context of Culture:
an Exploration of the Borderland Between Anthropology, Medicine, and
Psychiatry* (Berkeley, University of California Press).

Kleinman, Arthur, Peter Kunstadter, E. Russell Alexander, and James L.
Gale (1975), *Medicine in Chinese Cultures: Comparative Studies of
Health Care in Chinese and Other Societies* (Washington, D.C., US Dept.
of Health, Education, and Welfare).

Kwan, Lai-hung (1984), 'The Charitable Activities of Local Chinese Organizations During the Japanese Occupation of Hong Kong, December
1941–August 1945'. In David Faure, James Hayes, and Alan Birch (eds.),
*From Village to City: Studies in the Traditional Roots of Hong Kong
Society* (Hong Kong, Centre of Asian Studies, University of Hong Kong),
pp. 178–90.

Kwong, Luke S.K. (1979), 'The Chinese Maritime Customs Remembered:
An Appeal for Oral History in Hong Kong'. *Journal of the Hong Kong
Branch of the Royal Asiatic Society* 19:21–6.

Kwong, Paul C.K. (1989), 'Population and Immigration'. In T.L. Tsim and

Bernard H.K. Luk (ed.), *The Other Hong Kong Report* (Hong Kong, The Chinese University Press), pp. 369–380.

Lang, Graeme (1989), 'Oppression and Revolt in Ancient Palestine: The Evidence in Jewish Literature from the Prophets to Josephus'. *Sociological Analysis* 49:325–43.

Lang, Graeme, and Lars Ragvald (1988), 'Upward Mobility of a Refugee God: Hong Kong's Huang Daxian'. *Stockholm Journal of East Asian Studies* 1:54–87.

—— (1987), 'Official and Oral Traditions About Hong Kong's Newest God'. *Journal of the Hong Kong Branch of the Royal Asiatic Society* 27:93–100.

Lau, Muriel (1990), 'Would-be Migrants' Spirited Approach'. *South China Morning Post* (9 February).

Lau, Siu-kai (1984), *Society and Politics in Hong Kong* (Hong Kong, The Chinese University Press).

Law, Joan, and Barbara E. Ward (1982), *Chinese Festivals in Hong Kong* (Hong Kong, South China Morning Post).

Lee, L.T.H., and Board of Directors (1971), *One Hundred Years of the Tung Wah [Donghua] Group of Hospitals, 1870–1970.* (Presented to the Governor, Sir David French, in Commemoration of the Group's Centenary.)

Lee, Rance P.L. (1975), 'Interaction between Chinese and Western Medicine in Hong Kong: Modernization and Professional Inequality'. In Kleinman, et al. (1975), pp. 219–214.

—— (1980), 'Perceptions and Uses of Chinese Medicine Among the Chinese in Hong Kong'. *Culture, Medicine, and Psychiatry* 4:345–75.

—— (1985), 'Social Stress and Coping Behavior in Hong Kong'. In Wen-Shing Tseng and David Y.H. Wu (eds.), *Chinese Culture and Mental Health.* (NY, Academic Press), pp. 193–214.

Leeming, Frank (1977), *Street Studies in Hong Kong: Localities in a Chinese City* (Hong Kong, Oxford University Press).

Lethbridge, Henry (1969), 'Hong Kong Under Japanese Occupation: Changes in Social Structure'. In I.C. Jarvie and Joseph Agassi (eds.), *Hong Kong: A Society in Transition* (London, Routledge and Kegan Paul), pp. 77–127.

—— (1978), *Hong Kong: Stability and Change* (Hong Kong, Oxford University Press).

Lewis, I.M. (1989), *Ecstatic Religion: A Study of Shamanism and Spirit Possession* (second edition) (London, Routledge).

Lo, Peter W.K. (1991), *Wong Tai Sin Temple: Brief Introduction* (Hong Kong, Sik Sik Yuen).

Loomis, C. Grant (1948), *White Magic: An Introduction to the Folklore of Christian Legend* (Cambridge, Mass., The Mediaeval Academy of America).

MacInnis, Donald E. (ed.) (1972), *Religious Policy and Practice in Communist China: A Documentary History* (NY, MacMillan).

Marsh, Robert M. (1961–2), 'The Venality of Provincial Office in China and in Comparative Perspective' *Comparative Studies in Society and History* 4: 454–66.

Martin, Katherine Gould (1975), 'Medical Systems in a Taiwan Village: Ong-Ia-Kong, the Plague God as Modern Physician'. In Arthur Kleinman, Peter Kunstadter, E. Russell Alexander, and James L. Gale (eds.), *Medicine in Chinese Cultures: Comparative Studies in Health Care in Chinese and Other Societies* (Washington, D.C., US Dept. of Health, Education, and Welfare), pp. 115–41.

Meyer, Jeffrey F. (1982), 'The Sacred Truth Society (Sheng Li She)'. *Studies in Religion* 11:285–98.

Morgan, Carole (1987), 'A Propos des Fiches Oraculaires de Huang Daxian'. *Journal Asiatique* CCLXXV:163–91.

Moroto, Aiko (1976), 'Conditions for Accepting a New Religious Belief: A Case Study of Myochikai Members in Japan'. (Unpublished M.A. thesis, Department of Sociology, University of Washington, Seattle.)

Myers, John T. (1975), 'A Hong Kong Spirit-medium Temple'. *Journal of the Hong Kong Branch of the Royal Asiatic Society* 15:16–27.

—— (1981), 'Traditional Religious Practices in an Urban Industrial Setting: The Example of Kwun Tong'. In Ambrose King and Rance P.L. Lee (eds.), *Social Life and Development in Hong Kong* (Hong Kong, Chinese University Press), pp. 275–88.

Ng, Sek-Hong (1989), 'Labour and Employment'. In T.L. Tsim and Bernard Luk (ed.), *The Other Hong Kong Report* (Hong Kong, The Chinese University Press), pp. 119–43.

O'Callaghan, Sean (1978), *The Triads: The Mafia of the Far East* (London, W.H. Allan and Co.).

Ogura, Manabu (1980), 'Drifted Deities in the Noto Peninsula. In Richard M. Dorson (ed.), *Studies in Japanese Folklore* (New York, Arno Press), pp. 133–44.

Overmyer, Daniel L. (1976), *Folk Buddhist Religion* (Cambridge, Harvard University Press).

—— (1985), 'Values in Chinese Sectarian Literature: Ming and Ch'ing *Pao-chuan*'. In David Johnson, Andrew Nathan, and Evelyn Rawski (eds.), *Popular Culture in Late Imperial China* (Berkeley, University of California Press), pp. 219–54.

Pas, Julian (1984), 'Temple Oracles in a Chinese City: A Study of the Use of Temple Oracles in Taichung, Central Taiwan'. *Journal of the Hong Kong Branch of the Royal Asiatic Society* 24:1–45.

—— (ed.) (1989), *The Turning of the Tide: Religion in China Today* (Hong Kong, Oxford University Press, in association with the Hong Kong Branch of the Royal Asiatic Society).

Perera, Neil (1987), 'There Came a Plague Upon Their Houses'. *Hong Kong Standard* (June 11).

Preston, James J. (1980), *Cult of the Goddess: Social and Religious Change in a Hindu Temple* (Prospect Heights, Illinois, Waveland Press). (1985 reissue of the edition published in India in 1980 by Vikas Publishing House).

Pryor, E.G. (1983), *Housing in Hong Kong* (second edition) (Hong Kong: Oxford University Press).

Ragvald, Lars, and Graeme Lang (1987), 'Confused Gods: Huang Daxian (Wong Tai Sin) and Huang Yeren at Mt. Luofu'. *Journal of the Hong Kong Branch of the Royal Asiatic Society* 27:74–92.

Rhoads, Edward J.M. (1975), *China's Republican Revolution: The Case of Kwangtung, 1885–1913* (Cambridge, Mass., Harvard University Press).

Salaff, Janet (1981), *Working Daughters of Hong Kong: Filial Piety or Power in the Family?* (Cambridge, Cambridge University Press).

Savidge, Joyce (1977), *This is Hong Kong: Temples* (Hong Kong, Hong Kong Government).

Schoeps, Hans-Joachim (1969), *Jewish Christianity: Factional Disputes in the Early Church* [trans. by Douglas R.A. Hare] (Philadelphia, Fortress Press).

Scott, Jr., George M. (1987), 'The Lao Hmong Refugees in San Diego: Their Religious Transformation and its Implications for Geertz's Thesis'. *Ethnic Studies Report* V(2):32–46.

Seiwert, Hubert (1981), 'Religious Response to Modernization in Taiwan: The Case of I-Kuan Tao'. *Journal of the Hong Kong Branch of the Royal Asiatic Society* 21:43–70.

Sham, Francis and S.T. Cheng (ed.) (1988), *Predictions of Wong Tai Sin* (Hong Kong, Board of Directors [1987–88], Tung Wah Group of Hospitals).

Shum, Ka Cheong (1990), 'A Study of Qiu Qian at Huang Daxian Temple from a Sociological Perspective' [in Chinese], (Department of Religion, Chung Chi College, unpublished The Chinese University of Hong Kong).

Sik Sik Yuen (1971), *The Foundation Stone Laying Ceremony of Wong Tai Sin New Temple* (Hong Kong, Sik Sik Yuen, 7 October).

—— (1981), *Inauguration Ceremony, Fung Ming Lau and Nine Dragon Wall* (Hong Kong, Sik Sik Yuen, 26 November).

—— (1982), *The Opening Ceremony of Temple Library, Confucian Hall, and Yee Mut Hall* (Hong Kong, Sik Sik Yuen, 9 September).

Simpson, W.J. (1902), *Report on the Causes and Continuance of Plague in Hong Kong and Suggestions as to Remedial Measures* (Report to the Secretary of State for the Colonies, 22 December 1902).

Sinn, Elizabeth (1989), *Power and Charity: The Early History of the Tung Wah Hospital, Hong Kong* (Hong Kong, Oxford University Press).

Siu, Helen (1990), 'Recycling Tradition: Culture, History, and Political Economy in the Chrysanthemum Festivals of South China'. *Comparative Studies in Society and History* 765–94.

Smart, Alan (1985), 'The Squatter Property Market in Hong Kong: Informal Regulation and the State'. (Paper presented at the Centre of Urban Studies Research Seminar, University of Hong Kong.)

Smith, Richard J. (1991) *Fortune-tellers and Philosophers: Divination in Traditional Chinese Society* (Boulder, Colo. Westview Press).

Soymie, Michel (1954), 'Le Lo-feou chan'. *Bulletin de l'ecole francaise d'Extreme-orient* [Saigon] Tome XLVIII (1er semestre): 1–137.

Stark, Rodney, and William Sims Bainbridge (1987), *A Theory of Religion* (New York, Peter Lang).

Swart, K.W. (1940), *Sale of Offices in the 17th Century* (The Hague).

Terzani, Tiziano (1985), *Behind the Forbidden Door: China Inside Out* (London, Unwin Paperbacks).

Topley, Marjorie (1974), 'Cosmic Antagonisms: A Mother–Child Syndrome'. In Arthur P. Wolf (ed.), *Religion and Ritual in Chinese Society* (Stanford, Stanford University Press), pp. 233–49.

Topley, Marjorie, and James Hayes (1966), 'Notes on temples and shrines of Tai Ping Shan Street Area'. In *Some Traditional Chinese Ideas and Conceptions in Hong Kong Social Life Today* (Hong Kong, The Hong Kong Branch of the Royal Asiatic Society), pp. 123–39.

Tsai, Wen-hui (1979), 'Historical Personalities in Chinese Folk Religion: A Functional Interpretation'. In Sarah Allan and Alvin P. Cohen (eds.), *Legend, Lore, and Religion in China, Essays in Honor of Wolfram Eberhard on His 70th Birthday* (San Francisco, Chinese Materials Center), pp. 23–42.

Tsim, T.L., and Bernard H.K. Luk (ed.) (1989), *The Other Hong Kong Report* (Hong Kong, The Chinese University Press).

Tsui, Bartholomew P.M. (1991), *Taoist Tradition and Change: The Story of the Complete Perfection Sect in Hong Kong* (Hong Kong, Christian Study Centre on Chinese Religion and Culture).

Walsh, Anthony (1980), 'The Prophylactic Effect of Religion on Blood Pressure Levels Among a Sample of Immigrants'. *Social Science and Medicine*, 14B:59–63.

Wan, Mariana (1988), 'Life is All a Tale of Fortune for Wong Tai Sin's Mr Mak'. *South China Morning Post* (March 13).

Wang, Shih-Ch'ing (1974), 'Religious Organization in the History of a Taiwanese Town'. In Wolf (1974), pp. 93–103.

Watson, James L. (1985), 'Standardizing the Gods: The Promotion of T'ien Hou ('Empress of Heaven') Along the South China Coast, 960–1960'. In David Johnson, Andrew J. Nathan, and Evelyn S. Rawski (eds.), *Popular Culture in Late Imperial China* (Berkeley, University of California Press), pp. 292–324.

Welch, Holmes (1965), *Taoism: The Parting of the Way* (Boston, Beacon Press).

Weller, Robert P. (1987), *Unities and Diversities in Chinese Religion* (Seattle, University of Washington Press).

Werner, E.T.C. (1932), *A Dictionary of Chinese Mythology* (Shanghai, Kelly and Walsh).

Williams, C.A.S. (1960), *Encyclopedia of Chinese Symbolism and Arts Motifs* (New York, Julian Press).

Wolf, Arthur P. (1974), *Religion and Ritual in Chinese Society* (Stanford, Stanford University Press).

Wong, Luke S.K. (1970), 'Squatters in Pre-war Hong Kong'. *Journal of Oriental Studies* 8:189–205.

Wong, Shiu-hon (1979), 'The Cult of Chang San-feng'. *Journal of Oriental Studies* 17:10–53.

—— (1985), 'A Study of Wong Tai Sin' [in Chinese]. *The Journal of the Institute of Chinese Studies of the Chinese University of Hong Kong* XVI:223–39.

Yang, C.K. (1961), *Religion in Chinese Society* (Berkeley, University of California Press).

Youngson, A.J. (1982), *Hong Kong Economic Growth and Policy* (Hong Kong, Oxford University Press).

Index